KU-777-200

ROSS KEMP
WARRIORS
BRITISH FIGHTING HEROES

arrow books

Published by Arrow Books 2011

2 4 6 8 10 9 7 5 3

Copyright © Ross Kemp 2011

Ross Kemp has asserted his right under the Copyright, Designs
and Patents Act 1988 to be identified as the author of this work

This book is sold subject to the condition that it shall not,
by way of trade or otherwise, be lent, resold, hired out,
or otherwise circulated without the publisher's prior
consent in any form of binding or cover other than that
in which it is published and without a similar condition,
including this condition, being imposed
on the subsequent purchaser.

First published in Great Britain in 2010 by
Century
Random House, 20 Vauxhall Bridge Road,
London SW1V 2SA

www.randomhouse.co.uk

Addresses for companies within The Random House Group Limited can be found at:
www.randomhouse.co.uk/offices.htm

The Random House Group Limited Reg. No. 954009

A CIP catalogue record for this book
is available from the British Library

ISBN 9780099550594

The Random House Group Limited supports The Forest Stewardship
Council (FSC®), the leading international forest certification organisation.
Our books carrying the FSC label are printed on FSC® certified paper. FSC is
the only forest certification scheme endorsed by the leading environmental
organisations, including Greenpeace. Our paper procurement policy can
be found at www.randomhouse.co.uk/environment

Typeset by Palimpsest Book Production Limited,
Falkirk, Stirlingshire
Printed and bound by CPI Group (UK) Ltd, Croydon, CR0 4YY

Contents

Introduction

This book tells of the adventures and celebrates the courage and sacrifice of eleven truly remarkable British servicemen. The two bloody global conflicts of the twentieth century produced hundreds of thousands of heroic acts from two generations of men, who were obliged by history to abandon their everyday lives, leaving their families, homes and careers to answer their country's call to arms. Only three of them – coincidentally, the Navy characters – were regulars when war broke out; the rest were just setting out in the world on their chosen paths. The men honoured in these pages stand out as exceptional warriors and human beings even among the multitude of heroes that our country produced in the first half of the twentieth century.

Drawn from all walks of life and all corners of the United Kingdom, together they demonstrate the unity, sense of patriotic duty and local pride that marked the general spirit of the day. There are two infantrymen, a submariner, a Battle of Britain fighter pilot, a medic, a ship's commander, a Bomber Command flight sergeant, a Royal Marine Commando, a First World War flying ace and two men who today would be termed as 'Special Forces'. Their stories take place in the trenches of Flanders, the skies over Europe, the jungles of Malaya and Burma, the North African desert, the beaches of Normandy and Italy and the waters of the Mediterranean and the Atlantic.

Their memories are still honoured by the units and forces in which they served, but otherwise they have been largely forgotten. In July 2009, Harry Patch, 'the Last Fighting Tommy' of the First World War, passed away. He took with him the final living link to the Great War. It will not be long before the last servicemen of the Second World War leaves us as well, severing our living connections with that extraordinary period in our history. This book is about British warriors and heroes, but that is not to say that there weren't heroic acts performed in both wars by our allies and some of our enemies. If you meet a veteran from the last of the two world wars, look him in the eye, shake his hand and thank him for what he did for you. For they are the generation of men that sacrificed themselves so that we might live in peace and freedom. This book is written in tribute to all of them.

ARMY

Lieutenant Colonel Freddy Spencer Chapman

Freddy Spencer Chapman's story of sabotage and survival in the stifling heat of the Malayan jungle is surely one of the most incredible in the history of British warfare. Yet until very recently it had been largely forgotten. Field Marshall Archibald Wavell, one of Britain's most senior commanders during the Second World War, said Chapman's exploits were every bit as awe-inspiring as those of the lavishly celebrated T.E. Lawrence in the Arabian desert. Chapman, he said, was a shining example of a very British type of hero. 'This war has shown, as others have done before it that the British make the best fighters in the world for irregular and independent enterprises,' he wrote after the conflict. 'Our submarines, commandos and airborne forces . . . have proved that where daring, initiative, and ingenuity are required in unusual conditions, un-rivalled commanders and men can be found both from professional and unprofessional fighting men of the British race.'

Such was the havoc wreaked on their lines that, for a long period, the Japanese believed a force of two hundred highly trained commandos was at large and dispatched four thousand troops to hunt them down. In truth, it was one Cambridge-educated botanist, birdwatcher and adventurer, together with a couple of mates, who were causing all the trouble.

Chapman wrote an account of his experiences in a book called *The Jungle Is Neutral*, which caused something of a sensation when it was first published after the war. But overshadowed by the many stories of daring and heroism of our servicemen in Europe and the Middle East, Chapman slipped from public consciousness until *Jungle Soldier*, a new biography published in 2009 by the *Sunday Times* journalist Brian Moynahan, restored him to the position of eminence he so richly deserves.

'Colonel Chapman has never received the publicity and fame that were his predecessor's [Lawrence] lot,' concluded Wavell. 'But for sheer courage and endurance, physical and mental, the two men stand together as examples of what toughness the body will find, if the spirit within it is tough; and as very worthy representatives of our national capacity for individual enterprise, which it is hoped that even the modern craze for regulating our lives in every detail will never stifle.' That was in 1948.

The unorthodox nature of his childhood shaped Chapman the man. Born in 1907, he was orphaned after his mother died of blood poisoning when he was only a few weeks old and his father was killed in the trenches at Ypres in 1916. He was brought up by an elderly vicar and his wife in the Lake District. It was here that his rugged independence, resourcefulness, stamina and durability became evident. At prep school he regularly egged fellow pupils on to hit him over the head with a cricket bat 'to see how hard he could take it'. One of his teachers told his first biographer, Ralph Barker, that the wild young boy was 'completely fearless, no regard for danger'. He was beaten frequently, but that didn't bother him either. He liked pain. At Sedbergh, a tough public school in the heart of the wild Cumbrian countryside, he was given special privileges to indulge his love of the outdoors. Instead of playing organised sport, he was allowed to roam the barren hills and lush valleys. He began to push himself to extremes, trekking and climbing for hours on end, always opting for the most challenging routes. He learnt about wildlife, how to poach and how to find his way without a compass. By the time he had arrived at Cambridge University after winning a Kitchener Scholarship (for the children of servicemen), his character had been well and truly moulded out of the experiences of a lonely childhood spent fending for himself in the wilderness: tough, independent, fearless, spirited and at one with nature.

His appetite for danger manifested itself at Cambridge in the dangerous undergraduate pastime of night climbing. For no other reason than the sheer excitement of it, and without any equipment, he spent hours climbing the steep façades of buildings and the towers and spires of the colleges. After graduating from Cambridge, he needed no second invitation to join a research expedition in 1930 to the Arctic, where he developed a whole new range of survival skills. He ate the still-warm kidneys of a polar bear minutes after it was shot, he learnt to speak Inuit, and he fathered a son, Hansie, with his Eskimo girlfriend Gertrude, as he called her. He announced he was going to send Hansie to Sedbergh when the time came but tragically the boy died of flu the following year. Ever practical and completely unsentimental, when a bitch in his sledge team delivered pups he had no second thoughts about feeding them to the other dogs that were suffering from starvation after weeks of trekking over blizzard-blasted ice caps.

He returned to England in 1931 after a series of harrowing ordeals, including the death of the expedition leader, Gino Watkins, but twelve months later the pull of adventure was too great and he joined an expedition to Greenland where he would perfect his survival skills in some of the harshest conditions on the planet. He lost numerous finger and toenails to the cold, survived for an entire day in a sealskin kayak during a ferocious storm at sea and led a team for several weeks across a treacherous ice cap to rescue a stranded colleague. In 1936 he joined a five-man British mountaineering expedition to the Himalayas during which he and Sherpa Pasang Dawa became the first men to reach the summit of the 24,000-foot Mount Chomolhari. It was an incredible feat that almost cost him his life after the pair were caught in a violent snowstorm during their descent. Not until 1970 did another mountaineer succeed in reaching the summit of one of the world's most treacherous and challenging peaks.

On his return he took a teaching job in the Scottish Highlands, but when war broke out he joined the Seaforth Highlanders and served briefly as a fieldcraft instructor with SAS founder David Stirling. Their small unit soon merged with Special Operations Executive (SOE), the covert organisation set up by Churchill to wage irregular warfare. The idea was to train recruits in the dark arts of guerrilla tactics and techniques and then dispatch them to all corners of the globe, themselves to train local fighters to wreak havoc inside occupied territories. By September 1941, Chapman was appointed number two at a new Special Training School in Singapore. It had only been operational for a few weeks when, to the astonishment of the British colonial authorities, the Japanese, sweeping across south-east Asia, surged through Thailand and invaded Malaya from the north. The Japanese advance was rapid, forcing the British to retreat towards Singapore at the bottom of the long, narrow peninsula. The two British Indian Divisions deployed in the colony outnumbered the Japanese invaders but, with no protection from the air or sea, they stood no chance of holding out.

When the 'Japs' – as he referred to them in his diaries and book – entered the Malay capital Kuala Lumpur on 11 January 1942, Chapman disappeared into the mountain jungles with a small group of hastily trained guerrillas, a motley collection of British and Australian rubber planters, businessmen and servicemen. He was not to emerge again until May 1945. The malaria he was suffering from at the time was a mere foretaste of some of the virulent diseases that were to lead him to death's door over the coming years. The fact that he had never before set foot inside the jungle was of no concern to him.

The plan of Chapman and his 'stay-behind party', as these small units had been dubbed, was to carry out exactly what they had been training to do: wage a guerrilla war behind enemy lines. They took with them boxes of Tommy guns, revolvers, explosives, fuses, trip wires, ammo, grenades, whisky, cash, tinned food, biscuits, oatmeal, medical supplies, maps, books, compasses and parangs – the large, heavy Malayan knives used for hacking down vegetation and without which no man can move more than a short distance in the jungle.

With the Japanese still some distance away to the north, they were able to make the first leg of the journey in vehicles. Turning off the main route which ran north to south, they passed through many vast rubber plantations and began to climb through virgin rainforest along steep, narrow roads twisting with S-bends. This was an entirely unknown and new environment for the intrepid British adventurer and he immediately began to record his impressions and observations in the first of many diaries. As the party advanced along endless dirt tracks they crossed dozens of bridges over dangerously fast-flowing water and passed through little communities of tin-roofed huts, smallholdings and vegetable patches. The heat and humidity were oppressive, the forest alive with the chatter, song and whistle of birds, insects and monkeys.

Most of Malaya's infrastructure was located along a passage fifty miles wide running the length of the narrow country. The main roads, rail lines and communication networks ran through the strip, flanked by the natural boundaries of the Main Range mountains to the east and the rivers of the coastal plains to the west. It was here that the Japanese were setting up their bases while working their way south towards Singapore. Chapman's plan was to set up two camps on either side of the mountain region to use as bases from which the party would stage its attack on the Japanese. The locations proposed by local planters were only fifteen miles apart, but thick jungle lay in between and getting from one side to the other involved climbing over a steeply sided mountain, 6,431 feet high. Chapman planned to hack a path between the two. Setting off from one of the proposed bases, the plan was to rendezvous with another pocket of British resistance fighters at the other. He was accompanied by Bill Harvey, an Australian rubber planter, and Sergeant John Sartin, a British explosives expert at the Singapore training school.

Confident the three of them could complete the journey in five days, Chapman and his two colleagues set off in stifling humidity and heat, each carrying 25lb of equipment. Afterwards, he conceded it was 'a nightmare journey . . . the most unpleasant journey I have ever done. I had not realised that in the Malayan jungle a mile on the map may mean four or five on the ground . . .' The hillsides were almost impenetrable with vegetation and sharp thorns ripping their bodies and hands as they clung on to stop themselves from tumbling down slopes.

Not long after they had set out, heavy rain began to fall, bringing out the leeches that bit into their flesh by the dozen. By the end of the day, the three men were covered in blood from the bites and scratches. 'I had pulled off scores during the day and did not know any had crawled through until I felt the blood run down my chest,' he said. Chapman came to the conclusion that it was no good pulling off the parasites because they took a lump of flesh with them. He advised leaving them on so that they fell away on their own accord once they had their fill of blood. Highly poisonous snakes and scorpions were a constant threat. Mosquitoes were more a problem down in the valleys but high up it was the clouds of midges, whose bites felt like a severe nettle sting, that overwhelmed the men. The men's faces swelled up so much that they were unable to see for long periods of time. Sweltering by day, the temperatures plummeted at night, forcing the shivering men to huddle together for warmth. The three rapidly exhausted the small amount of tinned food they had brought and the rain quickly destroyed most of their perishable food. From the second day onwards, the men, burning up the calories at an incredible rate, had just one bag of oatmeal between them.

Chapman was as hardened and experienced an outdoorsman as any, but the going was as tortuous as anything he had ever known. The wet leaves of the jungle floor made it extremely slippery underfoot and all the more exhausting as they stumbled, slid and hacked their way through. With no light reaching through the canopy above their heads, day after day the men lived in constant gloom, struggling to see more than a few yards ahead of them. Without the movement of the sun or any landmarks to guide them, they were in danger of walking in circles. Chapman tried to work out their position by dead reckoning but he was forced to admit: 'I had absolutely no idea where we were . . . I realised the terrifying vastness of the Malayan jungle.'

Soaked through with sweat, blood and rain and the damp from the jungle floor at night, the men never dried out. Their heavy equipment rubbed away the skin, adding to the discomfort. The two Tommy guns each man was carrying caused particular irritation. 'The Tommy gun in the jungle is a source of considerable grief and bad language,' he wrote in his memoirs. 'It is far too heavy and is covered with knobs, swivels, handles, catches, guards and other protuberances which, however you carry it, scrape and bruise your hip bone, dig you in the ribs, and still more infuriatingly, catch on every twig and creeper in the jungle.'

By the ninth or tenth day – Chapman had lost count – they were almost out of oatmeal. All of them had lost a great deal of weight at an alarming rate. One of his companions had taken in six holes of his belt. But Chapman drove them on, clinging to his personal mantra: *There is nothing either good or bad, but thinking makes it so.*

On the twelfth day, they suddenly emerged into a clearing close to a village, more by luck than anything else. A few more days in the jungle and they would have been dead. In the sunlight, the first they had felt on their faces for almost a fortnight, they were shocked by each other's appearance. Bones protruded from their chests, and their skin was yellow and mottled with leech bites and shredded with cuts and scrapes. 'We must have looked the most awful desperadoes with our swollen features, emaciated bodies, twelve days' beard, and scarred hands and faces,' said Chapman. The locals were so terrified that they 'started to hurry their children into the jungle'.

Bad news was waiting for them. The other party of guerrillas were not at the camp, nor was their large store of food and tobacco supplies. They had been stolen by a criminal gang. To their relief, the robbers had left the heavier boxes containing weapons, ammo, medical supplies, maps and clothes. Four years later, Chapman discovered that the party had tried to reach Singapore but were captured by the Japanese and beheaded.

The three men rested for only one day before they went into action against the enemy.

The 'mad fortnight' is how Chapman described the period that followed as the three men set about disrupting the Japanese advance. Working in the small strip of open land running through the country, their operations were fraught with risk at every turn. The terrain was crawling not only with Japanese troops but also local informants. The latter were happy to betray them, either because they had been actively recruited by the Japanese or simply because they wanted to avoid the brutal reprisals being carried out by the advancing forces.

Chapman's attention to detail was rigorous. The three men covered themselves in dye, made from soot and coffee, so that they resembled Tamils, the tallest of Malaya's many ethnic groups. They camouflaged themselves out in the open and wrapped their Tommy guns so that they didn't reflect the moonlight. They even inserted fireflies and luminous centipedes behind a leaf in their torches so that, if the battery failed, they had enough light to read the map and wire up their explosives. Chapman taught the friendly locals at their camp to whistle 'The Lambeth Walk' and imitate the calls of the British tawny owl to make themselves known in the darkness. From their hideout in the jungle it took several hours to reach the sites of their planned attacks.

The first attack was launched on 1 February 1942 on two railway bridges outside the town of Tanjung Malim. As it was a gruelling three-hour walk from camp, the three-man party couldn't carry enough explosives between them to blow the bridges completely. Instead, they laid 30lb in the middle of the track with a pressure switch under the rail in the hope that, when the train detonated the charge, it would topple over and take the bridge with it. They laid up in the undergrowth close by and listened nervously as a train chugged out of the town and headed towards the bridge. Moments later, a huge white light burst through the darkness, derailing the train but failing to damage the bridge. Chapman and his two comrades slipped into the night as the local Japanese garrison rushed to the scene and began hunting the saboteurs. A further attack two nights later succeeded in derailing a troop train.

The third attack was more ambitious and more dangerous: to ambush a Japanese convoy on the main arterial road through Malaya. Hundreds of trucks passed along the road by day and night, providing Chapman and his men with rich pickings but placing them in greater jeopardy. In the more exposed terrain by the roadside, fleeing the scene would be more problematic if they were caught up in an engagement. They made a makeshift bomb by stuffing gelignite into a thick bamboo cane and connecting it to a pull switch. Placing it in the middle of the road, they retreated into the undergrowth and waited. Soon enough the headlights of three trucks cut through the darkness. When the first of the vehicles was directly over the bomb, Sartin tugged the switch. The bomb exploded in a flash and seconds later a second larger explosion occurred when the fuel tank caught, engulfing the vehicle in flames. The truck behind rammed into the back of it and the third careered off the road and crashed. The three men emptied their Tommy guns and hurled their grenades into the midst of the panicking Japanese before sprinting away into the night. The sabotage party was long gone by the time the stunned troops had regrouped.

The frequency and professionalism of the attacks convinced the Japanese that several hundred British and Australian commandos were carrying them out. Almost an entire brigade of men was dispatched to hunt them down. In spite of the risk of capture, for the next five nights Chapman, Harvey and Sartin stepped up their ambushes on convoys along the highway. They adopted the same, simple procedure each time: blow up the lead truck and then hurl grenades and home-made bombs into the following vehicles, strafe the column with machine gun fire and then slip away before the enemy had a chance to gather themselves and retaliate. The party often attacked from cuttings through hills where they had the advantage of height over their targets. Getting away was easier too as it took their pursuers longer to scramble up the steep embankments. During an attack the three men yelled and yodelled at the tops of their voices to give the impression that they were a far larger force than they actually were.

Chapman grew in confidence with every raid and at night they even began to slip through towns and villages where the troops were stationed. Chapman realised that the Japanese were not quite as good as they were cracked up to be, noting that they gave away their presence by smoking and chatting loudly. 'They didn't like the dark,' he said, adding, 'Jap sentries were the world's worst shots.'

Ambushes were launched at the closest range possible to ensure the target was hit. On one occasion they were so close to the enemy that a grenade bounced back from the canvas canopy of a truck and knocked Sartin unconscious for a few moments when it exploded close by. Infuriated by the relentless attack on their lines, the Japanese responded with a brutality typical of their conduct in the war. Of all the many minority ethnic communities in Malaya, the Chinese were the largest and, led by the communists, they were also the most active insurgents. The Japanese had been carrying out appalling atrocities against the

Chinese throughout this period. They are thought to have slaughtered six million of them by 1945 and it was the Chinese, predictably, who bore the brunt of Japanese wrath, with dozens of massacred in retaliation for the casualties caused by Chapman's sabotage party and the efforts of other guerrillas. The standard reprisal procedure was to burn down a village, march the inhabitants to a slaughter location and, while the women and children looked on, the men dug a mass grave. When it was finally ready they were all lined up along the edge and shot.

By Chapman's own estimate, over the two-week period he and his comrades detonated 1,000lb of explosives, threw over 100 grenades and inflicted between 500 and 1,500 enemy casualties. It was difficult to be precise but, from the feedback he received from the locals, Chapman estimated that they derailed 7 or 8 trains, damaged or destroyed 15 bridges, severed the rail lines in 60 places, and wrecked 40 military vehicles. Such was the success of the ambushes that the Japanese stopped using the roads at night. Earl Mountbatten, Chief of Combined Operations, later said the three men had inflicted more damage and disruption 'than a whole division of the British Army could have achieved'.

After the fourteen-day frenzy, Chapman's party was running out of explosives and fuses and the gruelling marches to and from the ambush sites were taking their toll. 'By now we were completely and utterly exhausted and our nerves could stand no more,' he said.

On 15 February, the day Singapore fell in what Churchill described as the worst defeat in British military history, Chapman and his comrades disappeared deep into the jungle to hide out at a former gold-mining camp. For good measure, they blew up one last train before leaving, watching from above as a huge bright flash and a deafening explosion erupted in the night, knocking the train from the rails and sending shrapnel flying in all directions.

On reaching the camp, Chapman turned on his wireless and heard the news that Singapore, recently fortified at enormous cost, had fallen. They were now trapped on the Malayan peninsula occupied by Japanese forces from top to bottom. Immediately they drew up rough plans to escape by boat to Ceylon, India or Sumatra. Back in the UK, he was registered as 'missing, believed killed'.

The only other British troops left on the Malayan peninsula, bar a few others who had fled into the jungle, were the thousands of prisoners of war caged in work camps in horrendous conditions. If captured, Chapman knew an even worse fate awaited him. As a saboteur, he would be tortured and beheaded. For the time being, Chapman had only one option: to try and evade the Japanese and survive in the unforgiving, dangerous world of the jungle, trying to ward off disease and the constant threat of betrayal by local informers.

Chapman, Harvey and Sartin teamed up with another 'stay-behind party' and together, on 13 March, they made a dash on bicycles under the cover of darkness to try and reach the coast. They were helped by Chinese guerrillas, but the breakout ended in catastrophe. At some point, the main group became detached from Chapman's party and ran into a Japanese patrol. A few managed to escape but most of them, including Harvey and Sartin, were captured. They were taken to a detention centre, chained, prodded with bayonets and denied food and water for two days. Eight of them managed to escape but were soon betrayed by locals. On return to the prison, they were forced to dig their own graves and were then beheaded.

Chapman, meanwhile, had fled back into the jungle with a Royal Navy Reserve officer called Clarke Haywood and trekked his way back to the Chinese guerrilla camp. Chapman grew to have great admiration and affection for the Chinese rebels. Though frustrated by the way they trained and operated as a unit, often over-complicating matters, he admired their loyalty and tremendous bravery. At enormous risk to themselves and their families, they went to great lengths to help and protect Chapman.

Soon after teaming up with the rebels, he and Haywood had set out on a mission by bike to collect equipment left at a previous hideout when they were confronted by a unit of Malayan policemen. As they pedalled away, Chapman was shot in the calf, ripping the muscle to shreds. Carrying boxes of explosives and ammunition on his handlebars, Chapman, though weak from blood loss, cycled through the night before they stopped to treat the wound. A Chinese guerrilla set about cleaning out the wound with a crude instrument made from bamboo sticks. The pain was so great that 'fortunately I fainted', Chapman recalled. The party then continued the final leg of the journey on foot through thick jungle. When they reached their destination the following afternoon, Chapman collapsed with a raging temperature. Convulsed by acute pain, cramps and fever and gasping for breath, of the days that followed Chapman said: 'I felt so ill that I thought I was going to die, so I started to write my will.' When he emerged from his delirium, Chapman thought he had been ill for two days. Haywood broke the news that it had been seventeen.

Now down to 100lb, Chapman had lost a third of his body weight. Less hardy characters may have seen the following period of time as a chance to rest and rebuild their strength – but Chapman had other ideas. 'I now had the most wonderful opportunity to study the natural history of the jungle.' And so for the next few weeks, weakened by ongoing bouts of dysentery and a chest infection, the botanist-adventurer spent his days identifying bird species and collecting specimens of plants to press which, eventually, he hoped to donate to Kew Gardens. 'I had always made a point of doing this in any country I ever visited for any length of time and I saw no reason why the presence of the Japs should prevent me now.'

Once he had regained his fitness, the Chinese planned to move Chapman and Haywood to a new camp where they would help train rebels. They set out on 9 July 1942 and, after a two-day trek through the jungle, they climbed into a Morris 8 saloon and set out along a main road. It was just as well that transport had been arranged because Haywood was now seriously ill and incapable of continuing much further on foot.

They made good progress at the beginning and Chapman was thrilled by the audacity of driving through enemy held territory in a British car, but disaster was soon to strike. Caught in the headlights of a Japanese troop truck, some of their Chinese comrades panicked and the driver swerved violently into its path, coming to a stop just in front of the truck. The party of rebels was outnumbered six to one. As Haywood and the six Chinese leapt to the left of the road, the Japanese poured out of the back of the truck and opened up on them, killing Haywood and the driver.

Chapman threw two grenades into the Japanese through a hail of gunfire, killing eight of them and injuring several others. He crawled under the Morris and then sprinted to the other side of the road, but as he disappeared into the darkness, he was hit by two bullets, one through the arm and the other along the side of his head. As he lay up behind a rubber tree, he had the presence of mind to bury his diaries with details of his own operations as well as those of his Chinese hosts. A short, intense battle followed with the Japanese adding mortar bombs to the strafing machine-gun fire. One mortar threw Chapman against a tree, leaving him dazed. Communicating with the tawny owl call, he linked up with one of the Chinese rebels and staggered into the hills.

His dysentery now forced him to stop at regular intervals to vomit and pass diarrhoea, his bullet wound to the arm was causing him agony, his face was caked in blood from the head wound and he was half dazed from the mortar blast – but Chapman had to keep going. For three hours, they crashed and stumbled through the trees as the pursuing Japanese raked the jungle with machine-gun fire. The camp to which they were headed was fourteen miles away; they had no water or food, no compass or map. But he later wrote of the incident: 'As long as a man is reasonably fit, the capabilities of the human body are almost unlimited.'

Hour after hour, through the night and the following day, he drove himself onwards, through thorn thickets and swamps, up and down steep, slippery hillsides. When they finally reached camp, Chapman collapsed with exhaustion. Told of Haywood's death, he noted that all his fellow countrymen and Western comrades were now dead or detained. From now on 'I saw no white men'. More significantly, they had been forced to leave behind all their supplies and what little comforts they had, including blankets, books and his treasured natural history notes and specimen collections.

For the next year, Chapman lived in the Chinese communist guerrilla camps helping to train the rebels. For a man of action, it was a frustrating time for the most part and he soon began to look for ways to occupy and challenge himself. Often he disappeared into the jungle for a few days at a time without a compass. Sleeping rough, he trained himself not to panic as darkness enfolded a world bristling with predators and poisonous creatures. He went barefoot and lived off the land. He hunted all manner of animals, mainly wild pigs, but also turtles, snakes and crocodiles. He became very fit, taking on as much physical work as possible to stay in shape and pass the hours. If there were heavy supplies to be carried up to the camp, he always volunteered his services, eager to prove he was every bit as effective as one of the hardened 'coolies'.

During one trek between camps, his legs were shredded by thorns and became infected. They became covered in ulcers, causing him intense pain and making movement all but impossible for six weeks. He had barely recovered when, knocked out by malaria once again, the guerrilla camp came under attack by Japanese and Sikh troops. A furious firefight followed with Chapman killing at least two Sikhs as the rebels faded into the jungle. For a week, six hundred enemy troops hunted for them, but the fugitives took to rafts on the fast-flowing rivers and slept in abandoned huts and shelters. Throughout their escape, Chapman suffered from a raging temperature and was delirious for long periods. At one point, he began to have violent convulsions when they were hiding in the undergrowth just as a Japanese patrol passed within yards of them. His teeth were chattering so loudly that the Chinese guerrillas had to gag him.

In October 1943, en route to the main guerrilla camp, he was struck down by blackwater fever, an extremely dangerous complication of malaria with a very high risk of death. Typically, it affects people who have been subjected to repeated bouts of malaria. Attacking the red blood cells, it causes anaemia, high fever and chills, racing pulse, black urine and excruciating pain. At times he convulsed so hard that he had to be pinned down. 'For a whole month, I was as ill as it is possible to be without dying,' he wrote. Today, treatment for blackwater fever includes intensive courses of drugs, full blood transfusions and complete bed rest, but even so the death rate is still about 25 to 50 per cent. Chapman had only bed rest and it is a measure of the man's physical and mental strength that, although already weakened by constant illness, he slowly began to recover.

By the end of 1943 he was eating normally again – or so he thought. At Christmas he was presented with a traditional dish by his Chinese hosts. He enjoyed it very much. 'I was told I had been eating Jap . . . I was quite interested to have sampled human flesh.' A few days later he was reunited with two British acquaintances, Richard Broome, a former colonial official, and John Davis, a chief policeman. The pair had managed to escape from Singapore and, after training with SOE, they had been reinserted into Malaya to instruct guerrillas. At first he was overjoyed to be back among compatriots but the next four months proved to be a frustrating period for Chapman. Most of it was spent sitting around in camp, running through daily drills and exercises at the request of his Chinese hosts. In April, a window of opportunity presented itself with news that a young British ethnologist, Pat Noone, had gone missing in the mountains to the north. Chapman immediately volunteered to lead a search party.

The only books of Chapman's diaries to survive his Malaya experience were those he made from this period. Today, the four notebooks, written up in his minute hand, are held in the Manuscript Collections department of Pitt Rivers Museum in Oxford. It's a thrilling experience to hold them in your hand

and imagine the man himself, filling up the pages as he sat holed up in the depths of the thick jungle, crippled with illness, Tommy gun over his lap, with the Japanese patrolling the area just a short distance away.

The first entries describe the fruitless search for Noone who, unknown to Chapman, had been murdered by a tribesman jealous of the Englishman's relationship with a beautiful young girl. His guides took him to a camp of Chinese guerrillas who were thought to know of Noone's whereabouts, but almost immediately Chapman realised the group were bandits, not guerrillas. After he found one of them going through his belongings, he discreetly packed up his rucksack with 45lb of kit and, once the camp had fallen asleep, slipped into the jungle and set off for the long trek 'home' to the friendly guerrilla camp he had left four weeks earlier.

The jungle in this area was almost impenetrable and after two days Chapman had advanced only a short distance from the bandit camp. The sound of aircraft overhead suggested that the Japanese had been alerted to his presence in the area.

His diary entry on 11 May reads: '. . . Tried to follow the ridge for an hour but had to give it up & return . . . Terrible going. Waterfalls . . . Pack very heavy & all the stumbling has skinned my shoulders . . . Very weary. Saw the track of a heeled boot? Could not be Japs up here. Saw 2 S [Sakai aboriginals] bathing & smoke of a camp fire. Hurray. Went cautiously close & suddenly saw a Jap . . . Tried to hide. Too late. Pandemonium. I had no weapon and could not run with pack. Completely dazed with exhaustion. About 5.30pm. 100 Japs. 100 Bengalis . . . They all gabbled killy-kollack, one hit me on my head with rifle butt – didn't hurt – they took my pack and searched me for weapons.'

To be captured by the Japanese effectively amounted to a death sentence. Chapman had to try and shake off his exhaustion and make a series of quick judgements. After being knocked around for a few minutes, he was taken into a tent for interrogation by a senior officer who spoke perfect English. When asked if he knew an Englishman called Colonel Chapman, he replied: 'Yes. He is my elder brother. Have you any news of him? I heard he had been killed in an ambush . . .'

Chapman told him a long-winded story about how he had been stuck in Malaya when war broke out, how he hated the Chinese guerrillas from whom he had managed to escape, how much of a pleasure it was to be back among civilised people again . . . The charm offensive and the great detail in his account gradually began to win over his interrogator. The clincher came when Chapman asked the status-conscious officer if he knew the whereabouts of two Japanese he had known at Cambridge, Prince Hashisuka, a keen ornithologist, and Kagami, a famous skier. His interrogator was impressed. He was soon apologising to his prisoner for not having any whisky to offer him and he congratulated him on his excellent Malay. 'We wished each other a very cordial good-night and soon there was no sound but the cracking of the fire and the heavy breathing of my bedfellows.'

Flanked by a Japanese soldier on either side of him in a dormitory tent, Chapman waited until they were asleep. When he saw the sentry outside disappear from sight, he made a dash through the opening in the canvas and shot into the thick vegetation of the jungle. He was free to live another day, but he now had another very serious, possibly lethal, problem with which to contend. He had no equipment: no maps, no compass, no weapons, no food, no anti-malarial drugs or other medical supplies. He had only '. . . my shoes, long trousers, blue pants, aertex vest, flannel shirt, handkerchief'. This may have been the appropriate dress for an evening drink with a wealthy rubber plantation owner, but it was completely unsuitable for a man facing the prospect of a fifty-mile jungle trek.

Chapman had no option but to set off. His infuriated captors would soon to be on his tail. He kept going for twenty-four hours despite having not slept for almost three days. When he did finally allow himself some rest, he covered himself from the heavy rain by lying under some banana leaves on the jungle floor. The next night he slept in a cave. He had no idea where he was. On 12 May he wrote in his diary: 'Very hard to keep direction but marked my track by bending twigs.' It was tough going, up and down steep gorges and hillsides through the dense vegetation with no parang to cut a path and nothing to eat but ubi [tapioca] leaves and unripe pineapples. To his horror, two days later he discovered that he had walked in a giant circle. 'In late PM came to my cave! Same river I followed up 2 days ago but different tributary . . . Much disturbed by brand new

S. [Sakai] tracks here. Found 2 small unripe pineapples . . . Not hungry but weak and light-headed. The ubi leaves made me drink all day. Slept well in cave. No snakes. V heavy rain 4 pm on.'

He knew the Japanese were close. The next day, 15 May, he recorded: 'Away 5.30. Found paper of Jap biscuits in track. Not here 3 days ago. Drank out of puddles in track . . . Found a track covered with Jap boot marks and cigarette papers.'

For the next ten days, Chapman continued his trek in what he hoped, rather than knew for certain under the dark canopy of the jungle, was a southerly direction. With little food to sustain him, Chapman grew weaker by the day. On 24 May, his mounting despair becomes evident: 'Terribly steep and thick . . . two terrible days.'

Chapman was falling ill and he knew that he had very quickly to find somewhere to hole up. Mustering the last of his strength, he staggered in the direction of a small hut he had passed earlier, crawling on his hands and knees for the last part of the journey. 'Very very exhausted. Realise I have fever. Retire to bed.' That was 25 May.

Chapman knew that he was now in very serious danger of dying. He was on his own, but for a handful of Sakai aborigines living close by. They were able to bring him water and ubi leaves from time to time, but they were too frightened of Japanese reprisals to make more than the occasional visit and they refused to carry an SOS message to the nearest Chinese guerrillas to alert his colleagues back at the main camp. It was not only a fresh bout of malaria from which he was suffering; he also had around two dozen leech bites and scratches on his legs that had become infected and turned into potentially fatal ulcers. Gangrene and blood poisoning were a serious risk if left untreated.

For day after day he swooned in and out of consciousness, forcing himself to get up, drink water, eat leaves and bathe his ulcerated legs. His diary entries reveal a man on the edge of death. Sweating and feverish, he lay in his jungle hideout, singing love songs and remembering old girlfriends. The diary entries reveal his rambling thought processes: 'Am often comatose but never I think delirious . . . Had to pee in coconut shell & throw it out, had to shit in leaves & throw it out . . . I just roared and roared with laughter. Tried to pray. Said Lord's prayer over & over but could not get beyond childhood picture of bearded old man sitting on clouds . . . Decided I had superb but not successful enough life . . .'

On the eighth day, alerted by the barking of a dog, he saw two Japanese and about a dozen Sikhs approaching his hut. They were just yards away when he managed to crawl though the back of the shelter into the jungle behind. He watched as they tried to burn the hut down, but it was too damp. Chapman spent another week immobilised by illness but little by little he began to recover and, on 9 June, the fever finally began to subside. The following day, emaciated and dizzy, he set off again. On he trekked, exhausted and racked with pain. 'Fell flat on my back in faint,' his dairy entry of 13 June reads. 'Bad fever all PM. Terribly hot & furious pulse. Could not eat.' Some good fortune finally came his way when, a week later, some friendly locals agreed to guide him to the nearest Chinese guerrilla camp. By then, illness had flared up again. 'Terrible pain behind eyes unless I lie down. Weak as old woman. Dizzy if I do anything. Pulse 80–90. No appetite. Sleep badly.'

The base, he soon discovered, was a traitor-killing camp where the communist rebels exterminated anyone suspected of collaborating with the Japanese. 'A marvellous secure place,' he recorded '. . . Very good lot of men. They have been hereabouts for years and have shot literally 100s of spies.' In his memoirs, he says it was over a thousand. They nursed and fed their British guest like one of their own and arranged for guides from his camp to come and escort him back. The trek took ten gruelling days, but when finally, on 25 July, over three months after leaving them, he staggered back among his friends, he was so thin and ill that no one recognised him at first.

The chapter in his memoirs describing the months that followed his return is entitled 'A Year of Frustration'. Chapman had had enough of the jungle, the serious illness, the heat and humidity, the tedium of training. He was now desperate to get out. He had been on the run behind enemy lines for two and a half years. He and his two British colleagues, Broome and Davis, had no idea what was happening in the world beyond. But in November 1944 they managed to rig up a wireless set and, to their joy, listened to the voice of a well-spoken British broadcaster announce news of Allied successes in Europe and the Far East. Hope hovered on the horizon.

In January 1945 he fell seriously ill again – as ill, he said, as he ever had been. The symptoms were the usual combination of high fever and chills, vomiting, intense headaches, swollen glands and almost unbearable cramps and pains. Suspecting Weil's disease from rat's urine, his colleagues were convinced he was going to die. His temperature rocketed to 105 and then hovered between 102 and 104 for several days. He was so ill that his diary lay unkept for three weeks.

During this latest bout, his colleagues managed to build a two-way radio and transmit a message to Ceylon. To their delight, five days later the set crackled into life and they received a reply. Soon afterwards, Allied planes began to drop supplies, including vital medical ones, as well as home comforts such as bacon, chocolate, rum and whisky. Among the supplies was a new anti-malaria pill called mepacrine that proved highly effective. Having been laid low by malaria for almost half the time they had been in the camp, from then on no one succumbed again. The Allied fightback was not just military, it was medical and logistical.

By the beginning of March, Chapman was fit enough to start doing exercises again but his recovery was slow. In mid-April, a plan was made to extract him and Broome by submarine from an island off the south-western coast of the peninsula. The Chinese were to provide a series of guides to take them there, but it was a journey fraught with danger at every turn.

They set off at dawn on 27 April to make the prearranged rendezvous on 13 May. The pattern was the same every day for ten days: hard trekking at night and lying up during daylight hours, but the final leg of the journey was the most perilous. To get to the island they had to go by sampan, a 20-foot wooden boat in which the single oarsman stood up to row. Setting out on the first of several fast-moving tributaries, guided through the watery maze by the oarsman, the boat was swept into the mighty Perak River which was so wide that Chapman couldn't see the banks on the far side. Transferring to a larger vessel, they paddled through creeks thick with overhanging vegetation and full of giant mosquitoes, crocodiles, and snakes curling over the branches above their heads.

At various points they were put ashore and forced to march through hideous terrain including mangrove swamps, and fetid, foul-smelling mud in which they sank up to their knees. Two days before the scheduled pick-up from the small island of Pangkor Laut, they set out at sunrise in a small fishing boat, operated by the guide. Dropped in a small sandy bay of the idyllic island, the two men darted into the trees that fringed the sands. They had enough rations to last a week, but no radio equipment to communicate with British forces. They had been told to hold out a white sheet during daylight to alert the sub waiting offshore. At 7.10 a.m. on 13 May 1945, they spotted a periscope. The men put out the white sheet, packed up their gear and waited until dusk for contact with their rescuers.

'. . . All set by 6,' Chapman wrote in his diary. 'No sign of ship since 3. Flashed [torch] 7–8.30. Get very tired of it . . . About 9.10 saw a shadow. 5 secs after heard a hail Ahoy! Saw appearing 2 men in boat. Collected gear & ran to edge . . . All OK. Then: "You'll have to swim, we have got no boat." I could not believe it. I made them repeat it! Swam out with gear on back. Phosphorescence. Easy: only 50 yds. Saw C. [conning] tower and 3" gun. Climbed up slippery side by line & over rail. Found a group of very tall, very young darkly bearded men in sarongs . . . Wardroom 6x6x7. 5 bunks, lot of sailors. Chart table. Air tubes. Couch. I sleep on campbed under table.'

It was five days after the war in Europe had come to an end and three and a half years since he had disappeared into the mountainous jungles of Malaya. Against all the odds, Freddy Spencer Chapman, posted 'missing, believed killed', was very much alive and well.

In recognition of his remarkable exploits and operational achievements, Chapman was promoted to lieutenant colonel and given a Distinguished Service Order and bar, but not the Victoria Cross that a great many people, including Earl Mountbatten, were convinced he deserved.

After the war Chapman married, had three children and returned to the teaching profession, becoming a headmaster at schools in Germany and South Africa, leaving the latter in disgust at the hardening of the apartheid regime. He ended up as warden of a hall of residence at Reading University. Forced to retire early owing to ill health, Chapman was suffering from one of the periodic bouts of depression that had dogged him since his days at Cambridge when he shot himself in the head in his office on 8 August 1971. He was sixty-four.

Captain John Randle

If a panel of experts was tasked with ranking the 182 acts of the
Second World War that led to the award of a Victoria Cross
based on the criteria of sheer guts in the critical moment of an
action, it would have a job on its hands to find one that topped
the deeds of John 'Jack' Randle of the Royal Norfolk Regiment.
His was an act of pure self-sacrifice that took place in May 1944
during the Battle of Kohima, a truly vicious, strategically crucial
encounter between British and Japanese forces on the India/Burma
border. Randle had already earned the equivalent of a regimental
blazer's worth of decorations for his actions over the previous
two days when, bloodied and muddied from helmet to boot, he
found it within himself to produce an extraordinarily selfless act

of valour. As he leapt from his position to carry it out, he must have known that his death was certain. His award was only ever going to be a posthumous one.

Before continuing, I have to declare an interest: In 1964 the Royal Norfolks merged with other regiments to become the Royal Anglians, a regiment very special to me. My father served in the ranks of the reconstituted regiment and I have twice had the honour of being embedded with them on tours to Afghanistan. Regimental loyalties aside, few could argue that the inspirational actions of Jack Randle do not merit inclusion in a book honouring some of our most courageous servicemen. The man deserves a full twenty-one-gun salute, not just a glowing write-up.

The stakes couldn't have been higher at the Kohima. Having gained control of Burma, the Japanese were massing in their hundreds of thousands, waiting for the final breakthrough that would allow them to stream towards Delhi and break the British in the Far East. For weeks, a small motley force of British troops had been fighting desperately to cling on to a small patch of land that controlled the only route in and out of India. Further down the road, a far larger force of British troops had been encircled in the plains of Imphal and their fate was tied to whatever happened at Kohima. The British were desperately trying to bring in reinforcements from India, but were hampered in doing so on many fronts. The RAF played a vital role in sustaining the British effort, flying thousands of sorties to drop supplies and equipment and attack the enemy.

By the battle's close, the RAF had flown in 19,000 tons of supplies, 12,000 men and evacuated 13,000 casualties and 43,000 noncombatants. Without their contribution, the British forces on the ground could not have fought on.

The first phase of the Battle of Kohima pitched 13,000 soldiers of the Japanese 31st Division against 1,500 men of the 4th Battalion The Queen's Own (Royal West Kent Regiment) supported by a few garrison troops from the Assam Rifles and the Assam Regiment. So close, so intense, so desperate was the fighting that on many occasions it became an old-fashioned hand-to-hand encounter involving knives, bayonets and fists. At one stage, the only territory that stood between the two forces was the tennis court in the grounds of the Deputy Commissioner's home. The losses sustained by the West Kents and their Indian comrades were dreadful, but still they refused to yield this key stretch of ground high up on a ridge. It has been said many times and without any exaggeration that the fighting at Kohima between 4 April and 22 June 1944 was the most ferocious experienced by any British forces over a sustained period throughout the entire six years of the global conflict.

While the West Kents battled to stand their ground against an overwhelming force, the 2nd Infantry Division, which included the Royal Norfolks, was many hundreds of miles away deep inside India. As commanders reacted to the rapidly unfolding emergency, the men of 2nd Division were transported by any means available to get them to the front as quickly as possible. The Japanese had cut the main road and the relief units did not have the luxury of time or even a suitable location in which to concentrate before going forward into battle as a coherent, well-organised force. They were sent straight into action unit by unit the moment they arrived.

Even when the British managed to retake the Kohima road and pour in reinforcements, they were still faced with a daunting challenge, first, to hold back an almost maniacal Japanese force hell-bent on breaking through to Delhi and, secondly, to drive them off the ridge dominating the surrounding area. Dug deep into commanding hillsides and well supplied with equipment and provisions, the enemy's position was extremely strong. It was going to take an almighty effort of will to dislodge a force prepared to fight to the last man. A direct assault up the steep hills was out of the question and the commanders opted to send one brigade to the east and one to the west to try and turn the flanks of the Japanese. The monsoon rain fell from the sky in sheets as the troops waded and hacked through mud and thick jungle up the slopes. But helped by the local Naga tribesmen working as guides, equipment porters and stretcher-bearers, the two brigades slowly crawled their way forward. On reaching the top, they took the enemy by surprise and, after a series of fierce engagements, overran their positions. The Royal Norfolks had played a key role in taking the flanks of the ridge – and without the customary assistance of a softening-up artillery bombardment. But one headland, laced with well-entrenched Japanese bunkers, continued to hold out.

John Neil Randle, a twenty-six-year-old who had known little else in his life but school and war, was commander of B Company of the Royal Norfolks' battalion. Those who witnessed the temporary captain's actions on 4 and 5 May say he had already earned his Victoria Cross before the critical action took place the following day. B Company were ordered to carry out a frontal attack at first light on 6 May to take the heavily defended Japanese positions. What few published or unpublished accounts there are of Randle's actions, all appear to be based on the citation for his Victoria Cross that was announced in the *London Gazette* six months after his death. In plain facts, it tells us everything we need to know about his sacrifice:

On the 4th May, 1944, at Kohima in Assam, a Battalion of the Norfolk Regiment attacked the Japanese positions on a nearby ridge. Captain Randle took over command of the Company which was leading the attack when the Company Commander was severely wounded. His handling of a difficult situation in the face of heavy fire was masterly and although wounded himself in the knee by grenade splinters he continued to inspire his men by his initiative, courage and outstanding leadership until the Company had captured its objective and consolidated its position. He then went forward and brought in all the wounded men who were lying outside the perimeter. In spite of his painful wound Captain Randle refused to be evacuated and insisted on carrying out a personal reconnaissance with great daring in bright moon-

light prior to a further attack by his Company on the position to which the enemy had withdrawn. At dawn on 6th May the attack opened, led by Captain Randle, and one of the platoons succeeded in reaching the crest of the hill held by the Japanese. Another platoon, however, ran into heavy medium machine gun fire from a bunker on the reverse slope of the feature.

Captain Randle immediately appreciated that this particular bunker covered not only the rear of his new position but also the line of communication of the battalion and therefore the destruction of the enemy post was imperative if the operation was to succeed. With utter disregard of the obvious danger to himself Captain Randle charged the Japanese machine gun post single-handed with rifle and bayonet. Although bleeding in the face and mortally wounded by numerous bursts of machine gun fire he reached the bunker and silenced the gun with a grenade thrown through the bunker slit. He then flung his body across the slit so that the aperture should be completely sealed. The bravery shown by this officer could not have been surpassed and by his self-sacrifice he saved the lives of many of his men and enabled not only his own Company but the whole Battalion to gain its objective and win a decisive victory over the enemy.

Jack Randle quite literally laid down his life for his comrades.

The battle for the ridge continued for the next ten days. Wave after wave of attack and counter-attack rolled back and forth in torrential monsoon rains across a terrain littered with broken bodies. It was painfully slow progress but inch by inch, hour by hour, the British and Indian troops gained the upper hand, finally seizing control on the night of 16 May when the 2nd Battalion The Dorsets, with the help of a tank that had been dragged up through the mud, drove the Japanese off the tennis court once and for all.

Most historians agree that the Battle of Kohima was the decisive encounter of the Burma campaign. Had the Japanese prevailed, it is highly unlikely that the tens of thousands of British troops at Imphal could have been relieved. Carnage or imprisonment awaited them. The defeat was the beginning of an overthrow that saw the Japanese rolled all the way back to the Burmese capital Rangoon where they had little choice but to surrender. The Japanese lost more soldiers in the campaign against the British and Indians in Burma than in any other theatre of the conflict in the Far East.

Earl Mountbatten described the encounter as 'one of the greatest battles in history . . . naked unparalleled heroism . . . the British/Indian Thermopylae'. Pictures of the ground over which they fought reveal a landscape similar to the worst battlefield of the Great War: a hell of tree stumps, waist-deep mud littered with mutilated bodies. The recollections of survivors are enough to make a grown man weep with pity and awe at the heroics of those who refused to surrender. Indeed, the bomber pilot Leonard Cheshire, a great war hero himself, actually did weep when he read of the courage of his old friend Jack Randle on those murderous slopes. Randle is buried in the Kohima War Cemetery in Plot: 2. C. 8. The inscription on the British war memorial in the hill town reads:

When you go home
Tell them of us and say
For their tomorrow
We gave our today.

Captain Noel Chavasse

On 22 July 1912, Noel Chavasse stood on the threshold of what promised to be a glorious career: an idyllic childhood lay behind him and, having just qualified as a doctor, a golden future stretched out before him. He had left Oxford with an athletics blue and a first-class honours degree, competed in the 1908 Olympics and he had just secured a post at the prestigious Royal Southern Hospital, providing medical care to the poor of his home city of Liverpool. For many years, his ambition had been to use his abundant natural gifts and privileged upbringing to help the less fortunate in society. Like his identical twin Christopher and their five siblings, the son of the Anglican Bishop of Liverpool had been brought up with a strong sense of civic and patriotic duty. Working as house surgeon under the renowned orthopaedic specialist Robert Jones in Toxteth, one of the most impoverished districts of Britain, was exactly the challenging opportunity he had set his heart on.

As his family toasted his latest success, little could they have imagined that in five years' time, almost to the day, the boy with the world at his feet would be crawling, blood pouring from several serious shrapnel wounds, through the cratered, corpse-strewn mud of Flanders. None who had met him, however, would be in the least surprised to learn that, ignoring his own injuries, the young medic was dragging himself through the hellish landscape in order to raise the alarm and find help for his wounded colleagues.

Out of the millions of men to serve King and Country in the most brutal war ever fought, Noel Chavasse was the only one to win the Victoria Cross twice. He never fired a shot or thrust a sword in anger, but this modest, conscientious, humorous young medical officer has a strong claim to be regarded as the most courageous man to have pulled on a British military uniform. Some display their valour in one bold action, others over the course of a campaign, but Chavasse showed sustained courage over a period of almost three years. That he lived for so long in the ferocious killing fields of Flanders was remarkable enough in itself; but the fact that he kept at his work, tending thousands of wounded men when so many of his colleagues had folded under the pressure, speaks of a man of superhuman strength of character.

In early 1913, war with Germany looming, Noel was accepted by the Royal Army Medical Corps (RAMC) and was attached, as surgeon lieutenant, to 10th (Scottish) Battalion The King's (Liverpool Regiment), a territorial unit known to all as 'the Liverpool Scottish'. On 2 August 1914, two days before Britain declared war, he said farewell to his colleagues, strode out of the Royal Southern and set off with the battalion for a training camp. He was never to return.

The first of hundreds of letters to his family soon began to arrive. Highly detailed and candid, full of strong opinions and good humour, the letters, currently held at the Bodleian Library in Oxford, offer an intensely powerful and moving insight into life in the trenches of Flanders, of boyish innocence wrecked by harrowing experience. By the time the reader reaches the last letter in the bottom of the archive box it is difficult to stop the lower lip from quivering and the tears from rolling.

The letters begin with great enthusiasm and a confidence that the patriotic young men of Britain will make short work of the 'Hun'. For the modern reader, knowing the horrors that were soon to be, this only makes his optimism and characteristic humour that much more poignant.

On 5 September he wrote to his father from the Liverpool Scottish camp in King's Park, Edinburgh: 'I find the officers much changed, even the most flighty of them are talking more seriously . . . they all think that the war will do England a lot of good, and that it wanted pulling up . . . Everyone here is trying to grow a moustache and so I am having a go too.' His main task at the camp had been to vaccinate the battalion against typhoid.

With the war almost three months in, Chavasse and his comrades were eager to get to the front and do their bit before the fighting was over. The widespread view was that the conflict would be short. As a territorial unit, the London Scottish were not expected to see any front-line action, but the men were keen to help support the regular troops. On 27 October Chavasse wrote to his bed-ridden mother from a camp in Tunbridge Wells to which the London Scottish had moved:

'We have today received unexpected but very excellent news. We have been ordered to France and we go on Friday . . . It is a great honour to be sent out so soon and we were getting rather disheartened over it.' Four days later, 829 men and 26 officers of the Liverpool Scottish boarded a troop train for Southampton docks from where they set sail for Le Havre.

As they moved up towards the front line, Chavasse's thoughts were focused not on the treatment of combat injuries, but on hygiene and disease. Potentially, germs posed a far more devastating threat than the German guns and shells. Tetanus, for which there was no vaccine, was a major worry. The bacterial infection was most likely to occur when an open wound became contaminated with manure or faeces. A prophylactic serum injected into wounded men offered the only protection. Obsessive about inoculation and cleanliness, Chavasse was one of the first doctors to use the serum as a matter of routine.

The men of the London Scottish were impressed by their

medical officer's almost obsessive attention to detail and devotion to their every need. From the moment the battalion arrived in France, Chavasse was on the hunt for supplies and equipment to make their lives safer and more comfortable. He proved to be highly resourceful in ordering, demanding and scrounging all manner of provisions and even buying them with his own money. He was also imaginative in the choice of supplies he acquired. He brought in gallons of castor oil to keep boots soft and administered foot massages after a long march. He got hold of a gramophone – then something of a rarity – to play popular tunes and keep up spirits in his dressing station. He even requisitioned a cow to provide a constant supply of fresh milk. His lively character and ardent commitment to the troops soon established him, in the words of one of the men, as the 'mascot' of the battalion.

In a letter to his father dated 17 November he played down the dangers that lay a few miles ahead and, with typical modesty, claims he lacked the courage to put himself in harm's way: 'I am behind at headquarters . . . where I sit waiting for wounded to be brought to me. I believe that doctors are not allowed in the trenchs [sic] so I really shall run very little risk during the war and I do not intend to run any risk at all unnecessarily; my blood is not heroic.'

The battalion moved into the front line for the first time on the night of 27 November. From their billets in the Belgian village of Westoutre, they marched up to the trenches to relieve the Highland Light Infantry, close to the demolished town of Kemmel, six miles south west of Ypres. In another letter to his father he describes his shock at the devastation in Kemmel. 'The town was a mass of ruins and absolutely deserted. There were large holes in the road where shells had burst, now ponds, the roads were dreadfully muddy. Everything is ankle deep in mud here . . .'

Noel and his orderlies prepared to deal with the wounded. The system set up by the RAMC was for stretcher-bearers to collect wounded and carry the worst cases to the Regimental Aid Post (RAP), the forwardmost medical position. After primary treatment, the wounded were then taken further back, first to the advanced dressing station, then beyond to the main dressing station. Those requiring specialist treatment were transferred to huge Casualty Clearing Stations and, if they were long-term casualties, removed to the sprawling Base Hospitals along the coast before being taken back to Britain. For four years, an endless procession of wounded men, over a million British and Commonwealth combatants, were to make their way through this system.

Noel's first patient was his friend and former schoolmate at Liverpool College, Captain Arthur Twentyman, who led the first company into action. He was hit in the chest by a bullet and died of his wound. Chavasse wrote to his father describing his efforts to recover Twentyman's body.

I feel very sad about it because I liked him the best of the lot and he had always been unbelievably kind to me . . . I miss him very much . . . A guide led us up to the trenches and we got sniped at a bit especially at one place where a German had a gun trained on a bit of the road . . . I took all the cover I could chiefly in wet ditches . . . I made my way to where the poor captain lay. At first the zip zip of bullets hitting the sandbags close to one's head was rather disconcerting, then it became just part of the general environment. At one place we had to get out and double past a gate – where a sniper lay in wait. I went by doing the 100 well within 10 secs. We got to the poor captain lying in the mud at the back of the trench. We fitted up a temporary stretcher with two poles and a great coat. Then we climbed out of the trench and 2 of us carried him back. This was the risky part because the moon was full & bright & we had to carry him along the back of the trench where there was a crossfire. He was dreadfully heavy . . . then we had to cross a ploughed field for about 400 yards . . . but we had to rest 5 times during this bit. During one of these halts we stopped where about 10 dead Frenchmen lay. One of them was in a shallow grave but there was enough left to take cover in.

Chavasse refers to running through the Germans bullets; it was his speed as a sprinter that would keep him alive on many occasions over the coming years, dashing across the no-man's-land before a sniper could secure a fix on him.

The letters home reveal Chavasse's astonishment at the conditions in which the Tommies were fighting and how quickly they reduced proud, smartly turned-out men into a bedraggled mass. He wrote: 'Our men have had a terrible experience of 72 hours in the trenches, drenched through and in some places knee-deep in mud and water. They don't look like strong young men. They are muddied to the eyes. Their coats are plastered with mud and weigh an awful weight with the water which has soaked in. Their backs are bent and they stagger and totter along with the weight of their packs. Their faces are white and haggard and their eyes glare out from mud which, with short bristly beards, gives them an almost beastlike look ... I have seen nothing like it. The collapse after running or rowing is nothing to it. Many, too many, who are quite beat, have to be told they must walk it. Then comes a nightmare of a march ...'

This is taken from his first major dispatch from the front line and it was just as well he didn't know that their experiences so far were nothing but a light introduction to the terror to follow.

Chavasse was soon dealing with a flood of blast injuries. 'These head injuries are very distressing as the men live for so long with frightful mutilations although happily they are unconscious,' he wrote. 'One man lost the whole of the side of his head and a large part of his brain, yet lived and was semi-conscious for two days ... his brother arrived with another Liverpool battalion at the front the day he died and about the first duty of the poor fellow on arriving was to attend his brother's funeral.'

It soon became obvious to Chavasse that the Germans were not the only enemy they were fighting. There were other, equally serious problems. In that first, very wet winter of the conflict, trench foot was the most pressing concern. At the time the condition was little understood and was known as 'frost bite'.

The scourge of the infantryman hit the British troops with a vengeance before Christmas. In the Kemmel section of the line, as in many others, there were no dugouts, duckboards or water-pumps, very few sandbags and there were no repairs made to the damage caused by constant shelling. The outbreak of it was not helped by serious supply problems to the forward lines and a severe shortage of effective clothing and equipment for the men. All efforts were going into simply holding the line. By the end of December, the Liverpool Scottish officers and ranks had been reduced from 855 men to 370. Of those thirty-two had been killed or wounded; the rest succumbed to trench foot. By the time the troops had reached front-line trenches they were already sodden and covered in mud, wading through it up to their waists for long stretches. They then spent days with their legs submerged in near freezing mud and water. When their boots were removed back in their billets days later, their feet were numb and swollen, occasionally gangrenous and needing the amputation of a toe or sometimes an entire foot. Blisters burst and became infected.

Long before any official efforts were made to combat the condition, Chavasse was writing home and asking for hundreds of pairs of warm socks. In a letter to his father from 'Dressing Station, Belgium', written in early March, he explained how he had successfully combated the problem. 'They get their feet dried & warmed & rubbed and a pair of dry socks put on, the result being that we have not seen any case of so called "frost bite".' Chavasse also arranged for great fires to be burning for them on their return from the front, sending out the lightly wounded to collect the wood.

Lack of food was a problem, too, compounding the misery for the Tommies up and down the line. No field cookers meant no hot food, only tins of bully beef and biscuits. All meals, including dixie cans of hot tea, had to be carried up to the front, often under falling shells over a mile or two of cratered, mud-thick terrain. Often it would never arrive but, if it did, the tea was invariably as cold as the mud in which the men stood.

At the same time, an infestation of body lice was afflicting the entire British Army, prompting Chavasse to step up his already determined efforts to raise standards of cleanliness. He collected dozens of tubs so that the men could have regular hot baths and wash their clothes. The lice were more than just a skin irritation, they robbed the already exhausted troops of their sleep. When a soldier scratched too hard and broke the skin, the eggs of the louse caused boils and impetigo. Towards the end of the war, doctors had worked out that 'trench fever', a severe flu-like condition that affected tens of thousands of men, was caused by the waste matter of the body louse.

Some advised that men should rub themselves and their clothes in petrol to ward off the lice but this practice was stopped abruptly when one man set fire to himself when striking a match, and ran through the camp in flames before dying. Noel put to work the walking wounded and any other free hands available to ensure his dressing stations were of the very highest quality. His heart-felt letters home pleaded for donations and helped galvanise the people of Liverpool to even greater efforts on behalf of their men in the front line. Soon the supplies began to arrive: clothing, field stoves and, later, even an entire field hospital. Liverpool was the only city during the war to establish and fund its own hospital in the war zone, staffed with its own citizens.

The casualties came thick and fast across Chavasse's treatment table. In a graphic but unsentimental letter home, he described his experiences on Christmas Eve in an inn converted into a dressing station: '. . . Four men staggered in with a stretcher & dumped it down in the middle of the room. A bugler holding a candle gave the light & we had to cut the filthy coat off the poor fellow, then we cut away the kilt, and so came upon the wound, a great slash in the back muscles. All I could do was to paint the wound with iodine, swab it with pure carbolic and bandage. We cut his boots and puttees off and a bugler rubbed away at his feet but we could not get them warm . . . After this, man after man arrived. One could really do little for them. The wounds one had to dress were not the clean punctures I had imagined gunshot wounds to be . . . to take an instance of a wound in the fleshy part of the thigh, the entrance wound was neat and punctured but the exit was a gaping burst, a big hole that I could put my fist into, with broken muscles hanging out . . .'

Experiences that in other circumstances would be considered remarkable were barely acknowledged in the chaos of the war.

In January 1915, he wrote matter-of-factly that the battalion had lost its two rugby heroes, a Scotland captain and an England international, who were buried next to each other in a Flemish churchyard. Both graves were later destroyed by shelling.

In March he wrote of a boisterous evening in his dressing station: 'In our room this evening there was a wild scene. A Captain and two Subs [subalterns] came in and we had a musical evening. The officers then tuned in with 12 miners and they all drank cocoa and very diluted brandy . . . Outside the door, there lay muffled up in their oil sheets, rigid and still, two poor men who had laid down their lives that morning – we are, I think, mercifully numbed, or who would ever smile here? They say that after three months an officer loses his nerve, from sheer nervous drain, but so far I have, please God, a good hold on myself . . .'

At the time of writing, the battalion had been moved forward into the Ypres Salient to prepare for a major offensive. When it came, the strain pushed Chavasse and the fighting men of the Liverpool Scottish to the limits of their endurance.

Ypres, or 'Wipers' as it was known to the British troops, is a small town that blocked the route to Calais. Road, rail and canals converged there making it an important transport and communication hub. The town soon attracted repeated attacks by the Germans, inspiring formidable defence by the British. The top brass decided that Ypres was to be held at all costs to prevent the Germans breaking out to the coast. To protect the once prosperous medieval cloth town, they built a salient of layered defences around it. Throughout the war, wave after wave of attack crashed upon the British lines of defences, wreaking death and destruction on an epic scale. Three major battles were fought in the Ypres Salient, including Passchendaele, causing between 300,000 and 400,000 British casualties (the figures have been a subject of dispute).

The Liverpool Scottish billeted in the St Eloi area, with half the battalion sent to the front-line trenches and the rest held in reserve in huts a few miles back. Shells rained down on the area throughout their stay as the Germans attempted – and eventually succeeded – in reducing Ypres to a giant pile of rat-infested rubble.

In a letter home, Noel wrote:

Every now and then there passes overhead a thunderous shriek, like an express train tearing through a small station. This is followed by a dull roar . . . I don't know what thunderbolts of wrath were hurled on the cities of the plains, but they could not have been more terrible than those forged by the Hun. We hear them pass over all day and we hear them crash and, looking over tangled and pockmarked fields, we can see great pillars of smoke and dust rising from the tortured city.

It is wonderful to see how quickly but how graciously Nature tries to hide the hideous scars made by man in the countryside. I have now lived for a month in a shattered village 400 yards behind our trenches. When we came at the beginning of April, all around was a stark, staring, hideous abomination of desolation . . . Now the shells of the houses are being veiled by blossom. In the rubbish flowers are forcing their ways up to the sunlight . . . Meanwhile, between the bursts of cannonade, the birds sing ever so sweetly and are building everywhere. I found a nest only yesterday in an old dugout . . .

But in the coming weeks there was precious little to cheer and at the beginning of the summer the battalion suffered its darkest day of the conflict since deployment. Officially called the 'first action of Bellewaerde', it is known to the Liverpool Scottish as the Battle of Hooge. The plan was to take enemy trenches between the Menin Road and Ypres–Roulers railway while the rest of 9th Brigade of 3rd Division pushed forward on either side.

Chavasse's account of what happened on 16 June 1915 is plainly distressing.

'. . . When we came out of the trenches, we were told we were to have 10 days' rest & that every officer was to have five days leave,' he wrote home, four days after the event. 'I put in for leave but next day all leave was cancelled & we were told confidentially that the battalion in a few days would take part in a charge on the German trenches.'

The battalion knew they were facing their most daunting challenge because when parsons arrived on Sunday 13 June, 150 men paraded for Holy Communion, 80 to Presbyterian Communion and 50 to Roman Catholic mass. 'I know every man was commending his soul to God,' added Chavasse.

We went up to the trenches from which we were to jump off on the night of the 15th. It was an eight mile march & the pipers played us for 4 miles. There was a tremendous stream of men along the road as a whole brigade was to attack. The men were in the best of spirits, & sang all the way – my stretcher bearers who had their number increased to 24 as usual making a joyful noise & had finally to be silenced by the Adjutant . . . At 2am a terrific bombardment began & went on till 4am, but I was so tired that I dozed through it. But at 5am I was woken up by the first batch of wounded coming down . . . they came down a long communication trench in a steady stream. Meanwhile the Huns began to put crumps and shrapnel down the road. Our CO arrived with an artery bleeding in his head which was troublesome to stop as we had to tie him down at the back as a crump landed too near the dressing station for safety . . .

Leaving three wound dressers at their station, Chavasse headed into the network of trenches to fetch a man reported to have fallen.

I found the trench blocked with men who had dropped exhausted trying to drag themselves down. The Huns were putting big shells into the trenches and making direct hits so that in places the trench was blown in . . . arrived back to find another crump had burst just outside our dressing station and killed four men next door and wrecked our place . . . slipped up to the trenches to see how our boys were getting on there and took with me, besides dressings, two bottles of lime juice and a sack full of water bottles left by wounded men. We found the top end of the communications trenches blocked by wounded men. I dressed 30 of them . . . our stretcher bearers who had carried very well all the morning were now lying exhausted. The wounded men of my battalion were lying out in the road in front of a mud wall, no protection at all against the crumps or the sun. One poor chap half naked was already blistered . . . I went up & down the trenches with my dressings . . .

. . . When I got out it was dusk so I went with a trusty man & searched for wounded (I knew where the charge had taken place.) We found most of them in a little coppice. They were so weak they could not call out. Their joy and relief on being found was pitiful and fairly spurred us on to look for more . . . It was awful work getting some out of these trenches and dugouts. It was hard to find men enough to carry them. I had to appeal for volunteers but they were deadbeat. Finally at dawn we got our last man away from a very advanced front. On getting back . . . we found that the RAMC had failed us and had not carried any of our wounded back. But fatigue parties took pity on the poor chaps and carried all away one by one except 11 [?]. Then I set to work to dress those we had carried in, got them arranged along the mud wall & then fell asleep sitting on a petrol tin.

The plan of attack had been for Chavasse's 10th Battalion Liverpool Scottish to take the first trench, with a separate battalion following up to take the second, before the 10th leapfrogged them and took the third. The total distance covered was just under 1,000 yards and the artillery was to bombard each trench before it was taken. But, as Chavasse explained to his father, the London Scottish became accidental victims of their own success as they charged into the hail of fire.

... as a matter of fact our chaps made such a splendid rush that they carried all three trenches in 15 minutes & even penetrated to the fourth line. A great many of our own fellows got wiped out by our own shells ... then for some reason the people on our right gave way and the Germans also began to come round on the left so our men were in the air at both ends and had to retire to the first line we had taken ... In this way a great many wounded fell into German hands, many of them great friends of mine ... The remnants of our battalion was relieved the same night, 130 men reached the camp out of 550 who had marched out the previous day and 2 officers, both lieuts [sic], left out of 22 ... Dreadfully saddened. I am missing jolly faces everywhere & it was dreadful to see our great big fellows strewn on the ground as common fodder.

The letter was signed as always 'ever your loving son, Noel'.

In only a few hours almost the entire battalion was wiped out. In truth, only a minority were captured or wounded; most of the missing were dead. A more eloquent description of the carnage at the Battle of Hooge would be difficult to find.

A long list of recommendations for awards was drawn up by the Commanding Officer but this was destroyed by a fire in Brigade HQ before it could be sent back to London. Chavasse was recommended the Military Cross but when, two weeks later, he was told that it was going to be announced at a church parade, he stayed away. One of the men reported seeing the medical officer sitting in a wood, crying, while his name was read out a few hundred yards away. But if he was suffering from trauma, it certainly didn't show in his letters just a couple of weeks after the slaughter. Once again they resonate with his determined spirit.

By this stage of the war, the hideousness of the fighting was taking its toll on the overworked doctors and many of them chose to leave the front – much to Chavasse's disgust. In a letter of 15 August 1915, he wrote: 'I'm afraid that a great many medical officers have relinquished their temporary commissions, most simply became "fed up" or upset because so many of their officer pals have gone. Very poor reasons one would think for deserting one's country. I don't think they will stand doing nothing for long.

'I am now in the proud position of being the only regimental doctor who has not broken down . . . I am very glad I am so fit because I have a tremendous attatchment [sic] to the regiment and could not bear to leave it.' In fact he was the only doctor left in the entire brigade that had arrived in Flanders nine months earlier. He was made Senior Medical Officer. 'The only qualification for it is existence,' he commented drily.

Chavasse was promoted to captain in 1915 but he had every reason to feel world-weary by the end of the summer. 'The Germans have been very lively around the Salient during the last week and you will be sorry to hear that the trenches captured by the British on June 16 have been recaptured again by the Huns ...' In the same letter he described how a German bombardment buried alive fourteen men when a trench system collapsed on top of them. The artillery attack had apparently come in response to a joke made by the Tommies about the Kaiser. A neighbouring battalion had put out a green flag with an insulting picture of 'a criminal lunatic still at large in Germany ... I hope and believed that these buried men are stunned by the shock and do not suffer the pangs of slow suffocation.' One man was pulled out alive but died despite artificial respiration.

The letters home gradually add up to a catalogue of carnage and misery reported by its author with great sympathy and unflinching fortitude and cheerful fatalism. Had he not been a great doctor and war hero, he would have made a brilliant war correspondent. There is barely a single letter from the front that does not carry news of dreadful deaths and injuries. In one dated 5 October 1915, Chavasse tells of going to the scene where a group of guards had been undergoing an inspection on a bridge when ' . . . a silent shell landed in the middle of them & blew them all to pieces . . . I had to go up and sew them up in blankets they were so terribly mutilated.' One of them was his close friend Captain McLeod.

In late September 1915, after reinforcements had arrived, the battalion was considered strong enough to launch another attack, not far from the fateful charge at Hooge. His fury at the pointlessness of trench warfare was now strongly evident:

I have been the witness of as gallant a charge as ever took place, which has ended, so far as we are concerned, in our line here being exactly the same as it was before; but two regiments at least are cut to pieces. I doubt if much attention will be paid to in despatches; yet it was the biggest thing that has happened since we came into this tortured spot, and as usual everybody responded to the call of duty, and blood was poured out like water, and lives cast away as carelessly as old boots. I am sick of seeing men sent out to die in the mud which is the mould of former battalions 'gone under', but it will always be a delightful honour to lend a hand to the wounded heroes, and so in spite of all, in a selfish sense, this has been the happiest year of my life.

At the start of 1916 the battalion was moved from 9th Brigade, 3rd Division to 166th Brigade, 55th Division – the numbers of the units giving some idea of the huge levels of recruitment and deployment of young British men to the front.

Chavasse was awarded the Military Cross on 14 January 1916, but there was no citation in the *London Gazette* owing to the loss of the Commanding Officer's recommendation and the sheer length of the list. He eventually received the medal from King George V at Buckingham Palace on 7 June, almost a year after the action at Hooge for which he was awarded the decoration. He rejoined the battalion at the front in time to mark the anniversary of that terrible day. Rats, he reported in his next letter home, were now the principal concern for the troops. Huge creatures without the slightest fear of man, they trotted around the trenches, feeding off men's rations, eating through their clothes and honeycombing the walls of dugouts with their lairs. Those who neglected to cut up all their food from home and keep it in mess tins soon found they didn't have any. Many hours were passed trying to kill the creatures with bayonets. By the end of the summer of 1916 a plague of flies was adding to the unpleasantness of life on the front line, and not least for the fallen men lying out with open wounds.

At the beginning of the summer the brigade moved into the Somme area but the London Scottish were not involved in the early stages of that brutal four-month battle of that name which claimed 400,000 British casualties. Of those, almost 60,000 fell on the first day. The middle day of the middle year of the Great War is unlikely to be surpassed as the bloodiest day in the history of the British Army, but the Liverpool Scottish had to wait five weeks to experience their own fresh horrors.

On 7 August, the battalion received orders to prepare for an attack on village of Guillemot. It was an ill-thought-out, hurried plan that ended in failure and slaughter. No guides arrived to lead them to the trenches; enemy shells fell among them as they waited. When they eventually arrived they had no more idea than the waiting troops where their jumping-off trenches were, and the battalion reached them with just minutes to go before the whistle sounded. The attack was to be made past a wood and a copse to capture the German front-line trench and then the village itself. It got underway beneath a massive German artillery bombardment and into a storm of heavy machine-gun fire. There was no 'softening-up' bombardment of enemy positions by British gunners, the barbed wire hadn't been cut, the flow of information from above was sketchy and the terrain unknown to the new arrivals. The brigade, in short, was entirely unprepared for a major attack.

Four times the Liverpool Scottish charged, four times they regrouped and rallied and, with their numbers falling with each charge, four times they failed to break the line in the face of ferocious resistance. Once again, the Liverpool Scottish suffered heavy casualties. Of the 20 officers who set out, only 1 returned in one piece; 5 were killed, 6 missing and 8 wounded. Of the 600 men, 69 were killed, 27 missing, and 167 wounded. The attack was made over the same ground that 30th Division had attacked ten days earlier with enormous casualties. 89th Brigade, which was part of that division, was comprised of three battalions of the Liverpool Pals, of whom 460 were killed and a further 600 wounded, captured or missing. As the Liverpool Scottish charged across no-man's-land they will have known many of the men decomposing on the ground.

Several witnesses reported Chavasse's remarkable bravery that night as he and his stretcher-bearers searched for the wounded, carrying them in, one by one, under heavy fire. With no regard for his own safety, Chavasse spent hours scouring the terrain with his electric torch, whistling and calling out the names of the missing as he walked and ran around the corpse-littered landscape as sniper fire and fusillades whizzed through the night air. It was an exhausting, gruelling business carrying in dozens of injured men, falling into craters, stepping on and over the dismembered body parts of friends and comrades. One stretcher-bearer found himself buried when a mud wall collapsed, but managed to dig his way out before he suffocated.

Chavasse was struck by two shell splinters in the back but though he described them as no more than superficial injuries, they were serious enough for him to be forced to take sick leave after the disastrous action.

He wrote home again the following week, giving an insight into the horrors of the battle. 'The flys [sic] out here are dreadful & the poor fellows wounds were full of maggots . . . we found and brought in 3 badly wounded lying about 25 yards from the Hun line but two have died since I am sorry to say. Then we started off again, but this time we went into the Hun trenches and got bombs thrown at us and a Maxim gun at us for our pains . . . We got away back to camp in the early morning very happy but my day was a bit spoiled as I found I had two minute spicules of shell in my back & as the skin was pricked I had to have a tetanus injection which makes one feel a bit cheap.'

Word on the grapevine reached his father in Liverpool that Noel had been awarded the Victoria Cross for his efforts during the battle, but the young medical officer was almost dismissive of this tremendous recognition, writing: 'I fear that honour is not given as easily as all that and recommending is not getting so I shall adopt the attitude of the doubting Thomas and till I see it in print will not believe. If it will give me a bit of extra leave it will be well worth having.'

He was gazetted on 26 October. Four of his stretcher-bearers were also honoured for their valour that day, two with the Military Medal, two with the Distinguished Conduct Medal. The newspapers in Liverpool burst with pride, the names of the local heroes toasted in the city's many pubs. His citation in the *London Gazette* read:

During an attack he tended the wounded in the open all day, under heavy fire, frequently in view of the enemy. During the ensuing night he searched for wounded on the ground in front of the enemy's lines for four hours. Next day he took one stretcher-bearer to the advanced trenches, and, under heavy fire, carried an urgent case for 500 yards into safety, being wounded in the side by a shell splinter during the journey. The same night he took up a party of trusty volunteers, rescued three wounded men from a shell hole twenty five yards from the enemy's trench, buried the bodies of two officers and collected many identity

discs, although fired on by bombs and machine guns. Altogether
he saved the lives of some twenty badly wounded men, besides
the ordinary cases which passed through his hands. His courage
and self-sacrifice were beyond praise.

Noel was granted sick leave to recover from his wound and
he rejoined the battalion on 7 September near Delville Wood in
the Somme area. Almost immediately he was back in the thick
of the carnage, out rescuing men and treating those brought in
to his dressing station.

'We did not have any worry from the Hun in front but the
passage through the wood, a truly dreadful place, was always
stormy,' he wrote on 26 September. 'I was filing along through
the wood behind the men who had finished their strongpoints
and trenches. A whizz bang hit a RE [Royal Engineers] man who
was about 4 men off me & he fell down with a yell. My SB
[stretcher-bearer] bent over him & found him bleeding badly
from the arm & he held the main artery . . . I found that the
arm was almost off & could never mend & was only a source
of danger. So I cut it off with a pair of scissors and did the stump
up. We had to do everything by the light of our electric torch
& when we got a stretcher it took us 2 hours to get him out of
the wood . . . He rallied well and I'm glad to say he's alright.'

Shortly afterwards Chavasse was unexpectedly transferred to a
small field hospital away from the front line and the London
Scottish. The move was seen as a punishment for critical comments
he had made about the Field Ambulance and the official attitude

to the treatment of venereal disease among the troops. Chavasse had written a report decrying the efforts of the Field Ambulance, saying they often failed to arrive and were incapable of dealing with mass casualties. Few men on the front line were better placed to make a considered judgement on the issue, but his candid comments – driven by his concern for the men – provoked a bitter response from his medical colleagues.

At the same time, instances of venereal disease were reaching epidemic proportions and the issue of how to tackle the problem had triggered a fierce debate. When a scheme was proposed to open a chain of officially authorised brothels, Chavasse expressed his objections in the strongest possible terms, saying it was the duty of officers, doctors and padres to take a lead and prevent the men going astray. Riled by his presumption to speak out against more senior medics, the authorities dispatched Chavasse on a week-long course on sanitation; these were usually attended by young medics fresh off the boat from England. Even VC winners, apparently, needed to be upbraided by the top brass from time to time. His removal from the front line, away from his men, was a painful experience for Chavasse. His letters home at this stage reveal almost a desperation to rejoin the Liverpool Scottish in the forward trenches, but, by Christmas 1916, he was back with them.

In February 1917 Noel was granted fourteen days leave during which two momentous events in his life took place. Firstly, he went to the investiture at Buckingham Palace to receive his Victoria Cross from the king. Secondly, and far more importantly for the young doctor, he finally plucked up the courage to ask his child-hood sweetheart Gladys to marry him. She accepted and he returned to the front thrilled at the prospect of his wedding later in the year.

The first letter home on his return is characteristically self-effacing and begins with news of a recent acquisition to help the men in the trenches: 'I have taken a jolly nice little fox terrier with me who I hope will help to settle the rat questions in the trenches. The investiture passed all right. The king seemed to be quite sincere and was certainly very kind . . . There were seven of us, 4 being NCOs and men & these really had performed marvels.'

Rats were not the only pressing issue for him to address on his return to the front line. Following a spell of freezing weather, he was greeted by a procession of men suffering a complaint unique to kilted regiments: frostbitten knees. The grim attri-tion of trench warfare continued to take its toll on the London Scottish over the following months. As the casualty figures mounted, fresh-faced recruits arrived and died, a sense of frus-tration, bordering on despair, begins to creep into Chavasse's letters home.

On 14 March 1917, he wrote: 'The battalion is being heavily worked now. I suppose as a military necessity and of course if it must be it is all right. But we are using up our human ma-terial and wearing it out rather badly just now, in our sector of the line. The men are being pushed to exhaustion and without respite and good fellows are beginning to crack up . . . Our

Higher Commanders are so aloff [sic] that I doubt if they & their staff are really in touch with or understand the battalions.'

The reference to men 'cracking up' touched on the increasingly controversial subject of how the authorities chose to react to what today we would call 'combat trauma'. Facing harsh punishment for cowardice and malingering, including the death penalty in extreme instances, hundreds of men, on the verge of mental collapse, had killed themselves or inflicted wounds in order to be removed from the front line. Though fearless to a fault himself, Chavasse had sympathy for the men he saw being pushed to the brink of breakdown. His reaction to these cases was both practical and kind-hearted. When he sensed that soldiers could take no more, he arranged for them to work for him at the regimental aid post or dressing stations, carrying out light duties. More often than not the men recovered their strength and returned to combat action. Elsewhere on the front line, other men were being led away and shot.

Amid the relentless carnage, once again it is to nature that Chavasse turns to for support. In a landscape of shattered tree stumps, mud and ruins, the sight and sound of nature, forcing its way through the devastation, filled him with joy, especially in the spring. On 7 March 1917, he wrote: '. . . The mornings are splendid just now and the birds are singing. My head leaps up whenever I hear a thrush & there are blackbirds and larks here & I hope some nightingales later on. I cannot tell you how the singing of birds affects me out here. It is quite uplifting, in the rather mournful surroundings, it gives a feeling of hope. I suppose we must be nearing the end of the war now. I hope so, even if it will be a bloody business. It cannot be any worse than what, in God's mercy, we have already been through.'

His mind was also preoccupied with thoughts of marriage and his career after the war. While he was mulling over a wedding at Christmas time, he was unaware that Gladys had applied for a special licence for them to get married in France later in the summer.

On 20 June, the Liverpool Scottish moved to Zudausques, a village west of St Omer, where they began preparations for what augured to be a major offensive to smash the German lines. At the time, Passchendaele was no more than a name on a map. Within a few months, it would become a synonym for mass slaughter. Almost one hundred years on, the name continues to send a shudder down the spine.

In a letter of 15 June 1917 Chavasse reveals that he had turned down an invitation to become a surgeon at a Base Hospital, where he would be removed from the dangers of the front line. He concedes he is tempted by the prospect of learning from the senior surgeons working there but he cannot bear the thought of leaving the men at the front. 'It's too comfortable. Such jobs are for the elder men. Young fellows like myself ought to be with the fighting men. And I am by no means done yet. In fact I'm settling down to this mode of living as my life work and don't look now for the end. And I don't think I could leave the lads here to fight it out while I luxuriated in a coast town. The infantry lad does not want to get hurt or killed any more than

I do. In fact one of their most popular chants as they trudge up to the trenches is – 'Oh my I don't want to die – I want to go 'ome' – So while [sic] should not I, who as it is have a softer time than they.'

The strain and sense of resignation to his fate becomes evident in his letters during this period. In the very last letter in the box of his correspondence held by the Bodleian, dated 2 July but resuming one that he began on 25 June, his handwriting is erratic, his thought processes less precise and the descriptions less detailed. Anxiety and doubt have risen to the surface. It may have been that he was working so hard that he was having to dash his letters off even more quickly than usual but the sense of pressure, foreboding and fatigue is palpable. The boyish vigour and sunny outlook has not been completely extinguished, but the repeated exposure to the horrors and miseries of trench warfare, the cries of pain, the hideous injuries and the growing litany of lost colleagues and friends was clearly taking its toll.

'I don't think I will get leave just yet but hope to get some, about Sept,' he wrote.

'I am very keen on leave as I want to settle up things. I am thinking that if the war does not get on any quicker then I shall take time by the forelock & get married somewhere about Xmas. I could probably get leave of a month then. What is your candid opinion of it. Gladys wants it very badly . . . I should like it for a lot of reasons but shall feel rather a fool after the war, a married man without a job. Still it's a bit pathetic to have to leave a bronze cross to a nephew, or cousin twice removed. I don't think I really earned it as many have had to do. I prize it more than I can say.'

The very last paragraph of an emotional letter confirms that he has turned down the cushy surgeon's job in order to stay in the front line: 'I have written to the base hospital & said that though I valued the offer very much, I thought I had better stay with the lads & would not apply. I felt rather depressed about it for about ¼ hour. Always your loving Noel.'

Two days later, his youngest brother, Aidan, was killed while out on patrol. Another brother, Bernard, joined the search party to find him in no-man's-land, but the body was never found.

On 20 July, the Liverpool Scottish marched up to the front and readied themselves for an attack against the heavily defended enemy positions on Passchendaele Ridge. An artillery bombardment killed one officer and eight men as they moved forward. Over the next few days, the casualties mounted as the Germans bombarded the British lines with mustard gas and high explosive shells. The Liverpool Scottish lost a quarter of their strength with 140 killed or incapacitated before the battle had begun. On 29 July, the battalion of 25 officers and 475 other ranks was called forward under a violent storm. Thunder boomed louder than the artillery guns, lightning flashed across the sky and a deluge of rain drenched the men to the skin as they squelched through the thick mud. Carrying two days' rations and full battle equipment, the march turned into a gruelling five-hour slog.

After a few hours' rest, at 3.30 a.m. on 30 July the men moved up to their jumping-off trenches. At first light, the whistle blew and the Liverpool Scottish scrambled over the top and charged across the swamp of no-man's-land, first down a slight slope and then uphill towards the ridge. As they poured forward into a hail of machine-gun fire, many of the enemy began to flee. The battalion was taking casualties but it was making spectacular progress. By 7.45 they had reached all their objectives and taken dozens of prisoners.

At the start of the attack, Noel Chavasse was deep underground in a massive dugout in the village of Weltje that he and his team had converted into the principal dressing station. Captured from the Germans, the cavernous structure could hold several hundred men and was so deep that it was safe from even the heaviest artillery shelling. It had its own electricity supply for lighting and water pumps.

Most medical officers would have stayed in the security of the dressing station throughout the attack, but that was never an option for Chavasse who liked to be as close to the front line as possible. As the battalion advanced and secured territory, Chavasse moved up behind them and set up an RAP in a captured trench near a farm. When he stood up to indicate to the troops the location of the new aid post, a shell landed close by and he was hit by shrapnel in the head. The wound was grave enough for him to have to go and get it dressed at Weltje. His twin brother Christopher, serving as padre a short distance from the Liverpool Scottish positions, later claimed that the blow had fractured Noel's skull.

With his head bandaged, Chavasse refused a request to be taken to a Casualty Clearing Station further to the rear, and ran back to his aid post at the front line on the Passchendaele Road. Shells screeched overhead, erupting across the hellish scene as stretcher-bearers continued to bring in dozens of wounded. Chavasse went straight back to work. When night fell, he took his torch and headed out with a search party into what had been no-man's-land just a few hours earlier. It was now in Allied hands and the Germans were shelling it as they retreated. The heavens had opened up again, drenching the combatants and turning the cratered terrain into muddy, bloody quagmire, littered with the dead and wounded. The stumps of trees, mutilated mules and horses, broken-down tanks and the cries of men in agony completed a scene of perfect desolation. Such was the Battle of Passchendaele, aka the Third Battle of Ypres.

Back at the aid post, Chavasse worked through the night treating the wounded, helped by some captured German medics, who applied themselves to their tasks with the same gusto as if they were treating their own. At one point, a shell flew past Chavasse and killed a man in a nearby room. Accounts differ as to how many injuries Chavasse had sustained in the course of his work during the battle. One man said the doctor had been injured three times (adding that he had won the VC four times over in separate incidents in a terrifying twenty-four-hour period). Others said it was as many as five injuries that he sustained. What is certain is that at some stage during the second day, he received a second wound to the head. He refused to be taken away for treatment, quickly bandaged up his own wound and, despite suffering intense pain, carried on tending to the others.

Incredibly, he carried on working into a third day when, in the early hours of Thursday 2 August, he suffered a third serious injury. On this occasion, the shell fell directly into the aid post. Chavasse was sitting on a chair leaning on a table, exhausted and trying to catch a few minutes' sleep while his dressers continued to tend the wounded. Everyone in the room was killed or wounded so badly that they were unable to move. Now carrying at least three, possibly five, serious wounds, including a heavily bleeding hole in his stomach, Chavasse crawled up the stairs and along what remained of the blasted trench. In pitch darkness he crawled and staggered along the lane, the mud caking his open wounds, to raise the alarm and call for help for the men back at the aid post. We know this from the accounts of several witnesses.

Stumbling across a dugout, itself full of wounded men of the Loyal North Lancashire Regiment, he was eventually taken away to a hospital specialising in abdominal wounds. The operation to remove the shell splinters from his stomach was successful and, sedated with morphine, he was comforted by a nurse who, by coincidence, he had worked alongside in Liverpool. But at one o'clock in the afternoon of 4 August, the third anniversary of the outbreak of war, Captain Noel Chavasse passed away. The news was a heavy blow to the war-weary Liverpool Scottish. The spirited doctor who had defied death for so long had finally run out of luck.

His funeral took place the following day and he was buried in a field alongside some of the men who had fallen in the attack. Exhausted, covered head to toe in mud, many of them suffering various degrees of injury, the entire battalion was there to pay tribute to the man who had nursed and tended to their every need for two and a half years.

His parents received the telegram informing them of the sad news on 9 August, a day after they had been informed that Bernard had been wounded in the knee. King George V wrote to the bishop and his wife to express his grief at the news of Noel's death, adding his concern for the fate of missing Aidan. The stoical bishop broke down in tears when he was told a month later that Noel was to receive a posthumous bar to his VC. The award was announced in the *London Gazette* on 14 September, 1917. It read:

Though severely wounded early in the action whilst carrying a wounded soldier to the dressing station, he refused to leave his post, and for two days, not only continued to perform his duties, but in addition, went out repeatedly under heavy fire to search for and attend to the wounded who were lying out. During these searches, although practically without food during this period, worn with fatigue and faint with his wound, he assisted to carry in a number of badly wounded men over heavy and difficult ground. By his extraordinary energy and inspiring example he was instrumental in rescuing many wounded who would have otherwise undoubtedly succumbed under the bad weather conditions. This devoted and gallant officer subsequently died of his wounds.

Chavasse's headstone in the military cemetery at Brandhoek in Belgium (plot 3, row B15) is the only one in the world engraved with two images of the Victoria Cross. His father chose the words for the inscription that appeared on the original stone. They read simply: 'Greater love hath no man than this, that a man lay down his life for his friends.'

Two other men have won the Victoria Cross twice and by extra-ordinary coincidence, Chavasse has a connection with both of them. Captain Arthur Martin-Leake, also a medic, won his first VC during the Boer War in 1902 and his second in Flanders in 1915. The first medical unit Chavasse passed through on the night he was fatally wounded was commanded by Lt Col Martin-Leake. The only other man to achieve the double honour was Captain Charles Upham, a New Zealander serving with 20th Battalion, 2nd Infantry Battalion, New Zealand Expeditionary Force (The Canterbury Regiment) in the Second World War. He won his first in Crete in 1941 and his second in the North African desert the following year. By coincidence, Upham's family was related to the Chavasse's.

Noel Chavasse remains the most heavily decorated serviceman in the history of the British Armed Forces, but he was not the only member of his family to distinguish himself in the Great War. All seven siblings served their country in either a military, medical or pastoral capacity during the conflict. Christopher, the padre, and

Bernard, the medic, both received the Military Cross. Christopher rose up the church hierarchy to become the Bishop of Rochester and died in 1961. Bernard became an eminent eye surgeon. He died in 1941. Aidan is one of 55,000 British soldiers who were 'missing, presumed dead' and have no grave of their own, and whose names are inscribed on the giant Menin Gate memorial at Ypres.

The eldest sister, Dorothea, ran the Birkenhead 'Comforts Committee' throughout the war, organising supplies for the troops. Edith and Mary, the family's second pair of twins, worked as voluntary nurses on the front line. Mary was mentioned in dispatches.

Sergeant Major Stanley Hollis

A cold breeze cut across the English Channel as the largest invasion force in history set sail from the south coast of England under the cover of darkness in the small hours of Tuesday 6 June 1944. Sergeant Major Stan Hollis of D Company The Green Howards sat among his men in the dimly lit bowels of the *Empire Lance* as it rode the waves of the choppy sea. The troopship was part of a mighty armada of 6,939 ships that included 4,126 landing craft and 1,213 combatant vessels. Arranged in 59 convoys strung out over 100 miles, they carried 195,000 seamen, 140,000 soldiers, 14,000 vehicles including 2,000 tanks and 10,000 tons of equipment. Over 20,000 men had taken to the air, bracing themselves to land in gliders or to be dropped by parachute behind enemy lines to cut German communications and seize key locations. In total, 11,000 aircraft were detailed to assist the landings. Some of those Allied planes continued months of deception operations by dropping tons of aluminium foil strips known as 'chaff' in the Calais area to fool Nazi radar operators into believing that an invasion was going to take place at the mouth of the Channel. The ploy was working as the ships cut through the heaving surf.

The 6th and 7th Battalions of the Green Howards, whose men were drawn from North Yorkshire and Teesside, were to lead the initial assault on King Sector, Gold Beach, at Arromanches. They were part of the 69th Brigade, 50th (Northumbrian) Division that had been handpicked by General Montgomery to spearhead the infantry assault. 'Monty' had witnessed the fabled fighting skills of one of Britain's oldest regiments for himself in North Africa – and he had been highly impressed by their brute tenacity and ability to soak up heavy punishment without complaint. After years of hard, exhausting combat in the Western Desert and later during the invasion of Sicily, not all of the Green Howards were overjoyed by the honour handed to them by the 'Hero of El Alamein'. Huge levels of casualties had been fore-cast for the first wave of attackers in Normandy. The more negative were predicting outright slaughter on a scale not witnessed since the Somme and Passchendaele.

Hollis was as battle-hardened a veteran as could be found in the British Army. Seriously wounded four times in as many years of fierce combat, his skull full of metal plates, he was a giant of a man in every respect. Just the sight of his huge physical frame, toothy grin and bright copper hair must have come as a reassurance to the nervous young troops alongside him as they tried to gather themselves in the countdown to the onslaught. A former fish shop worker and lorry driver from one of the tougher corners of Teesside, Hollis had an intolerance of fools and German soldiers alike. His rebellious streak had led him into a number of scrapes with authority, but he was loved and held in awe by officers and men alike. If there was one man you wanted at your shoulder on D-Day it was Stanley Elton Hollis.

Handed a plate of bacon and eggs, many of the men could do no more than poke at it with their forks, but the rocking of the ship was only party responsible for the churning of their stomachs. Violence on an unimaginable scale was about to be unleashed. As they waited for the order to board their landing crafts, some of the men busied themselves checking their weapons for the umpteenth time, a few were sick with nerves, others vented their anxiety in banter. A handful sat in silent contemplation, taking deep breaths and thinking of the challenges that lay ahead and of loved ones left at home. Like his comrades packed in alongside him, laden with equipment, Hollis just wanted to get the fighting over and done with and get back to his beloved wife, Alice, and children, Brian and Pauline.

When the troopship had reached its designated location off the French coast, the men filed up on deck and began to load up the landing craft that had been lowered alongside. Among the equipment were boxes of ammo, which they had been tasked to carry up to the high-water mark on the beach for the subsequent waves of troops. His company commander and old friend, Major Ronnie Lofthouse, handed Hollis a box. Hollis opened the lid to discover a stash of latex condoms. 'What's all these for?' he grinned. 'Are we going to fight them or fuck them?' In fact, they were to cover the Bren guns to prevent seawater damaging the firing mechanism.

Hollis and the Green Howards were to be among the very first Allied soldiers ashore. After negotiating a minefield, their first objective was to take out various gun emplacements, ensuring the safety of subsequent waves of troops. The main gun battery, the Mont Fleury, was set back a little from the beach on higher ground, giving it commanding views of the area. Containing four 122mm guns and supported by four 100mm mobile guns, the battery was protected by a garrison of German troops and was capable of wreaking havoc on the thousands of disembarking troops. On the ridge of the dunes, halfway between the beach and the Mont Fleury battery, lay a smaller but equally dangerous gun emplacement known as La Rivière. Its reinforced concrete casements housed large guns capable of strafing Gold Beach in both directions. It was imperative that both positions were silenced as quickly as possible to prevent 'Deliverance Day' from turning into Allied carnage. The second objective was to seize the heavily defended village of Crépon, three miles inland, defeating all resistance they encountered in the fields and farms in between.

The order came for the men to scramble down the nets slung over the sides of the troopship into the landing craft. Getting into the 40-foot-long boats was an awkward procedure that did little to soothe the nerves of the men as H-Hour approached. Weighed down with Bren-gun pouches, Sten guns, grenades, backpacks, mortars, medical supplies and boxes of extra ammo for the follow-up troops, some of the men became caught up in the netting as they tried to board the small boat heaving up and down in the choppy water far below them. There were about 20 to 30 men per landing craft, depending on the amount of equipment aboard. As soon as one was fully loaded it went round in circles and waited until the entire company was afloat and lined up facing the shore. It was one of the great spectacles in military history: thousand upon thousand of landing crafts, row upon row of them, column upon column, mile upon mile, rammed to their metal walls with tens of thousands of nervous young men, poised to launch the liberation of Europe. Many of them would not see another day.

At the green-for-go signal, the Royal Marine coxswains opened the throttles and the landing crafts began to accelerate towards the beaches. Behind them, 5 battleships, 20 cruisers and 65 destroyers laid down a colossal bombardment of the Nazi shore defences. Their aim was to destroy minefields on the beaches and enemy positions up to twenty miles behind while striking terror into the troops tasked with holding back the human tide about to wash ashore. Captain W. Synge described the shocking noise of the salvos: 'The naval bombardment was terrific,' he wrote in *The Story of The Green Howards (1939–45)*. 'Salvos from 15-inch guns of the dreadnought HMS *Warspite* sounded like express trains thundering overhead. Cruisers and destroyers joined in, and landing craft carrying 25 pounders fired unceasingly as they steamed ashore. In addition there were rocket ships, which came within a hundred yards of shore, and each of which fired off four salvos a minute of ninety rockets each.'

Hundreds of bombers joined in the assault as the coastline erupted in a wall of flame, smoke and debris. Devastating though it was, the bombardment was never expected to break the enemy. The aim was to make them keep their heads down and allow the disembarking troops some breathing space as they raced across the sand to seize their objectives. The decisive blows against the defenders were always going to be delivered by the infantry – and in this sector that meant the Green Howards and other components of the 50th Northumbrian Division, as well as the supporting tank units of the 4th/7th Dragoon Guards.

As the landing craft approached the shore, Hollis spotted what he thought was one of the machine-gun pillboxes they had been shown in the rolls of pictures taken by aerial reconnaissance aircraft during the countdown to the invasion. He picked up a Lewis machine gun and set about hosing the target with a full magazine pan of ammunition. In the urgency of the situation and the need to disembark, he accidentally grabbed the searing hot barrel of the weapon as he put it down, causing a huge blister across the palm of his hand that he described, only half jokingly, as the most painful of the wounds he suffered in five years of fighting. The 'pillbox', it turned out, was a harmless tram shelter.

Enemy machine-gun fire rang against the walls of the landing craft as the ramp was dropped and the men poured out into the water. The man in front of Hollis, his friend Sergeant Hill, whom he had fought alongside for most of the war, stepped out into a deep shell hole and, weighed down by his kit, disappeared beneath the landing craft and was chopped to pieces by the propeller. A number of others on the landing crafts, including three more experienced sergeants, suffered a similar fate or drowned. So intense was the noise of the bombardment and the enemy returning fire that Hollis couldn't make himself heard as he shouted instructions to his men, wading the 60 yards to shore. Shells and mortar bombs fell around the troops as they scrambled forward, hundreds of machine-gun rounds kicked up shoots of water and sand. Men were falling in their hundreds as similar scenes were acted out along the fifty-mile stretch of the invasion coast. Led by Hollis and Lofthouse, D Company dashed up the left-hand side of the beach into the hail of fire. Watching them storm ashore, the Royal Marine officer in charge of the landing craft glanced down at his watch. It was just after 7.30. Everything was going to plan.

As he raced over the sands to the ridge at the top of the beach, Stan Hollis didn't need to prove his courage to anyone. He was already a hero and an inspiration to his comrades and friends in the Green Howards, many of whom he had grown up with back in the North East. His nickname was 'the man they couldn't kill'. After enlisting as a territorial, on the outbreak of war he was mobilised and assigned to the 6th Battalion, one of twelve raised by the regiment during the war. In April 1940 they went as part of the British Expeditionary Force to France, where he was employed as the Commanding Officer's dispatch rider even though he had never before ridden a motorbike. In the chaotic withdrawal to Dunkirk, Hollis risked his life time and time again to relay messages back and forth between the units as they made their fighting withdrawal, often speeding through enemy-held territory with the rounds flying around him.

His comrades insisted that in any battle other than the mayhem of Dunkirk, Hollis's heroics would have been rewarded by the highest gallantry awards. He and five others were actually put forward for the Military Medal after they went to the rescue of a Welsh Guards brigade that had become trapped. Jumping into a truck and laying down a wall of fire with their Bren guns, they were able to create a small gap in the encirclement through which the guardsmen were able to fight their way out and escape.

Hollis was one of a total of 340,000 soldiers (200,000 British and 140,000 French) who were saved during the mass evacuation by the Royal Navy and a flotilla of civilian boats in what has since become known as the 'Miracle of Dunkirk'. Had the professional British Army been wiped out or captured, it is highly unlikely that the country would have been able to fight on against Germany. Some of the troops were able to embark on to the ships from the harbour's protective mole, but others had to wade out from the beaches, often waiting for hours to board, shoulder-deep in water and attacked by dive-bombing German fighters. Hollis was extremely fortunate to have made it as far as the beaches. While he was weaving his way through the traffic carrying another message from the rear, a mortar bomb exploded next to him and threw him from his motorcycle. Shrapnel splinters lacerated his body and shredded his uniform. Lying on the roadside unconscious, he looked like another fatality to the retreating troops passing by. His comrades in the 6th Battalion went back to look for him and helped him on to the corpse-strewn beaches. Still delirious with concussion, bleeding from his various wounds and virtually naked, he waded into the sea and started swimming out to the ships waiting offshore. He remembered almost nothing about being dragged aboard one of the vessels.

'Throughout the days of confusion and hazardous moves, one man, although not decorated on this occasion, will remain in the memory of those who fought with the 6th Battalion at that time,' wrote Synge. 'He was Pte. S. E. Hollis . . . he travelled along roads and through towns reported to be held by the enemy, and arrived sometimes at his destination only to find that the British troops had gone. Yet he always got through and brought back valuable information. He was always ready to go out again . . . His devotion to duty had an inspiring effect on the men of the Battalion . . .'

Back in England a few days later, Hollis and his mates went out for a drink in Bournemouth to celebrate their escape from France, but, on returning to camp, a zealous sergeant major from another unit put them on a charge of being drunk and disorderly. Their recommendations for the Military Medal were automatically dropped as a matter of procedure. His regiment, however, formally recognised the heroics he had performed, promoting him from private to full sergeant.

Hollis and the 6th Battalion went on to distinguish themselves in the desert campaign of North Africa. Hollis was captured by German troops after his unit's position was overrun following a lion-hearted defence against a much larger, better equipped force. General Erwin Rommel, commander of the German forces, is said to have personally congratulated Hollis and his comrades for their bravery. A less welcoming reception awaited him in the transit prisoner-of-war camp. Kicked and beaten by his captors, Hollis suffered a broken cheekbone and cracked skull, but it didn't prevent him from escaping back over British lines. During lengthy treatment in hospital, a metal plate was inserted in his face. His comrades were to say that the experience in the POW camp intensified his hatred of the Germans and turned him into an even more formidable and fearless figure on the battlefield.

During the Battle of El Alamein in 1942, the turning point not just in the North Africa campaign but in the overall Allied war effort, Hollis played his part when he risked his life to destroy a 60-ton Tiger tank that was holding up the advance of his company and hammering them with its mighty 88mm gun. Grabbing a 'sticky' bomb, he raced towards it in his lightly armoured Bren carrier, jumped out, broke the casing of the nitro-glycerine explosive, which was covered in strong adhesive, and stuck it on the side of the tank. Five seconds later, as Hollis accelerated away, a bright flash erupted in the darkness. The explosion killed the crew and disabled the huge tank, allowing

Freddy Spencer Chapman in Tibet, 1936. He developed a passion for adventure at an early age, following the death of his parents.

Freddy Spencer Chapman with members of the 1936 British Mission to Lhasa, Tibet. Chapman is second from left at the back.

Jungle in Malaya. This dense vegetation was typical of the terrain in which Chapman was operating behind enemy lines.

Allied tanks and troops on their way to the front line. On 4 May 1944 during the Battle of Kohima in North East India, Randle was ordered to attack a strongly defended Japanese position on a ridge.

John Neil Randle of the
Royal Norfolk Regiment
who laid down his life for his men.

Captain Noel Chavasse VC & Bar, MC. The inspirational Army doctor, seen here wearing the Glengarry of the Liverpool Scottish.

One of the many letters written home by Chavasse. He was a brilliant letter writer who painted a vivid picture of life in the trenches.

Medics treat British tommies in an underground forward dressing station in France.

The grave of Captain Noel Chavasse VC, Brandhoek New Military Cemetery, Ypres, Belgium. He is one of only three men to have been awarded the Victoria Cross twice.

Company Sergeant Major Stanley Hollis of the Green Howards, the only man to have been awarded the Victoria Cross for his actions during the D-Day landings, pictured after receiving his medal from King George VI at Buckingham Palace, 10th October 1944.

British and Allied troops hit the beaches in Normandy. Hollis's combat-hardened battalion of Green Howards were amongst the first ashore and overcame stiff resistance.

A portrait of Stanley Hollis wearing his VC by Albert Lembert. Hollis, one of 18 Green Howards to be awarded a Victoria Cross, was seriously wounded four times in combat.

his company to pour past it. Like many of his exploits in Dunkirk, his selfless act was not witnessed by an officer and, although no award could be recommended, it was always remembered by his grateful comrades.

Hollis had recovered by April 1943 when the Green Howards were put in the front line at the Battle of Wadi Akarit, the last major pitch battle between the Eighth Army and their German counterparts. He was leading his company from the front in a surprise night attack when he was forced to the ground by machine-gun fire that tore through his right thigh. Hollis lost a great deal of blood and the wound took weeks to heal but he was one of the luckier men, who took heavy casualties before the battle was won. He was injured again, this time in the left leg, shortly after he returned to action.

The following year the 6th and 7th Battalions The Green Howards were involved in the invasion of Sicily, a bloody campaign against some of Germany's crack troops, including thousands of elite paratroopers. Some of the fiercest fighting took place at the 400-foot-long Primosole Bridge over the River Simeto near Mount Etna, one of three key locations on which the advance of Allied forces depended. Aware of its strategic importance, the Germans mounted a tough defence and held out for weeks as both sides piled in thousands of troops. Attack and counter-attack ebbed and flowed and many casualties were sustained by both sides until the Allies finally prevailed. (Among the Green Howards' dead was the famous England and Yorkshire cricketer Captain Hedley Verity.) The battle was into its tenth day when

Hollis and his company from 6th Battalion reached the bridge and were immediately attacked by a fifty-strong German patrol. A desperate hand-to-hand struggle ensued before the Germans scattered, leaving two dead and one wounded. During the skirmish, Hollis threw a grenade at one German that bounced off his chest but failed to explode.

The Allied advance continued and two days later heavy fighting broke out around Catania airfield. The Green Howards were quickly into the thick of the action as the battle once again descended into brutal hand-to-hand combat. Crawling up a railway embankment, Hollis suffered several shrapnel and bullet injuries to his head and body when his company came under heavy mortar and machine-gun fire. His wounds were so serious that he was put on a ship and taken back for specialist treatment in the hospital at Philippeville in Algeria, where doctors inserted another metal plate, this time in his badly fractured skull. It took him three months to make a full recovery. The Green Howards lost many of their finest men in the bitter fighting through Sicily and by the time they returned to England they had seen more than their fair share of hard combat in the five years of the war to date. They were overdue a prolonged break from front-line action but their toughest challenge was yet to come.

'A' Company lost a good number of its men before it had even reached the shore, some to drowning, some to enemy fire, but the remainder made a fearless charge up the beach to overwhelm a German unit positioned behind the sea wall that had been lobbing grenades and spraying the beach with machine-gun fire. Hollis and D Company were on their left and they too had suffered badly under heavy mortar fire. Led by company commander Major Lofthouse, they advanced through a mine-field, following the path cleared by the platoon of assault pioneers. The small-arms fire had died down and mortar bombs were falling behind them as D Company left the beach and began making their way up the hill to a house with a circular drive, the first major landmark they had been told to head towards.

The leading platoons had passed the house and were making their way towards the Mont Fleury gun battery when a pillbox 100 yards to the right of the road began to open up on them. The flashing muzzles of Spandau machine guns were visible in the dark slits of the well-camouflaged concrete encasement, spitting out the rounds at a rate of 1,200 per minute. Hollis didn't need a second invitation. Seeing that the other platoon was in danger of being destroyed, he leapt up and charged the pillbox, firing his Sten gun from the waist as he sprinted across the rough grass. The muzzles of the Spandau machine guns immediately turned towards him, filling the air around him with a stream of fire. As he reached the pillbox he fired a burst through the firing slit and scrambled on to the roof of the small structure. Pulling the pin from a grenade, he leant over and posted it through the opening. As a dull thud shook the concrete, Hollis jumped to the ground and pushed open the door. Two Germans lay dead and two others staggered out dazed and wounded. Noticing a trench connecting the pillbox, he put a fresh magazine into his Sten gun and began to advance along it towards a second strongpoint. As he approached it, the door opened and fifteen Germans came out with their hands up. Pointing them in the direction of the beach, where prisoners were to be assembled, he rejoined D Company and they pushed on inland.

The first objectives, including the big gun battery, had been seized and secured within forty-five minutes of landing, but the Green Howards had suffered a number of fatalities in the process. The commander and sergeant of 16 Platoon were among the dead and Hollis was ordered to take command. He was handed the task of clearing the village of Crépon to allow the rest of the battalion to pass through. Meeting only light resistance, by eleven o'clock the village had been cleared and 16 Platoon were ordered to check out a farm lying a few yards to the west on the road to Bayeux. A sleepy rural scene greeted the troops as they fanned out around the farmyard and began checking the house and the outbuildings. Hollis took the house. Upstairs he found a ten-year-old boy, cowering and quivering in one of the bedrooms.

Moving on to the farmyard at the rear of the house, he edged along the side of the building before peering round the corner. He was greeted by the sharp report of gunfire that riddled the stonework a few inches from his face. On the other side of the farmyard lay an orchard and a large rhubarb patch, thick with plants ready for picking. Beyond that was a high hedge where Hollis could see two dogs sniffing around and wagging their tails. Hollis looked again – and his heart skipped a beat as he saw the muzzle of a 75mm field gun sticking out of the shrubbery. This was a weapon that could cause serious damage to the advancing troops and he immediately requested permission from Lofthouse to engage it.

Picking up a PIAT hand-held anti-tank weapon and accompanied by two Bren-gunners, Hollis crawled through the rhubarb patch before opening fire. The round fell short and the field gun was immediately swivelled in Hollis's direction. One of the advantages of the PIAT was that it did not emit any smoke when it was fired and thereby didn't give away the position of its operator. Unaware of the precise location of their attackers, therefore, the field-gun unit fired a round in the rough direction of the farmhouse. A shell burst against the wall of the house, sending masonry flying in all directions. At the same time a sniper had spotted the three men and opened fire, with one bullet cutting Hollis across the cheek as he gave the order to withdraw. When he got back, Hollis realised that his men hadn't followed him out. Hearing the burst of Bren-gun fire behind him, he realised they were still pinned down in the rhubarb patch. Hollis volunteered to go back in and get them and, grabbing a Bren gun of his own, he rushed back into the rhubarb patch in full view of the enemy who were firing on him as he advanced. On reaching his two comrades, he ordered them to pull back while he kept the enemy's heads down before making his own escape under heavy fire.

By nightfall, the 6th Battalion had pushed five miles inland and the Allies had captured a broad area of coastline – but at a cost of 10,000 casualties, 1,000 of which were suffered on Gold Beach. The Battle for Normandy continued throughout the summer in the complex terrain of the *bocage* network of high hedges and small fields. Hollis and the Green Howards were never far from the front line, involved in fighting as intense as any they had experienced in North Africa and Sicily. By that time, the Germans were finally overwhelmed; 200,000 soldiers on each side had been killed, wounded or gone missing. Hollis, still putting himself in harm's way, became one of the statistics on D-Day plus forty-eight. The Germans were mounting a furious rearguard action in what was known as the Falaise Gap as they tried to prevent their entire force from being surrounded – and either forced to surrender or slaughtered.

Hollis had assembled his company at their temporary head-quarters and was awaiting orders to move out when a mortar bomb landed in the middle of them. The man sitting right next to him was one of several killed outright by the blast, while Hollis and the others suffered serious injuries. Dozens of shrapnel splinters tore into Hollis, tearing his flesh and lodging in his head. His skull was badly fractured for the second time in the war, his face badly cut up and a leg damaged, but 'the man they couldn't kill' remained conscious throughout as he lay among his dead and dying comrades.

After emergency treatment in the field, he was evacuated to England for further surgery and a long period of recovery. This time there was to be no return to the front line. He was sitting in a hospital bed in Leeds, with yet another metal plate having been inserted in his skull, when he was informed that he had been awarded the Victoria Cross for his actions on the first day of the Normandy landings. Not only was he D-Day's only Victoria Cross winner, he had also been recommended twice for Britain's highest gallantry award: once for charging the pillbox and once for rescuing his men in the Crépon farmyard. Under the regulations, however, a soldier can only be awarded one medal for a day's action.

He received the bronze cross with the crimson ribbon from King George VI on 10 October, 1944. The end of his citation read: 'Wherever fighting was heaviest CSM Hollis appeared, and in the course of a magnificent day's work he displayed the utmost gallantry and on two separate occasions his courage and initiative prevented the enemy from holding up the advance at critical stages. It was largely through his heroism and resource that the Company's objectives were gained and casualties were not heavier. By his bravery he saved the lives of many of his men.'

Work was hard to find after the war – even for VC-winning heroes like Stan Hollis. He took jobs as a labourer and a gardener, but even a local newspaper campaign was unable to land him more lucrative employment. After a brief spell away at sea with the Merchant Navy, he finally found a settled career when he became landlord of the Albion in North Ormesby, a few miles from where he was born. As a tribute to the new landlord and the men he served with, the name of the pub was changed to the Green Howard. In his later years, the many wounds he suffered in the war returned to torment him. He had to have four bullets removed from his legs when the pain became intolerable and affected his movement. Equally excruciating was a piece of shrapnel that inched its way, over the years, from his shoulder all the way down his arm and into his hand, from where it was removed. There were still bullets in his feet when he died of a stroke in 1972, aged fifty-nine.

In 1981 his family was forced to sell his Victoria Cross, which fetched a record £30,000. The anonymous buyer turned out to be Sir Ernest Harrison, chairman of Racal Electronics, who bequeathed it to the Green Howards Museum in Richmond, North Yorkshire. In 2005, Harrison also put up the money to buy the tram shelter above Gold Beach that Hollis had raked with the Lewis gun as the Green Howards stormed ashore. A group of influential visitors with Green Howard connections, including Field Marshal Sir Peter Inge, a former Chief of the Defence Staff, had seen a 'For Sale' sign on the dilapidated, bullet-riddled shelter and bought it on the spot. It joins an older memorial in Crépon honouring Hollis and his comrades.

Lieutenant Colonel Blair 'Paddy' Mayne

It was going to be a first in British military history. The new irregular warfare unit was to launch a daring night-time raid on the airfields at Timimi and Gazala deep behind enemy lines along the North African coast. They were to be the first blows struck in Operation Crusader, the Eighth Army's offensive to push Rommel's Afrika Korps back out of Cyrenaica and relieve the Siege of Tobruk.

The raiding party, made up mainly of ex-commandos, was to be dropped by parachute close to their targets on the night of 16 November 1941. After gathering up their equipment containers they were to lie up and observe the airfields during the day to get an idea of how the enemy went about defending the locations. Under the cover of darkness, a few hours before the Eighth Army launched the main offensive, the sixty-five-strong force were to steal in and set timed explosives on the parked aircraft. The five groups of the raiding party would then trek into the desert and meet at a rendezvous (RV) point where they'd be picked up by the Long Range Desert Group (LRDG), specialists in desert navigation and transport.

Each of the five groups was to be flown in by their own Bristol Bombay aircraft. Powerful winds were blowing across Bagoush airfield when they arrived. The conditions, their RAF hosts explained with classic understatement, were far from ideal for parachuting. Even if the assault group landed safely, the reduced visibility caused by the swirling clouds of sand risked disorienting the raiders spread out over a wide area. The problem for the unit commander was that he knew there were plenty of critics back at Middle East headquarters (MEHQ) waiting for the first excuse to pan the controversial new unit as a waste of time, effort and resources. What's more, the commander had vowed to his men that they would never be subjected to the last-minute cancellations that had dogged so many operations in their commando days. At a hastily arranged meeting, he put the vote to his officers. The response was immediate and unanimous. The operation was on.

Each of the five sticks climbed aboard their aircraft and got down among an assortment of containers, packed with explosives, food, water and Thompson sub-machine guns. Tossed around by the strong winds for two hours over the southern

Mediterranean, the aircraft banked sharply and headed inland into a barrage of anti-aircraft fire. All the Axis airfields were only a short distance from the coast but the landmarks they used to guide them were obscured by the sandstorm below and the aircrews could make only a rough guess as to the location of the pre-arranged drop zones. The red lights came on and one by one the five sticks leapt out and were swept away into the darkness. Unable to see clearly below them, the men hit the ground hard and were dragged along by the powerful winds, many of them breaking and bruising limbs on the rocky terrain and shredding their flesh on the dense thorn bushes. Barely a man escaped uninjured.

It was immediately clear to the commanders that the mission was going to have to be aborted. Serious casualties had been sustained and they were unable to find many of the equipment containers scattered across the desert. After hours stumbling around in the dark looking for each other, the remaining raiding party began to make their separate ways to the pre-arranged RV point. For a day and a night, the injured men staggered through the desert valleys, or 'wadis' as they are known to the Arabs. On the second day, torrential rain turned the wadis into fast-flowing rivers, forcing the men up to the higher ground where the going was much harder. Soaked to the skin, shivering with cold, covered with cuts and gashes and nursing an assortment of sprains and fractures, the men from three of the five sticks struggled into the camp. They waited a further two days, but the two other groups failed to appear. Of the sixty-five men who had jumped, only twenty-two returned. The first operation carried out by the Special Air Service (SAS) had been an out-and-out catastrophe.

The three founding members of the SAS had all survived the first mission. David Stirling was the commander and inspiration behind the unit, while Paddy Mayne and Jock Lewes were the first men he recruited. Had they been killed or captured in the drop, the history of British irregular warfare might have been very different. It is unlikely that any of us today would ever have heard of the SAS. The new unit would have died at birth. As it was, they still faced a major struggle to survive after their disastrous debut. It had taken months of bureaucratic wrangling with the desk jockeys in MEHQ to persuade the authorities that there was a role for irregular warfare in the desert campaign. Dealing with 'layer upon layer of fossilised shit' was how Stirling described their efforts to get the unit up and running, all played out against a backdrop of sniping from the sceptical, gin-swilling 'lounge lizards' in the messes and bars of Cairo.

When they finally got the go-ahead, 'L Detachment, Special Air Service Brigade' was the name they were given, partly to deceive the Axis forces into believing the British had a parachute brigade in theatre and partly to give the impression that the new force was ten times larger than it actually was. Fitness, intelligence, composure under pressure and bottomless reserves of courage and audacity were the qualities Stirling was looking for in his recruits. In Robert Blair Mayne, known to all as 'Paddy', he had the very model of the character he wanted.

The giant Ulsterman, 6 foot 4 inches and 17 stone, came with a frightening reputation. By the time war broke out, he was a well-known figure in British sporting circles. He had won the Ireland universities' heavyweight boxing championship, earned six caps for the Ireland rugby union team and excelled on the British Lions tour to South Africa in 1938. At the start of the war he joined the Royal Ulster Rifles, but, eager to get into the action, he transferred first to the Cameronians and then No. 11 (Scottish) Commando. In June 1941 he proved his leadership skills and stomach for combat in a major Combined Operations raid up the Litani River in Vichy French-controlled Syria.

For many years the story went that Mayne was languishing under close arrest after striking his CO in the mess when Stirling used his famous diplomatic skills to have him released in order to join his new enterprise. It is almost certainly untrue, but it was the first of many myths and exaggerations that have distorted the memory of the man. Everybody had a story to tell in the pub or the mess about Paddy Mayne. Many of these tales have found their way into books and newspaper articles and today it is difficult to distinguish between the true, the half-true and the outright false. Another such story emanating from these early days of the war tells of Mayne beating up the BBC reporter Richard Dimbleby while out on a drinking spree in Cairo before laying out half a dozen military police sent to arrest him. The most recent and authoritative biography of Mayne proves that once and for all to be another falsehood. There are endless tales of heavy drinking, dark moods and violence. Many of these bar-room anecdotes are probably no more than unintentional fabrications that seek to add to the myth of an immense, complex character. The facts of the operations described here have never been disputed or questioned – and they need no pub talk to embellish or bring them to life.

Stirling, Mayne and Lewes knew they had to make a major impact – and make it quickly, or risk seeing their fledgling unit grounded before it was even up and running. As soon as they returned to base, they set about planning a series of spectacular raids on Axis airfields. The first was scheduled to take place in mid-December with Mayne leading a party of five against a major new air base at Wadi Tamet. After taking on board the painful lessons of the first operation, it was decided to abandon the use of aircraft and employ the Chevrolet trucks and jeeps of the LRDG instead. Capable of carrying large loads of water, fuel and equipment, the LRDG were able to stay out in the field for weeks, ranging hundreds of miles across the deserts of Libya and Egypt to radio back valuable information.

From their base at Jalo Oasis, 150 miles in from the coast, Mayne's raiding party set out in a small convoy of trucks, each with two mounted Lewis machine guns. With almost all the fighting in the North African campaign taking place in the narrow strip along the coast, only rarely did the LRDG encounter ground forces out in the desert. The main threat came from the air. Easily spotted in the vast canvas of the desert sands and scrub, with few places to take cover, they were constantly exposed to bombing and strafing.

Dropped at the RV point, the six men marched the last few miles through the cold winter air towards their target. They needed no reminding that another failure was likely to lead to the winding up of their organisation. Stealing through the airfield perimeter, they slipped past the sentries and began placing their Lewes time bombs with pencil fuses on the aircraft. When they discovered they were one bomb short, Mayne disabled the aircraft by using his great physical strength to rip out the instrument panel. The lightweight bombs, named after their inventor, the same Jock Lewes who was one of Stirling's first recruits, were designed to go off when acid in the fuses ate through and severed the wire, thereby triggering the detonation. As the last of the bombs was being planted, the alarm was raised and thirty Italian soldiers and airmen burst out of the airfield buildings, only to be cut down by withering bursts from the raiders' Thompson machine guns.

With both attackers and defenders using torches to communicate with their comrades, Mayne blew on his back-up whistle to gather his men in the confusion. Once assembled, they made a fighting withdrawal to the perimeter with the aircraft exploding across the airfield and the tracer fire whipping back and forth. As the sabotage group dashed away into the darkness, the raging fires they left behind were visible for miles around. Ten aircraft and several telegraph poles were destroyed but the most spectacular explosions were caused by the destruction of the petrol dump and the bomb store. The noise and flames from these eruptions were heard and seen by the LRDG patrol waiting six miles away. Mayne and his men had struck a major blow against the enemy. More importantly, they had struck a decisive one against their detractors back at MEHQ. L Detachment had proved it was a force to be reckoned with.

Official recognition was not long in coming. Although only a lieutenant at the time, Mayne was awarded a Distinguished Service Order – a decoration usually reserved for more senior officers. His citation concluded: 'He led this raid in person and himself destroyed and killed many of the enemy. The task set was of the most hazardous nature, and it was due to this officer's courage and leadership that success was achieved. I cannot speak too highly of this officer's skill and devotion to duty.'

Eager to capitalise on their success, Stirling and Mayne drew up plans for a follow-up raid on the Tamet airfield ten days later, on Christmas Eve. With the enemy now alive to the threat of British saboteurs, this one promised to be even more audacious and risky than the first. Mayne led the assault, as before marching the final few miles to the target from the RV point. As expected, security had been seriously ramped up with several groups comprising five or six guards strung out around the perimeter. Even so, they still managed to find a way between the positions without being spotted and set about placing their Lewes bombs as quickly as possible. One of the fuses detonated before the assault party had the chance to move out. Silhouetted against the glare of the raging fire from the explosion, the raiders came under immediate attack from all directions. The Italians encircled them and a desperate firefight ensued before Mayne and his men blasted their way through using grenades. As they melted away into the night to return to their RV, they left behind an inferno created by their destruction of twenty-seven Axis aircraft. Their joy was dampened, however, by news that Jock Lewes had been killed on returning from leading a separate raid when his jeep was attacked by a Messerschmitt Me 110.

As the Axis powers intensified their siege of Malta in the first half of 1942, Churchill put General Auchinleck, Commander-in-Chief Middle East, under increasing pressure to launch a new major offensive against the Afrika Korps in order to relieve the pressure on the battered island. With convoys unable to get through, the tiny British colony – the key to Allied success in the Mediterranean – was on the brink of starvation and collapse. The main problem in its defence was that Allied aircraft were stationed too far away to be able to offer air cover for the convoys. Churchill wanted Auchinleck to force the Germans back further west, thereby enabling Allied aircraft to be stationed within flying distance of Malta. L Detachment was to play its part in the offensive by mounting further raids against coastal airfields. On 8 June Mayne's raiding party was one of three that set out from Siwa Oasis, the main base of the LRDG. Their long-range escorts dropped them at their forward operating base in the rolling hills of Jebel Akhdar where they laid up and observed their targets in the dusty plains below. A group led by Stirling was to attack Benina airfield near Benghazi, and a unit of Free French targeted Berka airfield while Mayne's party headed towards a third base known as Berka Satellite airfield.

A combination of bad luck and lack of communication compromised Mayne's raid. The French unit launched their attack early which, combined with an RAF bombing raid on the Benina airfield, put all the air bases in the area on high alert. The other two L Detachment raids succeeded in destroying or damaging twenty aircraft as well as the same number of aero engines and some buildings. Mayne's group had penetrated the perimeter of Berka Satellite base, when the guards, more vigilant than normal, opened up on them before they could place their bombs. A fierce engagement with the entire garrison followed and Mayne had no choice but to order a withdrawal to the RV point. What followed highlighted the fearlessness and risks that Mayne and Stirling were prepared to take in the free roles they had been handed. Taking one of the LRDG open-back trucks, they drove down towards Benghazi to witness the damage they had caused. With Mayne at the wheel, Stirling next to him, five others behind them and making no attempt to disguise their British uniforms or vehicle, they drove straight up to an Axis roadblock. Usually, these checkpoints were manned by Italians but on this occasion there were a dozen Germans in attendance. One of them walked out into the road as the truck slowed to a halt.

Among the British raiders was a Palestinian Jew called Karl Kahane, who had once served in the German army. Kahane told the guard in fluent German that they were returning from a long operation and had captured the truck after defeating a British patrol. Raising his voice and swearing, he shouted that the reason he didn't know the latest password for the sprawling military base was because they had been in the field for so long. The suspicious guard walked slowly around the vehicle. Mayne cocked his Colt .45. The metallic clatter of more bolts and catches being unfastened in the rear of the truck was enough to persuade the sentry to let them pass. A few miles along the road, heading deeper into the enemy's midst, they came upon a camp made up of several buildings and tents where dozens of soldiers were milling around. The guards flagged down the vehicle as it approached the checkpoint. Mayne slammed his foot on the accelerator. Simultaneously, Stirling opened up with the mounted Lewis machine gun and the five others picked up their Tommy guns from the floor and blazed away from the back. Speeding away in a trail of dust, leaving a scene of carnage and chaos in their wake, they soon spotted lines of unattended military vehicles parked up at a depot. The temptation was too much. Leaping out of the truck, they quickly attached bombs to as many trucks and jeeps as they could before jumping back in and continuing their escape. They headed south across the coastal plain, chased by a column of armoured vehicles. Only when they climbed the steep escarpment leading to the hills did they finally manage to shake off their pursuers.

As the truck bounced and jerked over the rough terrain, one of the men in the back heard the sound of a timer on one of the bombs which had been activated by the violent jolting of the vehicle. As Mayne slammed on the brakes, the seven men leapt clear as the truck was hurled into the air by the force of the explosion. The fuel tank and ammunition quickly caught fire, reducing their only means of transport to a charred wreck within minutes. They had no option but to march back to the RV point, where, to their relief, the LRDG were still waiting for them. When the whole convoy returned to Siwa Oasis they found the base hastily packing up. Tobruk had been captured, Rommel was powering towards Egypt and the British were frantically digging in along the Alamein line to make a last-ditch defence of the Nile Delta and block Rommel from taking Cairo and the Suez Canal.

Undeterred by the chaos of reorganisation around them, L Detachment continued to mount attacks. Mayne's suggestion that the raiders approached their targets in jeeps rather than march the last few miles was adopted in their next operation. Acquiring a small fleet of their own vehicles, they mounted two Vickers machine guns and set off for Bagoush airfield. The thinking behind the new tactic was that it allowed them to get in and out of the target zone more quickly, but it also gave them an extra attacking option, as they proved to spectacular effect that night. Mayne led a party of six and succeeded in blowing up twenty-two aircraft, but he was annoyed that the fuses on eighteen other bombs had failed to go off. Back at the RV point, he and Stirling decided to make a second attack. Undeterred by the frenetic enemy activity in the area following the first raid, the two jeeps sped back into the airfield and raked the remaining aircraft with machine-gun fire, destroying twelve of them to secure their highest tally for a single night's raid so far.

After returning to Cairo to restock their supplies and acquire more vehicles, L Detachment planned a massive assault on Sidi Haneish airfield near the coastal town of Fuka. Reconnaissance reports suggested that dozens of aircraft had been moved to the airfield and it was quickly turning into one of the busiest of all the Axis bases. In a departure from their customary tactic of stealing in under cover of darkness, planting their explosives and then slipping or fighting their way out, Stirling and Mayne planned a more direct all-out attack involving most of the men of the unit. The plan was for two columns of eight jeeps, with Stirling's vehicle spearheading the whole formation, to crash through the perimeter and attack the parked aircraft before the enemy had the chance to gather itself and respond. Mayne was at the head of one column and George Jellicoe, the son of John Jellicoe, the former Admiral of the Fleet, at the head of the other, as the raiding party set off on the afternoon of 26 July. Never afraid of laying themselves open to attack from the air, they travelled in open formation, kicking up clouds of dust in the wobbling heat haze as they descended from the mountains on to the coastal plain. The forty-mile journey over rough terrain took almost five hours and they were forced to stop on countless occasions to mend punctures. They were bumping through the darkness, edging closer to their target, when the area right in front of them suddenly burst into light. The runway lights had been turned on as a German bomber, coming in low over their heads, prepared to land.

Suddenly exposed to the enemy, the raiding party attacked immediately. As the jeeps raced between the rows of enemy aircraft, the muzzles of twenty mounted Lewis machine guns and dozens of Thompson sub-machine guns spat their fire into the targets. The noise was deafening, the light blinding and there was pandemonium among the enemy as one aircraft after another burst into flames. The Germans fired back into the maelstrom but, before they had a chance to organise themselves, the jeeps tore away into the hills leaving the airfield engulfed in an inferno. In a few furious minutes, they had destroyed more than thirty aircraft – many of them the Junkers Ju 52 transports upon which Rommel relied for his supplies. It was a stunning success but it came at the cost of one dead and half a dozen wounded.

The raid had taken place during the final hours of the First Battle of El Alamein – a month-long struggle that succeeded in halting Rommel's advance on Cairo. Code-breakers had established that Rommel was now seriously short of fuel and tanks, thanks in no small part to the efforts of British submarine fleets in torpedoing enemy shipping. Keen to exploit his weakness, MEHQ put together ambitious plans for raids on the Axis-held ports of Tobruk and Benghazi.

As part of a deception ploy ahead of a much larger assault on Tobruk, Stirling was ordered to lead a large force of several hundred men from various special units in an attack on the harbour at Benghazi. Stirling's reservations about the operation's chances of success were borne out by events on the balmy September night on which it took place. On this occasion the enemy were waiting for them – no fewer than five thousand men. They had been tipped off. The assault group was to attack a military camp on their way into the town and all was quiet on the approach – until they reached the gates, when the enemy, dug in all around them, opened up. A frenetic engagement followed, ending with the British withdrawing in disarray having taken significant casualties. But the worst was yet to come.

At daybreak, the Germans took to the air and hunted down their attackers' jeeps and trucks, bombing and strafing them without respite all the way back to their lines. It was every vehicle for itself as the raiders scattered in all directions, many of them with serious casualties aboard as they bounced and lurched over the rough terrain, trying to seek sanctuary in the relative safety of the hills. By the time the dust in the desert had settled, four men lay dead, dozens were wounded and more than twenty jeeps and twenty trucks loaded with equipment had been destroyed or abandoned. Four of the most seriously injured troops had to be left behind with a medical orderly, to give themselves up. Through no fault of their own, the last significant operation of the original SAS in North Africa ended much as their first one had done – in disaster. But by then only a few were still questioning their value on the battlefield and, in spite of the setback, two weeks later L Detachment was given the full status of a regiment under Stirling's command. He was promoted to lieutenant colonel while Mayne, his right-hand man and most formidable operative, became a major. By the end of 1942, Montgomery's Eighth Army had Rommel on the run after their victory in the

Second Battle of El Alamein. Over the coming months the Afrika Korps and their Italian allies were driven out of Egypt and Libya into Tunisia where, facing annihilation, they finally surrendered and 250,000 men laid down their arms.

With British and Commonwealth forces in the ascendancy, it was all the more of a blow for the men of the SAS when Stirling, their founder and CO, was captured in January 1943. Their operations in the desert were in the process of being wound up at the time and their future role looked uncertain. The unit needed a continuation of the strong, single-minded leadership that had transformed it from a small, semi-independent group of raiders into a significant military force. There was only one contender to succeed Stirling: Paddy Mayne, the man who had destroyed more enemy aircraft than any other serviceman in World War II.

By early 1943, the SAS had ballooned into a far larger unit than its original members could ever have imagined at its foundation eighteen months earlier. As they packed up their equipment and prepared to leave the desert, the organisation was split into two parts, with the Special Boat Section (SBS) commanded by Jellicoe and the rest reconstituted and renamed as the Special Raiding Squadron (SRS), commanded by Mayne. The SRS headed to northern Palestine in the spring of 1943 to prepare for their invasion of southern Europe and Mayne wasted no time in stamping his authority on the men under his command. As a top sportsman, fitness had always been a priority. He understood better than anyone that in any hard-fought physical contest, military or sporting, the outcome often turned on which side had the edge in stamina and physical strength. Mayne worked his men to the point of collapse and, although they didn't thank him for it at the time, they later came to appreciate the ruthlessness of his regime when they were pushed to the limit in bitter struggles with their enemy. Malcolm James Pleydell, a young medical officer who had recently been attached to the SAS, said the Ulsterman's natural command and authority made him stand out even in a group containing so many strong personalities. Writing after the war of his first impressions of Mayne, he said he was: '. . . a quietly forceful and rugged leader who could be relied upon in an emergency; a man who was as ruthless as he was quick-witted in action'. As Allied attention turned towards an invasion of Sicily and Italy, Mayne was to be given plenty of opportunity to prove that ruthlessness in what promised to be some of the bloodiest fighting of the war.

At Port Said in Egypt, the SRS boarded the troopship the *Ulster Monarch*, a modified ferry that had once worked the Irish Sea, and were informed of their mission: they were to form the spearhead of the invasion of Sicily in Operation Husky. Their first task was to destroy a gun battery with three 150mm coast guns, sitting on top of Capo Murro di Porco, a few miles from the harbour of Syracuse on the south-east coast of the island. As the first major assault landing against an occupied coastline in the war, this was unknown territory for the Allies. Casualties were expected to be high. The Germans had some of their best troops stationed there while the Italians were defending their homeland.

When the invasion fleet set sail from Egypt the weather was calm but, as they drew within sight of the Sicilian coast on the night of 9 July, a strong wind was blowing and the sea was rough. Wave after wave of Allied planes roared overhead, dropping their payloads over Sicily and a series of bright explosions erupted into the pitch darkness. The nine landing assault crafts (LCAs) were lowered over the side into the heaving surf and within minutes of setting out for the shoreline the troops were soaked to the skin as the waves crashed over the sides. For the seaborne troops, the dreadful weather was an inconvenience; for the airborne units it was a disaster. As the landing craft lurched over the waves they picked their way through the debris of troop-carrying gliders that had fallen short of land and crashed into the water. The survivors, many of them injured, bobbed up and down in the water. Some were pulled aboard the LCAs, others were left to fend for themselves as the amphibious force, under orders to stick to the schedule, pushed on for their objectives.

The ramps of the landing craft were dropped and 264 men of the SRS stormed ashore. The standard commando tactic in a night raid was to light up the target with flares, hammer it with small arms and mortar and then creep up for the final assault. Mayne's approach was even more direct. He ordered his 29-man mortar detachment to attack the battery, causing chaos in the garrison dug in at the gun battery as fires broke out all around them. Mayne immediately exploited the mayhem by sending in two of his three troops, each comprised of about seventy-five men. To prevent reinforcements reaching the battery, he dispatched his third troop to attack a neighbouring farm, which was being used as a defensive stronghold by the enemy. They had expected a bitter, drawn-out struggle to seize the position, but within an hour of hitting the beaches Mayne's men had captured and destroyed the battery. A major threat to the invasion force and the fleet offshore had been neutralised. The butcher's bill made for stirring reading when news of the success reached the operation commanders offshore: four coastal guns, three anti-aircraft guns, one rangefinder and half a dozen heavy machine-gun positions had been silenced, over fifty enemy troops had been killed and over fifty had been captured. The SRS hadn't suffered a single casualty.

Mayne now had a free hand to proceed as he saw fit. The SRS and other units of the Commando Brigade involved in the vanguard of the invasion came under General Dempsey, commander of XIII Corps, who had been impressed by Mayne and his men when he had come to watch them in training. His respect for Mayne was expressed in his orders to him for the operation. Most components of such a large operation were given their objectives and told to await further orders on completing them. But recognising his potential for wreaking calculated destruction on the enemy, Dempsey gave the SRS commander permission to act at his own discretion. Mayne certainly wasn't going to pass up the opportunity for a further strike against the enemy.

Mayne had set up his defensive positions around Capo Murro di Porco awaiting a counter-attack when a second battery a short distance away began to open up on the Allied fleet. Mayne ordered an immediate attack. Racing across open ground into incoming fire, his men quickly overwhelmed a number of enemy positions in farm buildings along the way. They took dozens of prisoners and released some paratroopers captured earlier in the assault. The second gun battery was better defended than the first and on this occasion the SRS suffered casualties in the heavy fighting that erupted. Muzzles flashed and twinkled in the dark, mortars and grenades filled the air with the din of explosion. The defenders buckled under the speed and intensity of the attack, but Mayne wasn't finished. Noticing two further gun batteries firing their deadly salvoes out to sea, Mayne exploited the momentum that his men had built up and launched them forward once again. The enemy could offer little resistance against the rapid and ferocious assault. In a short time, they had rolled up the major defensive positions along the entire stretch of coast, destroying a further three coastal guns, eight anti-aircraft guns, four mortars, several machine-gun posts and an ammunition dump. By the time the SRS had linked up with the main forces of 5th Division the following day, they had killed over two hundred enemy and captured more than twice that number. The SRS had lost just one man and had two wounded. Thanks in large part to Mayne's tenacity and quick thinking, a brilliantly executed operation had far exceeded the expectations of even the most optimistic of the operation planners.

The SRS had more than earned their rest when they re-embarked on board the *Ulster Monarch* but they had barely changed out of their combat fatigues when Mayne and his officers were summoned to a briefing by the divisional commander, to be told they were going straight back into action. An enemy counter-attack had been beaten back and General Dempsey wanted to take advantage while his troops were on the front foot. The SRS were ordered to seize the heavily fortified harbour of Augusta, whose dockside facilities would help relieve the pressure on the port at Syracuse as the invading forces tried to get men and equipment ashore as quickly as possible. It was an off-the-cuff decision and the rough plans for the operation were drawn up there and then. In soldier-speak, they were going to be 'fag-packeting' it – i.e. making it up as they went along. This was just the sort of impromptu action that Stirling had imagined for his rapid reaction force and Mayne had proved earlier in the day that he was just the man needed to lead such a hazardous step into the unknown. Who dares win.

It was to be the first amphibious daylight attack of the campaign. The simplicity of the orders belied the complexity of the challenge: take the town and hold it until a larger force of infantry fights its way through to the town. The sun was starting to set when, in clear view of the enemy on shore, the LCAs were lowered once again over the sides of the *Ulster Monarch* at the mouth of the harbour. The 260 men, who had barely had time to reclothe, rearm and grab some rations, climbed aboard. As the ramps were lowered into the water, the men poured ashore into a shower of heavy machine-gun and mortar fire. The landing crafts responded with their own mounted guns while a British cruiser and two destroyers laid down a bombardment. Led from the front by Mayne, the assault group waded waist deep through the waves and clambered up the beach with rounds whipping around them. Splitting up into sections, the troops spread out through the town, clearing it house by house and street by street. 'This part of the operation was carried out very successfully against Navy's advice in broard (sic) daylight under heavy machine gun fire,' wrote Mayne in his report of the action.

The fighting was fierce and they took casualties along the way but, by nightfall, the guns had fallen silent and the last sniper had been cleared out of his hiding position. Mayne immediately probed the outer limits of the town and discovered it was heavily defended with mortar troops, light tanks and heavy machine guns. Armed with only small arms and a few mortars, his unit stood no chance against such a formidable arsenal of weapons. Faulty radio sets were a constant problem throughout the campaign and Mayne was unable to contact the naval support ships to call in a bombardment. Taking the cautious option, he decided not to commit his men against such overwhelming firepower. Instead, he established two defensive positions on key bridges and waited for the inevitable counter-attack. To the relief of the exhausted unit, who had lost two men and had eight wounded, it never materialised and the following afternoon they were relieved by a large force and ferried back to the *Ulster Monarch*.

The outstanding performance of the SRS in Sicily was recognised in the award of seven medals for the unit. One Military Cross and five Military Medals were won, while Mayne himself received a bar to his DSO. The citation is worth recording in full:

Operation 'Husky', Sicily, On July 10th 1943 & 12th July 1943, Major R.B. Mayne carried out two successful operations. The first, the capture and destruction of a coastal defence battery on Capo Murro Di Porco, the outcome of which was vital to the safe landing of XIII Corps. By nightfall 10/7/43, SRS had captured three additional Btys, 450 prisoners as well as killing 200 to 300 Italians. The second, the capture and hold of the town of Augusta. The landing was carried out in daylight, a most hazardous combined operation. By the audacity displayed the Italians were forced from their positions in masses and most valuable stores and equipment was saved from certain destruction. In both these operations it was Major Mayne's courage, determination and superb leadership which proved the key to success. He personally led his men from the landing craft in the face of heavy machine gun fire and in the case of the Augusta raid, mortar fire. By these actions he succeeded in forcing his way to ground where it was possible to form up and sum up the enemy's defences.

Of more importance to the CO was the fact that he had proved that the SRS were a flexible unit, capable not only of small covert raids on unsuspecting targets, but also large-scale assaults against heavily defended positions. Regular or irregular, by land or sea, day or night, small scale or large – throw them any challenge, no matter how tough, and Mayne and his small unit of crack troops would carry it out.

As the Allies slowly ground down the resistance in Sicily, the

Germans retreated over the Strait of Messina to continue the fight on the mainland. It had been a truly bloody contest with the British bearing the brunt of the 25,000 Allied casualties, but the fight for Italy had only just begun. When the commanders drew up the plans for the next stage of the campaign, no one in SRS was surprised to learn that once again they were to be used as shock troops in the first wave of the invasion. Specifically, they were to capture and hold the old coastal resort town of Bagnara, fifteen miles north of the city of Reggio on the toe of Italy where they were to cut off German communications and await the arrival of the main units of the Eighth Army.

The assault was meant to take place under cover of darkness. In the small hours of 4 September the seven landing craft in which they were launched suffered a spate of mechanical and navigational problems that threatened to scupper the operation. When they did finally make it ashore it was dawn, they were three hours late and half the 243 men of the squadron were still somewhere out at sea. Fortunately, the landing was unopposed and half an hour later the rest of the men made land. The three troops and mortar detachment immediately spread out and advanced up the steep, winding roads to the town above the beach. Taking one German position completely by surprise, A section from No. 1 Troop captured twenty-eight men and wounded five, but any hopes that Bagnara was going to be a walkover for the British were quickly and painfully extinguished. Now alive to the danger, the Germans opened up from their higher positions on the most forward of the squadron sections with Spandau heavy machine guns and mortars, killing two and wounding half a dozen. Undeterred, Mayne pushed 3rd Troop through the town, where they forced back a German unit to the mouth of a road tunnel dug into the hills. In the engagement that followed, ten Germans were killed and three wounded. 'Prisoners questioned told us that they were completely unaware of our landing and were taken by surprise,' Mayne recorded. 'It can therefore be presumed that had our landing taken place at 0200 hrs as intended the whole position would have been cleared with much less casualties.'

With resistance inside the town mopped up by midday, the main threat lurked in the surrounding hills above where the bulk of the Germans had withdrawn behind some well-fortified positions with commanding views of the battlefield. Mayne and his men dug in and waited for the counter-attack. Once again, to their surprise, it never came and the following day advance units from the Green Howards arrived to relieve them. The SRS counted five men killed and thirty nine wounded at Bagnara – many of those attributable to communication failures caused by the poor quality of wireless sets in the hilly country. But casualties were light compared to those they were to suffer in their next, and last, operation in Italy.

The following month, General Montgomery turned to the SRS and the commandos of the Special Service Brigade as the Eighth Army tried to break what was known as the 'Termoli Line' a long way north of Bari. Operating alongside No. 3 and No. 40 Commandos plus support units, the SRS were sent in to seize two key bridges outside the town of that name. Their capture would assist the advance of the 78th Division up the Adriatic coast.

Operation Devon was launched on 3 October when two hundred men of the SRS put to sea in an LCI, a larger version of the LCA, but as at Bagnara there were problems that threatened to torpedo the operation before they reached land. The LCI was grounded and the troops had to wait several hours to be ferried ashore in a flotilla of smaller LCAs, delaying and disorganising the schedule laid down for the assault. When they finally hit shore they received a ferocious welcome from a far larger unit of battle-hardened German paratroopers. 'B' section from 3rd Troop was captured after it became cut off as fighting continued throughout the day. German resistance was well organised and typically dogged but by the evening Mayne's men had seized their objectives and, having been relieved by the Lancashire Fusiliers, he withdrew his troops into the centre of town for the night. One dead, three wounded and two dozen captured was the hard-earned cost of their success, but their casualty figures were a fraction of those suffered by the Germans.

Such was the importance of Termoli to the German strategy of holding back the Allied advance that on this occasion it was a question of when, not if, the counter-attack came. Constant sniper activity the following day was just a foretaste of the onslaught that was brewing behind the scenes. With all their supply lines still open, the Germans were able to bring in major reinforcements together with tank and artillery units. The Allied efforts to supply their troops were seriously compromised. A large number of bridges had been blown by the enemy and the problem was made considerably worse when torrential rain swelled the rivers and played havoc with the pontoons laid down by the engineers. What's more, unknown to Mayne and the commando units in the town, a German observation post had been set up in a church tower with commanding views of the Allied positions.

When the attack came the next morning, it was every bit as ferocious as they had feared. The first phase of it was delivered from the air and it was followed by a massive artillery barrage. Orders arrived from Commando Brigade HQ for Mayne's squadron to take up defensive positions at various points in the defensive line. As the men scrambled into action and the local population ran for cover, huge explosions rocked the town, sending up giant plumes of smoke, fire and debris. One SRS section had just climbed aboard a German truck they had commandeered when a shell landed in the back, killing eighteen men, fifteen of them outright. An Italian family that had been looking after the section, feeding them and washing their clothes, was waving the soldiers off when the mortar landed. Mother, father and daughter were killed instantly but the young son had suffered hideous wounds to his chest and abdomen and was running around screaming. Realising that the boy was mortally wounded and had no chance of survival, one of the SRS survivors put him out of his agony with a bullet. Two other SRS men were killed and several others wounded in a separate incident.

Against such overwhelming firepower the situation looked desperate for the squadron and the rest of the Commando Brigade. With only sea behind them, there was nowhere for them to withdraw. The Germans were closing in and the British lacked the hardware to resist the merciless blitz. Alarm was turning to panic in some sections of the line and the brigade commander, Lieutenant Colonel John Durnford-Slater, even threatened to shoot some of his anxious officers and men if they didn't steady themselves and stand firm.

In the late afternoon, some of the pressure was relieved when the forward observation post, which everyone had suspected but no one could pinpoint, was finally located. It was a lone German operating from the church tower and he was riddled with machine-gun bullets as he tried to flee over the building's roof. But the major breakthrough came the following day when engineers finally managed to lay a pontoon over the swollen river, allowing a Canadian squadron of Sherman tanks to join the battle. If anything, the German attacks were even more intense than the previous day and the SRS fought desperately to hold their section of the front under extremely heavy mortar fire. At one time the enemy pushed within a few dozen yards of their positions, killing an SRS captain in the process, but they were beaten back after the squadron's own mortar detachment finally silenced their German counterparts. The SRS hadn't yielded a yard in the onslaught and by mid-afternoon a British infantry brigade joined the attack, killing off German hopes of retaking the strategically crucial town. The SRS and the rest of the Commando Brigade had played the central roles in a glorious victory, but it had been a close run struggle.

Mayne and his men ended 5 October burying their comrades and friends. Not since the first disastrous operation in Libya had the squadron suffered so many casualties in a single day. In all, the operation had cost the SRS the lives of twenty-one men with twenty-four wounded and twenty-three missing, presumed captured. In its own dogged, brutal way, the battle at Termoli was as impressive as any of the squadron's many remarkable successes thus far. It may have lacked the daring and almost exotic glamour of their North Africa raids, but for sheer guts in the face of overwhelming enemy firepower it was second to none. Mayne wrote in his diary: 'It is a good sign that although the fighting of 5th/6th was an all out attempt to regain Termoli . . . and the enemy had ample forces and heavy support to smash the light forces which were there, he was unable to do so.' To emphasise the point, he underlined the last six words.

Their courage didn't go unnoticed. A week later, General Dempsey paid Mayne and the SRS a visit and delivered a stirring farewell address. Jettisoning the usually reserved language of senior commanders, the Commander of XIII Corps heaped extravagant praise on a unit that only a couple of years earlier was looked down upon by some in higher military office as a ragtag group of cut-throat bandits.

It is just three months since we landed in Sicily and during that time you have carried out four successful operations. You were originally lent to me for the first operation – that of Capo Murro di Porco. That was a brilliant operation, brilliantly planned and brilliantly carried out . . . The landing at Termoli completely upset the Germans' schedule, and the balance of their forces, by introducing a threat to the north of Rome. They were obliged to bring to the east coast the 16th Panzer Division, which was reserve in the Naples area. They had orders, which have since come into our hands, to recapture Termoli at all costs and drive the British into the sea. These orders, thanks to you, they were unable to carry out. It had another effect, though. It eased the pressure on the American 5th Army and, as you have probably read, they are now advancing . . .

. . . In all my military career – and in my time I have commanded many units – I have never yet met a unit in which I had such confidence as I have in yours. And I mean that!

In a long, detailed speech Dempsey laid out what he considered to be the factors that raised the unit above all others he had commanded. Recognising their unique operational capacity and advanced combat skills, he also spelt out the strict conditions under which he would put them into the field, saying a commander should 'never use you unless the job is worthwhile. That is to say, unless the effect to be gained more than compensates for the risk taken in putting you in; and there is always considerable risk in using troops like yourselves.'

In a way, his words were an official acknowledgement that in a very short space of time the squadron had made itself indispensable to the British armed forces. Although he didn't mention Mayne by name, the implication – and it needed no pointing out to his military audience – was that no unit could perform to such high standards unless it served under an exceptional commander.

With typical modesty, Mayne spoke of the pride in his men that he felt listening to the general. In a letter to Malcolm Pleydell, he said: 'General Dempsey, the Corps Commander, paid us what, I imagine, were the highest compliments paid to any unit. Among other things he said we were the best crowd he had ever had under his command. I think he is right, too; the lads have done well!'

On returning to the UK to join the preparations for the invasion for France, the SRS underwent a fresh reorganisation of its structure. It was renamed 1 SAS Regiment and Mayne, promoted to lieutenant colonel, was to be its commander. As the man who had taken part in more SAS operations than any other, his appointment was almost a matter of procedure and, as the CO, his role inevitably came to involve a great deal more organisation and planning than he had been used to while leading operations from the front in North Africa and Italy. In the different circumstances facing them across the Channel, the role of the regiment had changed, too. It was no longer like the early days in the desert when half a dozen of them would disappear into the night with a machine gun and a few bombs. Fighting behind enemy lines in France, in among the local population, was fraught with even greater risks. Inevitably, they were forced to change their *modus operandi* and their CO was never going to be able to take part in as many front-line operations as he had in the past. With so many units in the field, spread over a wide area and working in conjunction with the Resistance, it was important for Mayne to play a more withdrawn, supervisory role. It was, of course, not in his warrior nature to stand too far off the action and Mayne saw plenty more of it as the Allies gradually pushed the Nazis back into Germany in the eleven months following the Normandy landings.

Of the 2,000 SAS soldiers in the field 300 were lost, many of them tortured and executed under Hitler's infamous order to kill British 'commandos' who had been wreaking so much havoc across Europe. With their comrades in the Resistance, the SAS accounted for over 7,000 enemy killed, almost 5,000 captured and an immeasurable amount of physical damage to the infrastructure of the German war machine. They destroyed dozens of trains and scores of rail wagons, they caused 30 derailments and cut the tracks at over 160 locations; 750 vehicles were destroyed or captured and 400 bombing targets were passed on to the RAF.

The British recognised Mayne's contribution by awarding him a second bar to his DSO. His citation concluded: 'It was entirely due to Lt. Col. Mayne's fine leadership and example, and due to his utter disregard of danger that the unit was able to achieve such striking success.' French recognition of his work came in the form of admission to the Légion d'honneur and the awarding of the Croix de Guerre with palm.

Following Stirling's capture, Mayne had done more than anyone to raise and maintain the highest standards demanded by the squadron and it is a source of great sadness and regret to his former comrades and many other supporters that his last acts in the field became contaminated with controversy. In all other circumstances what happened on 9 April 1945 on the outskirts of the Saxon city of Oldenburg would be a cause for celebration and pride. That the events of the day are not seen in that positive light has nothing to do with Mayne himself, but with a mysterious figure in the higher reaches of the military hierarchy. First, the facts.

Mayne was ordered by the General Officer Commanding of the 4th Canadian Armoured Division to lead his regiment, consisting of two armoured jeep squadrons, and clear a path through German lines for Canadian armoured cars and tanks, causing as much mayhem among the enemy as possible.

During the action, Mayne received a wireless message informing him that the lead squadron was under heavy fire and the squadron commander had been killed. Mayne made straight for the scene of action. Hereon the story is best told in the very detailed recommendation for an award put forward by Brigadier J.M. 'Mad Mike' Calvert:

From the time of his arrival until the end of the action Lt. Col. Mayne was in full view of the enemy and exposed to fire from small arms, machine guns, sniper rifles and Panzerfausts. On arrival he summed up the situation in a matter of seconds and entered the nearest house alone and ensured the enemy here had either withdrawn or been killed. He then seized a Bren gun and magazines and single-handedly fired burst after burst into a second house, killing or wounding the enemy there and also opened fire on the woods.

He then ordered a jeep to come forward and take over his fire position before returning to the forward position where he disposed the men to the best advantage and ordered another jeep to come forward. He got into the jeep and with another officer as rear gunner drove forward past the position where the Squadron Commander had been killed a few minutes previously and continued to point a hundred yards ahead where a further section of jeeps were halted by intense and accurate enemy fire. This section had suffered casualties and wounded owing to the heavy enemy fire and the survivors were unable at that time to influence the action in any way until the arrival of Lt. Col. Mayne.

The Lt. Col. continued along the road all the time engaging the enemy with fire from his own jeep. Having swept the whole area with close range fire he turned his jeep around and drove down the road again, still in full view of the enemy. By this time the enemy had suffered heavy casualties and had started to withdraw. Nevertheless they maintained intense fire on the road and it appeared almost impossible to extricate the wounded who were in a ditch near to the forward jeeps. Any attempt of rescuing these men under those conditions appeared virtually suicidal owing to the highly concentrated and accurate fire of the enemy. Though he fully realised the risk he was taking Lt. Col. Mayne turned his jeep round once more and returned to try and rescue these wounded. Then by superlative determination and displaying gallantry of the very highest degree and in the face of intense enemy machine gun fire he lifted the wounded one by one into the jeep, turned round and drove back to the main body.

The entire enemy positions had been wiped out, the majority of the enemy having been killed or wounded leaving a very small percentage who were now in full retreat. The Squadron having suffered no further casualties were able to continue their advance and drive deeper behind the enemy to complete their task of sabotage and destruction of the enemy. Finally they reached a point 20 miles ahead of the advance guard of the advancing Canadian Division thus threatening the rear of the Germans who finally withdrew.

From the time of the arrival of Lt. Col. Mayne his gallantry inspired all ranks. Not only did he save the lives of the wounded but he also completely defeated and destroyed the enemy.

He was recommended for the VC by a brigadier, a major general and a general and it was signed off by none less than Field Marshal Bernard Montgomery. As endorsements went, they didn't come much higher than that, but the recommendation was downgraded to a third bar to his DSO. The citation clearly shows that someone has crossed out the letters 'VC'. Who did so and why is still not known today, but then, as now, people felt that Mayne had been the victim of a serious injustice.

Major General Sir Robert Laycock, Chief of Combined Operations after the war, wrote a short, moving letter to Mayne, making clear his views on the matter.

My Dear Paddy, I feel I must drop you a line just to tell you how very deeply I appreciate the great honour of being able to address, as my friend, an officer who has succeeded in accomplishing the practically unprecedented task of collecting no less than four DSOs. (I am informed that there is another such superman in the Royal Air Force.)

You deserve all the more, and in my opinion, the appropriate authorities do not really know their job. If they did they would have given you a VC as well. Please do not dream of answering this letter, which brings with it my sincerest admiration and a deep sense of honour in having, at one time, been associated with you.

A campaign has been ongoing ever since for Mayne to be awarded a retrospective VC. A signed petition was presented to the Queen on her Golden Jubilee and three early-day motions have been put forward in the House of Commons. The last of these, in 2005, was signed by more than one hundred MPs of all parties and stated: 'This House recognises the grave injustice meted out to Lt Col Paddy Mayne.' The Government minister of the time, however, said it would be wrong to reverse the decision, made for whatever reason, sixty years earlier.

After the war Mayne, who never married, returned to his hometown of Newtownards in County Down and resumed his work as a solicitor. On 13 December 1955, he died at the wheel of his red 2.5-litre Riley Roadster, when he crashed it at speed into a railing after returning from a night of poker and drinking with friends.

ROYAL MARINES

Lieutenant Colonel Herbert 'Blondie' Hasler

On the afternoon of 21 September 1942, a tall, athletic figure with a receding hairline and a magnificent moustache strode into the Headquarters of Combined Operations in Richmond Terrace, Whitehall. (Acting) Major Herbert 'Blondie' Hasler of the Royal Marines, holder of an OBE for his actions in the Norway campaign two years earlier, had come to discuss possible operations for the small specialist unit he commanded. An expert in small-boat handling, Hasler was based in Eastney Barracks, Southsea, where he and his unit of thirty-four men carried out a series of exercises and tested new equipment in the many harbours and creeks of the local coastline. It was his task to develop plans for attacking shipping in Axis-controlled harbours and the Prime Minister Winston Churchill himself was demanding that CO start implementing some of the dozens of operations that had been proposed.

These were dark days for the British. Despite victory in the Battle of Britain, the country's Armed Forces and their Commonwealth allies were being squeezed on all fronts in every theatre of the global conflict. Until the country generated the operational capacity to launch a concerted fightback, Churchill had turned to irregular warfare as a way of causing maximum disruption with minimum resources.

Hasler was handed a paper entitled 'Frankton'. Committing it to memory, the twenty-eight-year-old made the ten-minute walk across St James's Park, ordered a drink at the bar of the Royal Ocean Racing Club, and started writing. It wasn't quite written on the back of a napkin or a cigarette packet, but the document he presented on his return to HQ was not the most sophisticated to have passed over the desk of Lord Mountbatten, the newly appointed Director of Combined Operations. But what it lacked in format it more than made up for in its crystal clarity and breathtaking ambition. The initial reaction was one of scepticism bordering on disbelief. Hasler was proposing a long-distance canoeing raid to blow up Axis shipping in Bordeaux harbour.

After the closure of the Trans-Siberian Railway, all trade between Germany and Japan now had to go by ship. Axis ships were known to be operating out of Bordeaux, running the Royal Navy blockade to transport vital equipment to and from the Far East.

Thousands of tons of rubber as well as specialist oils and metals, vital to Hitler's war machine, had been arriving at the French city along the Atlantic coast in the south-west of the country. On the return leg, the ships carried tons of goods to assist the Imperial Army's occupation of south-east Asia, including radar parts, communication equipment and special chemicals. Lord Selbourne, the Minister for Economic Warfare, had written to the Deputy Prime Minister Clement Atlee to express his anxieties about the matter.

Bordeaux's location sixty miles inland up the River Gironde ruled out a conventional assault by sea or air. Beyond the reach of surface ships and submarines, an RAF bombing raid was also out of the reckoning as it would have been impossible to pick out the individual targets in among the dozens of other ships and then hit them with pinpoint accuracy. The alternative of saturation-bombing the dockyard would risk the lives of thousands of French civilians and destroy a major source of their livelihood.

It was for these reasons that the commanders inside COHQ sat up and read Hasler's outline plan with great interest. In broad brush, the mission looked straightforward enough. Hasler's sabotage team would be dropped by submarine off the French coast, paddle up the Gironde and, after laying magnetic limpet mines on the blockade runners in the harbour, paddle back downriver and escape overland to the relative safety of neutral Spain. The simplicity of the proposal belied the enormous complexity and challenges of executing it.

For a start, the Gironde was a fast-flowing river flanked by mudflats, thick reed beds and overlooked by the famous vine-yards of the region. It was patrolled by German navy boats and worked daily by dozens of local fishermen. The mouth of the estuary had been heavily mined both by Germans and the RAF, but the position of the explosives had not been mapped accurately. There were also powerful tides and inshore currents to contend with.

Lord Mountbatten thought the risks were so great that he didn't expect any of the raiders to return, and he was especially worried about the escape phase. With the Germans on full alert after an attack, there was no chance of the raiders being picked up by sub off the coast. The only option was travel overland with the help of Resistance escape organisations, but, covering between 250 and 500 miles, depending on the route they took, it was a journey fraught with hazards. The French Gendarmerie was under orders from the Vichy Government to assist the Germans and there was a serious risk of betrayal by local collaborators.

Mountbatten and other senior commanders in CO were adamant that Hasler himself should not go. As a leading authority in his field he was, they argued, too great an asset to risk losing. Hasler was furious and mounted a vigorous rebuttal of their arguments, saying that he was the only man with the skills of seamanship and navigation to lead the operation. He added that if the operation failed in his absence it would jeopardise similar projects in the future. Above all, however, he didn't want to lose the respect of his men by staying behind while they put their lives in danger. He cited SAS founder David Stirling as an example of a Commanding Officer of an irregular unit leading hazardous raids from the front. He concluded by asking: 'If I am not allowed to go on this operation what type of operation will be permissible for me?'

On 29 October, a conference with Mountbatten and three others chiefs at COHQ took place in Richmond Terrace to discuss the matter. It was, by all accounts, a lively meeting at the end of which Mountbatten sighed and said: 'Much against my better judgement I am going to let you go.' Originally, Hasler suggested using three two-man canoes, each carrying two men but Mountbatten increased the force to six.

The following day the outline of the plan, which had barely changed since Hasler had hastily drawn it up in the bar of his club, was forwarded to the Chiefs of Staff Committee for their approval. A week later they were given the green light and the sabotage party, handpicked by Hasler, headed to Scotland to begin their training.

Other than Hasler, none of the other eleven men had any experience of canoeing. They were tough lads drawn from inner cities who had made it through the rigorous qualification tests to join the Royal Marines, but they had no experience of handling a boat. Those with any such experience had been quickly snapped up by other elements of the Armed Forces. Hasler chose the men out of a group of forty, who had volunteered for 'hazardous' operations. Among other qualities, they had a willingness to learn and a bottomless capacity for physical punishment. Conscious that fitness was to be crucial to success, the training programme he put them through was as rigorous as any they had experienced. The party included one lieutenant, a sergeant, two corporals and seven Marines.

Much of the training exercises were, inevitably, carried out in the canoes which they would use in the raid and which had been designed with feedback from Hasler himself. The cockle (Mark II) was a semi-collapsible, two-man craft capable of carrying 150lb of equipment and it was sturdy enough to ride out rough water. At 16 foot long, it was possible for the canoes to be launched from the torpedo-loading hatch of a submarine. The men's long waterproof jackets had elasticated bottoms which allowed them to be stretched over the cockpits to act as spraydecks. Buoyancy bags were inserted into the bow and stern to keep it afloat when swamped. The only propulsion came from the muscle power of the two men wielding the paddles and it took great strength, stamina and skill to handle them for more than a short period. To travel sixty miles in three nights, through enemy-held waters, was a tall order even by Hasler's high standards.

Equipment in each canoe included three pairs of paddles, an escape kit, compass, torch, camouflage net, matches, waterproof watch, camouflage cream, two grenades, eight limpet mines, placing rods for applying them below the waterline, an assortment of fuses, rations for five days per man, 2½ gallons of drinking water and a small box of medical supplies, including a box of Benzedrine – an amphetamine stimulant widely issued to servicemen, especially night-time bomber pilots, to help them stay awake.

The unit moved to Margate where they carried out a full-blown exercise on the Thames Estuary that was designed to simulate the raid as much as possible in waters and terrain that closely resembled those of the Gironde. In Hasler's own words, the trial run was 'a complete failure' and he feared that the operation might be cancelled as a result. To his great surprise, however, Mountbatten expressed delight at the disaster, saying that, having learnt valuable lessons from their mistakes, the saboteurs would not now make them in the operation proper.

Back in Scotland, training continued with even greater intensity for a few more days. The necessity of having to lay up for at least three nights before launching the assault meant that the raiders had to have an extremely efficient packing system. It was vital that they were able to reach down and identify, with the touch of a frozen finger, every item they carried with them. Over and over in the dark, to practise operating at night, they stowed and restowed their equipment in the canoe's cargo bags until they were completely familiar with the location of every item, down to the last matchbox. The exercises also included learning how to fuse and set the limpet mines in the dark while sitting in a wobbling canoe. There was target practice with Colt .45 pistols and Sten guns and simulated combat with the famous 'Commando dagger', the seven-inch, double-edged Fairbairn-Sykes Fighting Knife, which they were to use if ever compromised by a German sentry or other hostile. The men were taught basic French to help them in their escape. Only Hasler spoke the language passably. At this stage no one in the unit had the faintest idea what they were training for. Rumours abounded that they were being sent to Norway to attack German warships in the fjords.

The operation planners anguished over the question of what the Marines should wear. Three weeks earlier Hitler had issued his infamous commando order, declaring that all British saboteurs, whether in uniform or not, were to be summarily shot after interrogation. Some felt the force should wear civilian clothes to facilitate their escape but Hasler was appalled at the suggestion. His men would fight as Royal Marines, he thundered, and, if necessary, they would die as Royal Marines. Hasler got his way and Royal Marine flashes and rank badges were sewn into the cockle suits.

The submarine that was to drop the party was HMS *Tuna*, commanded by Lieutenant Dick Raikes, a highly regarded character with a DSO to his name. In addition to his great composure under pressure, his first-class navigational skills would be a great asset when it came to reading the flat, featureless coast around the mouth of the Gironde in the dark. The question of where to launch the raiders was critical to the success of the operation. Hasler's ideal dropping-off point was unfortunately located right in the middle of the RAF's randomly laid minefield.

Another vexing question was who to pair up in each boat.

The strain of the training exercises had led to flare-ups and confrontations among the men. Tension under such great pressure was inevitable and even a healthy sign in some respects, but, as they prepared to depart, Hasler knew it was vital that there was a strong sense of companionship in each of the canoes. Each man relied on his partner for their survival. Marine Bill Sparks, a boisterous Cockney with a keen sense of humour and a bit of attitude about him, had clashed with one or two of the others during training and he was difficult to pair up. The Royal Marines have a tradition of encouraging individuality in their men but, in this type of operation, mutual trust and a spirit of cooperation were essential. Hasler, who rated Sparks as a canoeist and combatant, decided the most sensible option was to take him as his number two.

The raiding party was divided into two divisions, each with its own targets in the large harbour. Being cockle canoes, the name of each boat began with the letter 'C'.

A Division comprised Major Hasler and Sparks in *Catfish*, Corporal Laver and Marine Mills in *Crayfish* and Corporal Sheard and Marine Moffat in *Conger*. B Division was made up of Lieutenant Mackinnon and Marine Conway in *Cuttlefish*, Sergeant Wallace and Marine Ewart in *Coalfish*, and Marine Ellery and Marine Fisher in *Cachalot*.

In the morning of 30 November 1942, HMS *Tuna* pulled out of Holy Loch into the mouth of the Clyde and headed south into the Irish Sea. It was now that Hasler, summoning the other eleven men of the party, revealed the nature of their mission.

They had thought they were going on another training exercise. There was surprise and excitement that France was the destination. Hasler spoke at length about the details of the operation. Nothing was written down for fear of incriminating the men if caught. Everything had to be memorised.

The launch was to take place on the night of 6/7 December. In the afternoon, HMS *Tuna* closed towards the coast, twenty miles south of the mouth of the estuary at the southern end of the minefield. Observation of the coastline proved challenging, even for the expert Lieutenant Raikes with all his local knowledge. The sky was overcast and he was unable to make a sun-sight. The distant coastline offered few clues to their location. With so many potential hazards awaiting the raiders, it was essential that Raikes made a positive navigational fix before the operation could be launched.

With tension among the dozen Marines mounting by the hour, the sub commander was conscious of the deflation and frustration he was to cause when he informed Hasler that the launch was going to have to be postponed. The two men had quickly developed an excellent working relationship, but each had his own agenda. Raikes was unwilling to risk his boat and crew; Hasler knew that his schedule of attack depended on the movements of the tide and the weather. What made the postponement all the more frustrating was the fact that a lovely mist blanketed the coast to cover their approach. Unfortunately, it was the mist that was preventing Raikes from establishing exactly where they were.

The following day, the young lieutenant edged the sub closer to the coast, but they had to proceed with the greatest caution. Dozens of fishing boats were heading in and out to sea while German air patrols swept the coastline. The RAF's poorly laid mines made it essential that Raikes was absolutely certain that he was going to launch Hasler's force in exactly the right spot and at the right time so that they hit the incoming tide at the right moment. In the late afternoon, the twelve men took their supper and prepared to disembark. Raikes and Hasler shook hands and made an arrangement to have lunch at the Savoy Grill on 2 April.

After a final talk from Hasler, the men blacked up their faces and loaded their weapons as HMS *Tuna* rose to the surface about four miles from the coast. It was just after seven o'clock and, to Hasler's dismay, a bright moon shone from an almost cloudless sky. The six canoes, each weighing a hefty 250lb, were lowered from the torpedo loading hatches on slings on to a flat, calm sea. Searchlights swept the sea from a promontory further up the coast, and, although the powerful beams didn't reach the disembarkation position, it was an uncomfortable reminder of the obstacles that lay ahead.

Cachalot was damaged as she was lifted out of the hatch and had to be withdrawn from operations. It was a cruel anti-climax for Marines Ellery and Fisher. After eight weeks' intensive training, and with adrenaline coursing through their bodies, they waved off their comrades and climbed back into the sub.

It was just after eight o'clock when the formation of five

cockles paddled off towards the mouth of the Gironde. All went to plan for the first few hours but, just before midnight, the ten men began to feel the power of the flood tide below them and heard waves breaking along the shore. To their alarm, soon afterwards they made out the unmistakable rushing sound of a tidal rapid that had not been marked on their Admiralty charts. The breaking waters were far stronger than any in which they had trained back in Britain. Hasler and Sparks in *Catfish* took the waves head-on and then waited on the other side for the other four. Only three appeared. There was no sign of *Coalfish*, or of Wallace and Ewart.

Suspecting they had capsized and were swimming for shore, after a short wait Hasler gave the order for the remaining four cockles to press on. It had always been the plan that if one canoe lost contact with the others they were all to make their own way to the target. Wallace and Ewart did make it to shore but they were captured and were summarily shot under Hitler's commando order. What nobody was to know until long after the event was that neither man yielded a scrap of information under interrogation by the Gestapo. It was their courage under what has to be assumed was a brutal inquisition that saved the survivors from the same hideous fate they were to suffer.

The remainder of the party had only travelled a short distance further when they entered a second, more violent tidal race. The churning waters battered the little boats as the men struggled to keep them upright. When they emerged on the other side, exhausted from the effort, Moffat and Sheard were clinging to the upturned *Conger*. All the fears of the planners were being realised as the operation threatened to founder so soon after it had been launched. There was no chance of righting the canoe and so the decision was taken to scuttle her and try to tow the other two men to their first laying-up point. But already having to propel over 400lb of weight, including their own body mass, the canoeists struggled with the additional load. Chilled to the bone in the cold December water, the two men acted like anchors on the canoes. When a lighthouse at the Pointe de Grave was turned up to maximum power, the raiding party was lit up and clearly visible from land. Hasler had no other option but to press on and leave the men to swim ashore and try and make their own way to safety. Moffat drowned and his body was found on a beach eighty miles to the north. Sheard's body was never found.

With the raiding party now well behind schedule and in danger of failing to make land before sunrise, Hasler ordered the three remaining canoes to split up and take the quicker route closer to the shore. As individuals, they were less likely to be spotted than in formation. But when they reached their pre-arranged rendezvous point, there was no sign of *Cuttlefish*, carrying Mackinnon and Conway. They waited a short while but, with dawn almost upon them and with no chance of reaching their chosen laying-up point, they turned into the mouth of the estuary and, clinging to its western bank, began to search for a suitable place to come ashore. The Gironde Estuary cuts into the landscape at a roughly 120-degree angle and the two canoes – *Catfish* and *Crayfish* – were now heading in a south-easterly direction towards their target sixty miles inland.

The sun was up when they spotted a sandy beach with some scrubland behind a location known as Pointe aux Oiseaux. They had barely hidden their boats under the camouflage nets when half a dozen locals arrived on the scene. Unable to set out again until almost midnight, there was little the four men could do but smile at them and hope for the best. Hasler urged them to keep their silence and was reassured when one of them returned later with a loaf of bread.

Behind them lay the famous vineyards of the Médoc region, but the luxury of a fine claret was very far from their own experience as they lay, muddied and shivering, chewing on biscuits and sucking sweets for energy. The rest of the day passed uneventfully and just over twelve hours later they began the exhausting task of dragging their fully laden canoes over the glutinous mudflats down to the waterline to await the incoming tide. It was a bitterly cold night under a clear sky and ice had begun to form on the canoes when they finally got afloat.

Forced to lay up twice to negotiate the tides, on the second occasion daylight was breaking when once again they were forced to abandon plans of reaching their chosen site and opt for any suitable position they could find. This time they were even less fortunate with their choice of location but with the sun up they had no alternative but to scramble up the steep, muddy banks of the Ile de Cazeau on to a marshy, exposed field. With no natural cover in which to hide, the four men covered the canoes with the camo nets and then sat as still as possible for the entire day, listening to the aircraft patrolling above their heads and praying they weren't spotted. Unable to leave the cover of the camouflage, they were forced to eat and sleep in the cockpits of the canoes. To relieve themselves they had to lean over the edge of their canoe.

According to the original plan, the attack was to take place that night but, several miles short of where they hoped to be by this stage, Hasler decided to edge closer and launch the attack twenty-four hours later, when they would have time to catch the ebb tide after laying the mines. What the main raiding party didn't know was that Mackinnon and Conway from *Cuttlefish* were laid up three miles along the island. It was just as well that they decided not to launch their attack that night either – probably for the very same reasons that Hasler's party delayed their attack. In the event, it transpired, years later, that their canoe was holed when they launched for the final leg of the approach and they were forced to make a run for Spain. They managed to get twenty miles south of Bordeaux when they were taken in by apparently friendly locals who then betrayed them to the Germans. They too were executed according to Hitler's commando order.

Having spent their fourth night laid up in long reeds within a few minutes' paddle of their targets, the four men of *Catfish* and *Crayfish* gathered themselves to deliver the *coup de grâce*. At just after half past nine, on yet another painfully clear night, the men set the fuses of the limpet mines to a nine-hour delay. With the lights of Bordeaux twinkling on the banks of the river, the two cockles slipped from the reeds and headed for their respective targets. Hasler and Sparks stuck to the west bank and headed for the docks a little to the south. Laver and Mills headed straight across the water to the two cargo ships berthed directly opposite them on the eastern side. With the dockside ablaze with lights and sentries patrolling overhead, the four men paddled as quietly as they could.

Hasler and Sparks passed four ships before they drew alongside the cargo ship *Tannenfels* and lowered three of the magnetic limpets below the water surface and attached them to the hull, and then a further two on a German minesweeper, known as a *Sperrbrecher*. Turning back the way they had come to deal with the final targets, a cargo ship named *Dresden* and a fuel tanker, they had to pass between the two and were almost crushed when movement in the water squeezed the two vessels together, but they still managed to place their mines on them. It was time to withdraw.

When they emerged from the shadows of the ship into the open water, their paddles gently pulling at the surface of the water, a sentry leaning over one of the ship's railings shone his torch on them. They immediately froze as the beam bore down on them. Whether it was the camouflage of the boat, the weakness of the light or the confusion of the sentry, they were able to drift under the bow of the boat and out of sight without the sentry identifying them. After five minutes, the torchlight had gone and they slipped out into the river.

Carried by the powerful tide, *Catfish* made good progress and had passed the Ile de Cazeau when, by chance, they came across Laver and Mills who were in good spirits after successfully laying their limpets on two cargo ships, the *Alabama* and the *Portland*. After continuing together for a period, the two cockles went their own way, as planned. At low tide, just before dawn, about twenty miles from the scene of the attack, Hasler and Sparks dragged *Catfish* ashore on the eastern bank, took out their escape equipment, slashed the canoe's buoyancy bags and pushed her out into the estuary. The cockle refused to sink, as did *Crayfish* a little further along the estuary. Both canoes were found by German search parties later in the day.

Mills and Laver had reached the village of Montlieu-la-Garde, about twenty miles inland from where they had come ashore, but after a night in a farm building they were arrested in the village by French police, handed over to the German authorities and suffered the same brutal fate as their four other captured comrades.

Hasler's own ordeal was just beginning.

Back in Whitehall, gloom filled the corridors of Combined Operations headquarters. With no news from Hasler, the assumption was that all the men had been captured or killed and that the raid had been a tragic failure. They had picked up a German announcement declaring that a sabotage party had been captured and eliminated on the Gironde, and, although they knew not to take German news bulletins at face value, it was not a story their propaganda machine would have run unless it had at least some basis in fact. It was not until 25 January, six weeks after the raid, that all members of the force were reported as 'missing' and next of kin informed by telegram. Hasler's mother noted later that the wording of the message was almost exactly the same as the telegram that had informed her of her young husband's death in 1917. Lieutenant Arthur Hasler, of the Royal Medical Corps, was one of 423 men lost when the troopship SS *Transylvania* was sunk by a torpedo in the Mediterranean.

Few back at Eastney, the Royal Marines' barracks in Portsmouth, or at COHQ, held out much hope for the re-appearance of the raiding party, but there was some positive news. Preliminary aerial reconnaissance suggested that the raid had gone ahead and been at least partially successful. The images showed that a number of ships appeared to have been sunk or suffered severe damage. A full picture of the raid's success did not emerge for several more months when it became clear that Hasler and his men had pulled off a spectacular success.

As the four raiders fled through the French countryside the German troops and French dockers arrived at the quays for work to be greeted by a series of huge explosions. As a result of faulty timer mechanisms, all the limpets went off at different times over a six-hour period, starting at seven in the morning. The erratic nature of the detonations added to the chaos and confusion in the dockyards as emergency workers and engineers battled to save the stricken ships. French firemen, hostile to their German occupiers, added to the damage by flooding some of the burning vessels with more water than was strictly necessary. The *Dresden* sank, while the *Tannenfels*, *Portland* and *Alabama* were all holed at various points and suffered extensive fire damage. They were eventually repaired, but it was to be many months before these ships, so important to the Axis war effort, were back in action. Hitler, naturally, was infuriated that Britain's commandos had once again got the better of his forces.

Hasler and Sparks were none the wiser about the damage they had inflicted as they jogged in the dark up the vineyards that tumbled down towards the water's edge. They had been told to head to the town of Ruffec, about seventy miles north, where they were to link up with a Resistance cell that would arrange their passage out of the country. By heading north, the hope was that they would throw off their hunters, who would be expecting them to head south towards the Pyrenees. Passing through the rolling hills of Cognac country, the trek was likely to take them as long as a week but for the time being the most pressing concern was to get as far from the scene of the sabotage as possible. They were exhausted, ravenous and plastered in mud, and wanted nothing more than a hot meal and a good long sleep, but they knew they had to keep going. The German and Vichy French authorities would quickly work out what had happened in the dockyard and immediately dispatch search parties to comb the surrounding area.

On the second day of their escape, the two men decided to take a chance and knock on the door of a remote farmhouse to ask for some old civilian clothes. Their first two efforts had been rebuffed by suspicious occupants, perhaps fearing that the two men were German *agents provocateurs*. At a third house they were luckier and a farmer's wife had no hesitation in handing over some old clothes. After forty-eight hours of walking and sleeping rough, the two men finished the last of their rations of biscuits and oatmeal cakes. From now on, they were going to have to rely on the trust and generosity of the locals for their sustenance and survival. They also needed proper shelter after a week without getting more than an hour or two's sleep each day. Cold, wet and run down, there was a great risk of them falling ill and not being able to carry on. Inevitably, any contact with the civilian population was going to expose them to the risk of betrayal and certain death at the hands of their captors.

Once again, they were rebuffed by surly farmers in their first attempts, but at the end of the day they were taken in by a woodman and his young family and treated to lavish hospitality by their impoverished hosts. At first, the woodman was downright hostile and did not believe they were English, but, after showing him their silk escape maps and a British box of matches, the Frenchman, an avowed communist, laid on a feast of roast chicken, vegetable soup and wine. They were given hot water to wash in, comfortable beds and coffee and bread in the morning. The family listened to the BBC every night and Hasler promised to send them a secret message via the radio to let them know they had returned safely. For two more days they tramped through the rain, sleeping in hay barns, until they finally stumbled into the sleepy town of Ruffec. Having paddled one hundred miles up the Gironde, they had now marched the same distance in equally trying conditions, and, racked by exhaustion and hunger, they trudged through the alarmingly quiet streets.

How the commandos were to make contact with the escape organisation based in the town had been left to their own initiative. Inevitably, communication between the French Resistance and the British authorities was kept to the bare minimum, partly out of fear of compromising the local guerrillas and their sympathisers and partly because there were not sufficient amounts of equipment in the field. Seeking a cheap bistro in which they would be made welcome, and dressed in rough clothes and smelling like cattle, Hasler and Sparks now faced the most hazardous challenge of their escape thus far. They were going to have to approach somebody and reveal their identity. Whether that person was to turn out to be friend or foe was in the lap of the gods.

After peering through the windows of several bistros, Hasler opted for one of the least expensive ones with only a handful of customers. The middle-aged Frenchwoman who served them appeared to show no interest in her grubby, unshaven customers from out of town, and the two Englishmen ate their broth and bread in a tense silence. When paying the bill, Hasler slipped a message inside the folded franc notes. The message stated openly that they were British soldiers on the run and needed help in their escape. The minutes ticked by as the two fugitives waited to discover if Hasler's gut instincts about the place had been correct. If he was wrong, they would both most likely be dead by nightfall.

The woman walked back to their table and placed the change down in front of Hasler. Among the notes and coins was a scribbled reply telling them to stay put while she closed up the restaurant. Five minutes later, the room had been cleared, the owner locked the door and led them through to meet her husband in the kitchen. It was immediately obvious that they were in the care of people they could trust. They were given a room for the night and another meal and the woman laundered their clothes and gave them a tub of hot water. Later, two Resistance men came to interrogate them and, finally satisfied by their story, left for the night. The following day, a baker's van arrived and they were driven to a remote location in the woods where they were handed over to a young guide. Without delay, the Frenchman started jogging and the two Englishmen followed. They had not the faintest idea where they were being taken. Their fate was no longer in their own hands.

After a short distance, the three men reached a remote farmhouse where they were introduced to a respectable middle-aged couple with a young family. The house into which they were welcomed was more comfortable than the ones they had experienced so far and the meal they were presented with was of the very highest standard of French home cooking. Their hosts, the DuBois, were quietly spoken, modest people but their rules were strict. The two men were to stay in their double room, day and night, except when nature called, when they were allowed to cross the farmyard to the outbuilding where the pit-toilet was housed. They ended up staying for three weeks and, though comfortable, warm, superbly fed and well rested, the two commandos became almost wildly impatient and claustrophobic. In addition to the enforced inactivity, the two men came to realise that, beyond a shared interest in all things military, they had absolutely nothing in common and nothing to talk about. The seeds of mutual resentment bordering on dislike were sown in that quiet, well-furnished bedroom. It didn't help matters that the two men had to share a bed.

In the first week of the new year their hosts explained the reason behind the delay in moving them further along the escape route: the agent, known as 'Marie-Claire', was in hospital after being knocked down by suspected collaborators. The following day, her son, Maurice, arrived and explained, in perfect English, about his mother. He relayed the further bad news that the escape route to Spain over the Pyrenees had been jeopardised and that the Resistance were in the process of establishing a fresh route and a new chain of trustworthy contacts.

The two commandos, now almost chubby after the generous hospitality they had received, thanked their courageous hosts, who had risked their lives and those of the family to hide them. For many French people in the Occupation, the BBC Overseas Service was their only connection with the world beyond their borders, a valuable medium of more reliable information about the progress of the war as well as a source of hope to help carry them through the dark days of Nazi domination. Just as the woodman had done, the couple asked Hasler to send them a coded message over the wireless on their return.

Presented with two ancient, rickety bicycles, the two commandos followed the smiling nineteen-year-old guide along a series of country lanes for over twenty miles before they reached the small town of Roumazières. Without identity papers, the next leg of the journey was fraught with danger, but Maurice assured them they could carry it off. If challenged, he advised, they were to pretend to be from Brittany where many of the rural people still did not speak French. They were to take the night train to Lyons, France's third largest city, which was far to the east of their original escape route, but where a safe house had been arranged while a new route to the Pyrenees was established.

Hearts hammering against their ribcages, the two men waited on the crowded platform as the steam train chugged into the station. When Maurice gave them the nod, the pair followed him into a packed compartment where they took their seats and settled down for the long night journey. To their relief, nobody challenged them or tried to engage them in conversation and shortly after sunrise they disembarked and strolled into the city as if they were tourists in peacetime. Until recently Lyons had been unoccupied and the Germans had yet to impose the rigorous security clampdown that they had in other French cities.

They were taken to the apartment of the mysterious 'Marie-Claire' and were astounded to discover that Maurice's mother was a striking Englishwoman with a cut-glass accent and an outspoken, engaging manner. Her real name was Mary Lindell and she had grown up in Surrey. Decorated for gallantry under fire while working as a nurse in the First World War, she showed the same fearlessness throughout her life. After marrying a French aristocrat, the Comte de Milleville, she settled in France and after the invasion began working as an agent with the Resistance, helping dozens of British servicemen escape over the border to Spain.

She is remembered as one of the bravest and most colourful characters in the Resistance and there has been a book and a film about her remarkable life. She was not, however, the most discreet operative and barely made an effort to disguise her English origins – of which she was extremely proud – or her contempt for the Germans and the French who sided with them. It hadn't taken long for the Gestapo to catch up with her. She was tortured and sent to prison, but managed to escape and reach London where she was recruited by British intelligence organisation MI9 and flown back into France. She had arrived back in Lyons just six weeks before the launch of Operation Frankton. Her leg was still in plaster from the hit-and-run accident when Hasler and Sparks met her. At first both men were overwhelmed by her powerful personality and Hasler was lost for words when, minutes after arriving, she handed him a razor and told him to shave off his lavish moustache.

After breakfast, she took them across town by tram to a secret location where they had their photographs taken and were given identity cards. Marie-Claire was leaving for Switzerland later that day and Hasler quickly wrote her out a coded message to be relayed to COHQ that gave a summary of the raid. When the message finally arrived in London via the Special Operations Executive (SOE), six weeks later, it came through as an unintelligible jumble of words that resisted all attempts to decipher it. In the end, a bright young Wren called Marie Hamilton, a new arrival at the organisation, succeeded in cracking it, to the delight and mild embarrassment of her superiors. For Hasler and Sparks, the period that followed was as exasperating as their long confinement in the bedroom of the farmer's house, only this time they spent a full month entombed in various safe houses under strict orders never to leave the premises.

They were transferred to the port of Marseilles on the Mediterranean coast where they spent a further three weeks in an apartment used as a transit house for escaping servicemen, mainly RAF bomber crewmen who had managed to bale out of their aircraft after being shot down. At least here they had the company of fellow Britons, but it was a small property with up to a dozen men in it at times, and the atmosphere was often claustrophobic and restless. Everyone was desperate to get back to England, but, aware that dozens of French men and women were putting their lives on the line to help them, they sat and waited to be summoned without complaint.

As each day passed, more food was consumed and no exercise was taken, and Hasler began to fear that their deteriorating fitness levels were going to present a serious problem when – if – they ever managed to reach the Pyrenees. Walking over the rugged, snow-capped mountains, which reach 11,000 feet at their highest point, was no stroll in the best of circumstances, but to tackle them when completely out of shape was likely to push the two men to the limits of their capacity for physical and mental punishment.

There had been no prior warning when, on the first day of March, Hasler and Sparks, along with two airmen, were spirited away from the flat and put on a train to Perpignan, the small medieval city close to the Mediterranean coast. Here, they were transferred into the back of a delivery van in which they crouched among wooden crates as the old vehicle bounced and lurched over the winding, potholed roads and climbed slowly through the foothills at the eastern end of the mountains. The air was cold when they were told to disembark and, led by two Basque guides, took the first steps in a gruelling ten-day hike. Hasler's fears over their fitness were soon borne out. Even though the party skirted the highest peaks, the altitude took its toll on the two unfit Englishmen. But without water and barely any food, dehydration and lack of energy soon threatened to get the better of the two men. They were deeply embarrassed at not being able to keep pace with their wiry, tough guides.

Both men had become accustomed to the most extreme

physical hardship and severe tests of their stamina during their training – and in the raid on Bordeaux itself – but for several days they feared that they would not be able to go on. Incredibly, wine was the only liquid refreshment carried by the guides and the two Englishmen took to drinking straight from streams, ignoring the warnings and protests of their companions. Night after night, they slept in caves and gulleys, shattered by the exertions of the day. The effort became harder with every step and it reached the point when they were forced to stop every few minutes to slow their pounding hearts and gather their breath. Hasler had feared that their problems were likely to be compounded by the cold when they reached the snowline, but, in the event, the snow turned out to be their salvation. Melting it in their mouths, they quickly began to rehydrate and their strength began to return as they started the descent into Spain, buoyed by the knowledge that they had crossed the border into a neutral country. They were still not entirely safe, however. Franco's Spain remained a dangerous place and if captured by the police they risked imprisonment or deportation.

From the small town of Bandolas they were driven the sixty miles to Barcelona in the back of a truck loaded with porcelain toilets. On arrival, Hasler immediately wrote to his mother to let her know he was safe. It was 12 March, more than three months since HMS *Tuna* had slipped out of the Clyde. Hasler found his way to the British Consul in Barcelona, where officials contacted COHQ to confirm his identity. Two weeks later, he was flown out of Gibraltar by the RAF and arrived back in London on 2 April – the very day he had promised to meet *Tuna*'s commander at the Savoy Grill. Bill Sparks' return to the UK was more eventful. On reaching Gibraltar, he was arrested.

Unable to corroborate his far-fetched story, Sparks was returned to England on a troopship and put behind bars in a train carriage by the military police on his arrival. Realising the police had failed to lock the door, he walked out of Euston Station and went to see his father in the East End. Two days later, he turned up at COHQ in Whitehall where he was received with greater warmth. He returned to duty with the Royal Marines, serving in Burma, Africa and Italy. He was awarded the Distinguished Service Medal for his actions in the Bordeaux raid. In 1946 he took a job as a trolley-bus driver with London Transport and ended his working career as a garage inspector. In 1988 he was forced to auction his eight medals in order to stay in his Sussex retirement home. The anonymous bidder bought them for £31,000 with instructions that they were to be kept in the vault at Sotheby's so that Sparks could wear them whenever he wished. He died in 2002, aged eighty.

'Marie-Claire' continued to help repatriate British servicemen but at the end of 1943 she was captured at Pau railway station and tortured once again. Attempting to jump from the train taking her to Paris, she was shot in the face and skull and, still gravely ill, imprisoned in Ravensbrück concentration camp where she survived

Warriors

further barbaric treatment to see out the war. She became friends with Hasler and Sparks after the war. Her youngest son Ocky died in a concentration camp, but Maurice and her daughter, who also worked for the Resistance, survived.

Keeping his word to his French hosts, Hasler made it one of the first tasks on his return to send the cryptic messages via the BBC. He was soon back at work planning new irregular operations. He was awarded the Distinguished Service Order for the Bordeaux raid. There were many at Combined Operations who felt that he and Sparks deserved the Victoria Cross, but the nature of the operation did not meet the strict criteria for the award, which included having to carry out their act in the face of the enemy. 'I feel sure that there have been few decorations that were more deserved,' Mountbatten wrote in a personal letter to Hasler. After the war, while he immersed himself in competitive sailing and the invention of nautical equipment, the story of Operation Frankton soon became public knowledge. His raiding party was dubbed the 'Cockleshell Heroes' – a term he always loathed. It is said that he rarely talked about the raid, considering it to be no more than a minor episode in Britain's overall war effort.

Exactly how much impact the sabotage of the ships had on the Germans can never be fully evaluated, but for sheer daring, courage and tragedy there are few raids in the history of irregular warfare that can match the Bordeaux raid. In France, Hasler is revered as much as he is in Britain. In 1984 a memorial to the raid was unveiled at the HQ of the Special Boat Service in Poole. Made from local Purbeck stone, it is engraved with the words of Lord

Mountbatten and reads: 'Of the many brave and dashing raids carried out by the men of Combined Operations Command none was more courageous or imaginative than Operation Frankton.' Hasler died in 1987, aged seventy-three.

RAF

___

Captain Albert Ball

At 5.30 in the afternoon on 7 May 1917, Captain Albert Ball led a formation of eleven light-brown SE5 biplanes into the menacing skies above northern France. The weather conditions were not ideal for flying, let alone for aerial combat. Cecil Lewis, another brilliant young pilot who would make a name for himself during and after the war, described the scene: '. . . the May evening is heavy with threatening masses of cumulus cloud, majestic skyscrapes, solid-looking as snow mountains, fraught with caves, valleys and ravines . . .' Below, the bloody Battle of Arras was into its fifth and final week. Tens of thousands of young men on both sides of no-man's-land lay dead. The decisive breakthrough for which Allied planners had been hoping had yet to materialise.

Warriors

Somewhere over the Cambrai–Douai road, four red German Albatros D111 fighters burst from one of the thick cumulus clouds and ambushed the British formation. The attackers belonged to the unit commanded by Manfred von Richthofen, aka the Red Baron. Germany's celebrated flying ace was on leave at the time and, in his absence, his brother Lothar was handed temporary command. A furious dogfight ensued with over a dozen planes at a time weaving in and out of each other's paths and filling the fading light with thousands of rounds. Planes spiralled from the air, smoke pouring from their tails, others spluttered back in the direction of their airfields, too damaged to continue the fight. The scene was little different from any other that had taken place over the shell-blasted terrain of Flanders over the preceding months and years: dozens of brave young men in their newfangled flying machines circling, diving, climbing and strafing each other in a crazy, noisy, almost choreographed aerobatic spectacle. The combatants were so close that at times they could look straight into each other's eyes and hear their shouts.

As darkness began to descend and the drizzling rain was threatening to turn heavier, the visibility deteriorated, the formations became fractured and the dogfight splintered into a series of smaller contests. In the skies above Loos, Captain Ball dived to attack a German straggler in what was likely to be his last engagement of the day, possibly even of the war. Any day now, he was expecting to be withdrawn from the front line. The senior commanders of the Royal Flying Corps were eager that the leading Allied fighter ace of the conflict should finally be removed out of harm's way. No airman had earned his right to a less hazardous role in the war effort more than the twenty-year-old national hero from Nottingham.

Ball squeezed a short burst of Vickers machine-gun fire towards the red biplane with its distinctive black cross emblazoned on its wings and fuselage and, followed by one of his colleagues, chased the German into a towering black cloud. When the aircraft re-emerged, heading west towards the village of Annoeullin, Ball was right on the tail of the struggling German. With petrol spilling from his riddled tank, the Albatros crash-landed in the field below. The pilot, Lothar von Richthofen, stepped out of the cockpit of the stricken machine completely unharmed. As he strode away from the wreckage, his leather great coat tugging in the breeze, he saw Ball's SE5 climbing slowly before disappearing back into the black cloud. What happened next remains a mystery that is unlikely ever to be solved.

The son of a plumber who would rise to become the city's mayor and a knight of the realm, Albert Ball was born in Nottingham in 1896 and brought up on the outskirts of the city. When war broke out in August 1914 Ball, still two weeks shy of his eighteenth birthday, joined hundreds of thousands of other young Britons answering Field Marshal Kitchener's famous call to arms. His country certainly *did* need him, but as he waited his turn in the long queue of volunteers no one could have guessed that the short, fresh-faced teenager with the shy smile would emerge from a war of so many heroes as one of its very greatest. He looked more like a choirboy than a warrior.

In September 1914 Ball was enlisted as a private soldier in the 2/7 Battalion Nottinghamshire and Derby Regiment, better known as the Sherwood Foresters. Within days of joining up he was promoted to sergeant, and then almost as quickly to second lieutenant, on the dubious basis of his experience in the Officer Training Corps at Trent College, Long Eaton, Nottinghamshire. After undergoing his training, Ball spent the rest of the first year of the war preparing other new recruits for the front line. Desperate to be sent out to France, he quickly became frustrated with the monotony of drills and exercises. A keen cyclist, he transferred to the North Midlands Divisional Cyclists' Company in the hope that it would speed up his deployment, but with little use for bicycles in the mud of Flanders, his prospects of action began to look even slimmer. Like so many men who had joined the stampede to sign up, Ball became convinced that the fighting was going to be over before he was called into action. The idea that he might be able to fight the Germans in one of those extraordinary new flying machines hadn't even crossed his mind – until he was sent on a platoon officers' training course close to Hendon aerodrome, the centre of the country's rapidly growing aviation services.

Aviation was to the Edwardians what space exploration was to subsequent generations in the 1950s and 1960s. It was a magical, exciting new experience that quickly captured the public's imagination after the Wright brothers had launched the first powered flights in 1904. By 1911, the British Army had seen the potential for aerial reconnaissance and set up Air Battalion, Royal Engineers, made up of fourteen officers and 150 other ranks. At its formation, no one for a moment ever imagined that the aircraft might be used in a combat capacity. The following year, the battalion was replaced by the Royal Flying Corps, a much larger unit altogether, but, as war loomed, its role was still regarded as a purely observational one. The sheer thrill of the flying experience itself was enough to persuade thousands of young men to sign up and seek transfers to the Corps. So long was the waiting list that Arthur 'Bomber' Harris, head of Bomber Command in the Second World War, later recalled how he had to work all his family connections in the military to engineer a transfer.

The stampede to join was all the more remarkable given the well-known risks that came with the job. Even before an aircraft was designed to carry a machine gun, flying was a lethal business. Of the 14,000 pilots killed in the war, half died in training. Though they improved dramatically as the conflict progressed, at the outset of hostilities the planes were so flimsy, unwieldy and cumbersome that the pilots, buffeted by wind and cloud, had to put all their efforts into simply trying to keep them steady. Today, we take the ease, comfort and safety of it for granted, but in the earliest days flying was an extremely hazardous – and often terrifying – enterprise.

At the start of the war, the planes in which they trained had room for only one seat, so when a man took to the skies for the

Aero Club Pilot Certificate – effectively a flying licence – and he immediately put in a transfer request to join the Royal Flying Corps. It was accepted and on 26 January 1916, eighteen months into the Great War, he was awarded his pilot's wings. By then, the dead already running into the millions, the nature of military aviation was almost unrecognisable from its pre-war incarnation.

At the start of war, Germany had the largest air fleet with 246 aircraft and 7 airships, France had 160 and 15 airships. Officially Britain had about 180 but in truth only a third of them were fit for front-line duties. The first British planes deployed were a motley fleet of BE2s, Avro 504s, Farmans and Blériots. As they descended over the Channel like a rabble of big butterflies wobbling in the wind as they came in to make a bumpy landing on the fields of northern France, no one had much of an idea what roles these unwieldy flying machines were going to play.

Every plane that started the war was entirely unarmed and not designed to accommodate any form of weapon. They were delicate structures without the capability to act as a gun platform, let alone a bombing machine. There was also great mistrust of aircraft within the hidebound elements of the military's top brass.

The earliest aviators were often maverick daredevils, not unquestioning Tommies who did what they were told.

Within a few weeks, however, thanks to the brave young men at their controls working it out for themselves in the air, these flying machines had become a vital element of the battlefield. Their role was purely observational and they would remain the eyes of the infantry until the very last shots of the conflict were fired. They mapped the network of enemy trenches, reported major movements of troops and equipment and helped direct artillery fire. With the introduction of aerial photography, the aviators became an even greater menace to the troops on the ground. Realising the threat that the aircraft posed to them, the infantry on both sides began filling the air with machine-gun and rifle fire and anti-aircraft artillery shells from 3-inch guns mounted on trucks. Without any markings in the opening stages, the planes were also at risk from being shot down by their own troops. The Germans hastily daubed theirs with black crosses, the British with red, white and blue roundels.

An 'Archie' barrage, as the British pilots dubbed the artillery fire, was a terrifying experience for all pilots, especially the new arrivals. The noise of the shells bursting all around their wooden and cloth machines was deafening and the shock waves buffeted them like powerful gusts of wind. With no built-in means to defend themselves in the early days, pilots made their own arrangements, stowing shotguns and revolvers in the cockpits, and firing at enemy pilots like Wild West cowboys on horseback. In the absence of any official instruction, the pilots and engineers on the ground fell back on their own resourcefulness and imagination to adapt to the conditions and get the upper hand in this very new form of warfare. Some of the improvisations were ingenious. Louis Strange, a highly decorated pilot who fought in both world wars, found a way of installing a Lewis machine gun in his plane. Others followed his example but, forced to fire almost at right angles to the direction in which they were flying, it was an unreliable and inaccurate method of attack.

The fighter pilot came into existence to protect his colleagues carrying out observational roles, but fighting soon became an operational role in its own right. Both sides had fighters in the air to act as escorts and, when they encountered each other, a dogfight ensued. Once this became the pattern in the skies, an arms race was launched by both sides to design the most effective combat aircraft. Domination of the skies swung back and forth but overall the Germans probably shaded this behind-the-lines engineering and manufacturing competition. Over the months and years an endless stream of new models appeared overhead, with varying degrees of success.

In the Second World War, an aerial fight was a fleeting affair. The speed of the Spitfires, Hurricanes and Messerschmitts meant that an engagement tended to last no more than a few seconds. In the Great War, a dogfight was far longer. With their unsophisticated weapons systems, slower speeds and limited manoeuvrability, the planes circled and climbed to try and get into a position from which they could get away their rounds. Carrying only a few hundred rounds at a time, the pilots had to be careful not to squander their ammo. Nimble flying skills and an extremely strong nerve were the qualities needed to triumph in aerial combat. It was said that a pilot could always tell when he was up against a cool-headed expert if the man fired at him only with short squeezes. The new recruits, over-excited and frightened, tended to pump off their rounds in longer bursts.

Unlike the impersonal slugging match taking place in the cratered mud below, the relationship between the air combatants was almost chivalrous. If an engagement had finished in stalemate with both planes out of ammo, the pilots often used to wave goodbye to each other with a smile. When Oswald Boelcke, one of the German pilots, died in a mid-air collision, his British rivals flew over his grave and dropped wreaths.

The appointment of Hugh 'Boom' Trenchard in the summer of 1915 as the commander in the field of the Royal Flying Corps had led to a far more aggressive strategy in the air. He was determined Britain would achieve supremacy and he ordered his pilots to actively hunt out and engage enemy aircraft. In Albert Ball, he had the very model of his perfect pilot.

On 18 February 1916, Ball was posted to 13 Squadron at Marieux, France, to fly the two-seater BE2s, a poor aircraft dubbed 'Fokker Fodder' by those who flew them. Pilots were losing their lives at such a rate in these machines that most of those sent over the Channel to replace them were virtually untrained. For the more senior pilots it was heartbreaking to see the procession of young lads arriving at the squadron HQ with their new uniforms, proudly wearing their recently awarded wings. Many were sent straight into action and were killed within a day or two. In the chaos of the war, with its appalling turnover of men, there was simply no time to sit through lectures and spend weeks honing their skills in practice flights. There were no textbooks and manuals. They just had to get on with it.

Ball was soon flying patrols, directing artillery shoots and carrying out escort duties. He was up against the single-seater monoplane Fokker E1, which was also an unexceptional machine in most regards but it was more manoeuvrable than the BE2 and it held one lethal capability: a machine gun mounted in front of the cockpit that fired through the propeller's arc at a rate of six hundred rounds per minute. In spite of the inferiority of his aircraft, Ball's observer often had to restrain him from breaking away to fight the more powerful German machines. Strictly, his role was noncombative but Ball showed his appetite for the fray at the end of each patrol when he dropped down as low as he could and strafed the enemy lines with his machine gun.

There were few dangers that could unsettle him. On 20 March 1916, his engine failed on take-off and the aircraft slammed back to earth. Ball walked away from the wreckage without a scratch.

Ball was desperate to fly fighters and his wish was finally granted when he transferred to 11 Squadron in early May. It wasn't long before he was into the thick of the action he had been craving. On 15 May, flying a Bristol Scout, he opened his victory tally when he shot down an Albatros C two-seater reconnaissance machine. The following day he wrote to his brother Cyril and sister Lois, opening with news of a shocking end to the day of his first official triumph in aerial combat:

I have just lost such a dear old pal, Captain Lucas. He was brought down by a Fokker last night about 5pm. Now don't show Mother and Dad this letter, and I will tell you about the fights.

The Fokker came up behind the BE from the rear. It opened fire, and at once hit Captain Lucas who was the observer. Lieutenant Wright was the pilot and such a fine chap. He kept at his job, although he was hit in the shoulder. Fifty shots the Fokker fired but Lieutenant Wright got over our side and landed, walked out a few yards then fell down. Captain Lucas died in a few hours. The machine was brought back this morning and I am not exaggerating when I say it was soaked in blood and full of bullet holes. No 11, my squadron lost six machines yesterday, and one crashed today . . .

Now for a bit of cheerful news. I was on patrol yesterday morning on my British [sic] scout. I was at 12,000 feet and saw a Hun at 5,000. It started off and I went after it, catching it up when 20 miles over its lines. It took 120 shots to do it in, but in the end it went down upside down. I got back but was Archied badly . . . In the afternoon I received orders to fly a new French machine. Did well on it, so they are now getting one for me. This means I shall be on one of the best machines England and France can give a pilot so I hope for a good run.

He was referring to the new French-built Nieuport 16 Scout, a far more agile plane than the ones he was used to but, like a fine horseman with a new mount, it didn't take him long to get a feel for it. He quickly proved himself to be a natural fighter pilot, aggressive and almost recklessly courageous.

On 29 May, shortly after eight in the morning, he dived in his Nieuport on a German LVG two-seater, emptied half a drum into its fuselage and watched it plunge towards earth. Shortly afterwards, spotting another LVG being escorted by two Fokkers, he climbed above them and followed them at a distance. Two more Fokkers arrived on the scene but when the four escorts eventually went their own way, Ball pounced on the larger aircraft. Closing to within 50 yards, Ball emptied his ammo drum, turned away to put a fresh drum on the Lewis and then came back for the kill. As the rounds raked the fuselage, the German aircraft began to nosedive but it wasn't finished yet. As it fell away, the observer continued to fire from the rear cockpit, riddling Ball's plane with eight rounds. The damaged LVG was forced to land and Ball turned for home, harassed by artillery fire as he crossed over enemy lines, with one round hitting his tail.

On 25 June, as part of preparations for the Somme offensive, launched on 1 July, Ball destroyed an observation balloon behind German trenches, dropping phosphor bombs. During the mission, he was hit by anti-aircraft fire which damaged his engine but he managed to stagger back. Two days later his engine was knocked out by an artillery shell, but, again showing his exceptional cool under fire, he managed to glide the aircraft back over the German trenches to safety. This type of experience was becoming routine for the daring teenage aviator and he was astounded to be told on the eve of the Battle of the Somme that he had been awarded the Military Cross. Gazetted on 27 July, his citation read:

For conspicuous skill and gallantry on many occasions, notably when, after failing to destroy an enemy kite balloon with bombs, he returned for a fresh supply, went back and brought it down in flames. He has done great execution among enemy aeroplanes. On one occasion he attacked six in one flight, forced down two and drove the others off. This occurred several miles over the enemy's lines.

On 1 July 1916, unimaginable slaughter was wrought on British lines in the bloodiest day of the country's military history. There were more British casualties on that dreadful day – 62,000 in total – than in the Crimean, Boer and Korean wars combined. Ball watched the carnage from above, and was convinced he saw his former regiment the Sherwood Foresters charging across no-man's-land. Of his 627 former comrades, only 90 returned.

The following day was a significant one for Ball. At 5.30 in the afternoon, escorting four other planes across enemy lines in his Nieuport, he clashed with a formation of six Germans in Roland CIIs. Ball dived on one and strafed it with a full drum from his Lewis machine gun, sending it spiralling to earth. A second German suffered a similar fate at the hands of Ball's comrade, prompting the rest to flee the scene. Continuing the patrol, Ball spotted a German two-seater, an Aviatik C, and crept down on it unnoticed. When he was just 20 yards away he pulled the firing cable of his Lewis gun, but it jammed. Now vulnerable himself, Ball dropped below the German, rolled the Lewis gun back on its rail so that he could operate it manually and riddled his target. The German fell like a stone and broke into a thousand pieces as it smashed into the field. By accident rather than design, Ball had fallen upon a method of attack that was to become his standard *modus operandi* for the rest of his war: closing on the enemy from below and strafing the underside of its fuselage at point blank before banking away at the last second before collision. It was an approach fraught with risk, but it was highly effective.

In less than three months, Ball had accounted for two heavily defended observation balloons and nine enemy aircraft, either shot, driven or forced down or sent down out of control. The method of recording combat 'scores' in the First World War was a contentious, complicated business, which, even today, sends aviation buffs into a tailspin. At the heart of the argument lies the question, what constitutes a victory? A plane that has been completely destroyed, one that has been damaged, or forced to land? The issue is largely irrelevant with Ball and the other great aces such as Mick Mannock and James McCudden. By whatever criteria you adopt, they accounted for great numbers of enemy aircraft.

The stress of daily, close-quarter combat and the death of so many of his comrades soon took its toll on the fresh-faced nineteen-year-old. In a letter of 10 July to his sister, he wrote: 'Yesterday, four of my best pals went off, and today one of our new chaps has gone over, so you can guess we are always having to get used to new faces . . .'

But he felt no bitterness towards the men sending his friends to an early grave. In a letter to his father dated the same day, he wrote: '. . . You ask me to "let the devils have it" when I fight. Yes, I always let them have all I can but really I don't think them devils. I only scrap because it is my duty, but I do not think anything bad about the Hun. He is just a good chap with very little guts, trying to do his best. Nothing makes me feel more rotten than to see them go down, but you see it is either them or me, so I must do my best to make it a case of them.'

Every man had his own way of fighting his inner demons. The greatest fear for a pilot was burning to death after his machine had caught fire. Most carried revolvers to shoot themselves in the event of their petrol tank igniting. Many suffered nightmares; most drank heavily. Some suffered breakdowns, went mad, or even took their own lives both during and after the conflict.

In his 1934 book *King of Air Fighters*, a superb biography of Major Mick Mannock, another VC-winning ace, Ira Jones, wrote: 'Those who have survived the war must have had to fight an even greater battle in the effort to return to normal. How many have failed! Peace had stripped these veterans of their last resources of emotional reserves. We meet them daily, men who faced death and untold horrors in the war, beaten and cowed by the remorseless struggle for existence, unable to harness their shattered emotions to the stresses and strains of civilian routine, and fleeing defenceless into the gutters of the world's highways.'

Many of the pilots immersed themselves in more leisurely, gentle activities as an antidote to the terrifying experiences in the air: poetry, music, schoolboy pranks or, in Ball's case, gardening. He built himself a small wooden hut close to the aircraft hangar and dug some plots in which to plant flowers and vegetables.

In a letter home that summer of 1916, he attaches as much importance to his labours in the garden that day as to his hair-raising experiences in aerial combat, writing:

Will you do me the great favour of sending me one packet of marrow seeds, one of carrots, and a good big packet of mustard and cress? Also, I would like a few flower seeds, one packet of sweet peas, and also a few packets of any other flowers that will grow quickly.

I have only just missed being done in today. I was on the seven o'clock patrol and I saw over the lines a lot of trans-ports in a wood. I went over the lines to have a good look, so that I could report the place, but the old Huns did not like it. They surrounded us with shells from their Archie guns and at last we were hit. One of my cylinders was smashed off, also the machine got a few through it. Only just missed my leg.

I got up at 6am. It was raining so I could not fly. However I got my tools and set to work on my garden, for rainy days are just right for setting seeds. In three hours I just managed to dig a piece of ground 12 feet by 6 feet. In this I planted green peas. I hope to get in a few rows of beans tomorrow, if I have time to dig up another piece of ground.

In mid-July, shattered from near-continuous combat since arriving at the front, Ball asked his CO for a couple of days' rest to let his nerves recover. His request was interpreted as a plea to be removed from the fighter squadron and he was transferred to No. 8 Squadron that specialised in coordinating artillery fire and in bombing raids – humdrum tasks for a tenacious fighter pilot. Ball was appalled. 'Oh I am feeling in the dumps!' he wrote home. Some interpreted the move as a way of putting Ball in his place. He had upset his superiors by openly criticising the capability of some aircraft and, on his own admission, his success had made him a little big-headed.

The following weeks, however, were not without danger and excitement. At the end of the month he was tasked with dropping a French spy deep behind enemy lines. It was dusk and, with most aircraft grounded for the night, the solitary plane attracted the notice of every anti-aircraft gun in the vicinity. When he landed the plane in a field, the agent refused to get out. Ball took off again and made several further landings but the Frenchman wouldn't budge. Ball had risked his life for no reason and he returned to the aerodrome in a fury. The following day he received a personal message from Trenchard, thanking him for his brave effort.

On 14 August 1916 – Ball's twentieth birthday and a month after he had been transferred – the CO of 11 Squadron telephoned and asked him to return to his old fighter unit at the Bellevue aerodrome. He had also been promoted captain and appointed commander of A Flight. Best of all, though, he was given a Nieuport Scout for his personal use between squadron patrols. Ball was as thrilled by the prospect of a return to true combat as he was by the thought of seeing his allotment again. 'You bet I shall get my own back now!' he wrote home. 'And won't it be OK to see my garden again?'

Ball was straight back into the fray, delighted to be in his single-seater again. On his second day back, he wrote home: 'Dearest people, Hello am back in my dear old hut again. All is OK and my garden is fine ... I went up this morning and attacked five Hun machines. One I got down and two I forced down. After this I had to run because all my ammunition was used. However, I got back with only two hits on my machine.'

On 22 August, Ball scored a hat-trick, thought to be the first in the Royal Flying Corps, when he attacked seven Roland reconnaissance and escort aircraft, sending three of them crashing to earth in forty-five minutes. In the first attack he closed to within 15 yards of his target before opening up, with the second to just 10 yards before veering away at speed. Three Germans then closed in on Ball, each firing with their rear and front guns. Ball went straight at the nearest of his attackers and unloaded an entire drum of ammunition as he swept to within 7 yards of his target. The German aircraft dropped to earth in a trail of smoke before crashing through the roof of a house in a village.

His ammunition exhausted, Ball was forced down to 2,000 feet by the four remaining Rolands now on his tail, but he made it back to Bellevue where he quickly rearmed and refuelled and took off again. Almost immediately he encountered three Rolands and went straight for them. The four planes filled the air with hundreds of rounds as they went at each other before the Rolands turned towards their lines. Low on fuel and ammo, and with his aircraft riddled with bullets, most of it superficial damage, he turned for home. Still fifteen miles behind German lines, Ball ran into a formation of '14 Huns'. In the ensuing engagement, his windscreen was cracked in four places, his mirror shattered, the spar of the left wing broken and he ran out of petrol. He managed to glide the plane back over Allied territory and landed it in a field. Shattered by the day's ordeals, he lay down by his shredded aircraft and fell asleep.

On his return to the squadron he was met by the news that 11 Squadron had been amalgamated with 60 Squadron, commanded by the formidable figure of Major Smith-Barry, he of the Gosport tube and one of the great pioneers of British aviation. Recognising Ball's exceptional combat skills, Smith-Barry effectively handed him a free role to cause as much havoc as he wished. The licence to roam brought spectacular results. The last two weeks of August saw Ball dispatch sixteen enemy aircraft in one manner or another. Surviving dozens of dogfights was a remarkable achievement in itself, but Ball now had more victories to his name than any other pilot in British or French forces and his reputation had reached the highest levels of command. A general visiting the squadron's HQ at Izel-lès-Hameau at the end of the month told Ball: 'I am putting your name on a big board in the trenches to frighten the Huns!'

Five of those triumphs came on a single day, 28 August, when he used his preferred tactic of closing to within yards of the target from below to devastating effect. It is not difficult to imagine the terror of the German airman suddenly looking over his shoulder to see Ball's Nieuport on the verge of ramming him and then feel a full drum of bullets hammering into his fuselage.

Explaining the effect his tactic had on the enemy, Ball wrote: 'If a scout [aircraft] attacks a large formation of hostile aircraft, I think it is best to attack from above and dive in among them, getting under the nearest machine. Pull gun down and fire up into hostile aircraft. If you get it, a number of hostile aircraft will put their noses down and make off. Don't run after them but wait for the hostile aircraft that don't run, and again take the nearest machine. If they all run, wait for a bit and take a straggler. One is nearly always left behind. Go for that and give it a drum . . .'

On the final day of the month, setting out on a private mission after completing his official squadron work, Ball decided to 'beard the lion in his own den'. He crossed over the trenches and sought out the nearest German airfield. Spotting twelve Rolands taxiing in a field below, he dived on them and opened up, forcing them to scatter and take off in all directions. It was twelve against one as Ball locked on to his first target, closed to within 15 yards, pumped half a drum into the fuselage and watched it spin away wildly. Weaving in and out of the circling Germans, Ball latched on to a second aircraft and dispatched that, too. The Germans were responding with withering fire of their own. The rounds sliced through Ball's machine and a sustained burst from one of his pursuers knocked out his engine. It seemed that the balloon had gone up for Britain's leading fighter ace. He was out of ammunition and his aircraft had no power, but Ball wasn't quite done. Pulling a revolver from his coat pocket he emptied a clip of bullets at the chasing plane. Ball's machine began to lose height as he tried to glide it back to safety. Crossing low over the German trenches, he passed through a storm of machine-gun and rifle fire before managing to bring his trusty, robust Nieuport safely to ground. Exhausted by the heart-thumping exhilaration of the engagement, once again he lay down by his plane, like a cavalry-man by his horse, and fell into a catatonic stupor.

On his return to the airfield the following day, he learnt that he had been awarded the Distinguished Service Order for his recent efforts. He left for England in the morning for two weeks' leave. Expecting a quiet period of relaxation, he was surprised to find himself fêted wherever he went. By and large, the British were more reticent about using their fighter aces as propaganda tools than either their allies or the Germans, but Ball was an exception to this rule. With his handsome, boyish features and winning smile, he was extremely photogenic, and though he was so shy he could barely speak in public, the newspapers loved him.

On 11 September he wrote to his mother from the Charing Cross Hotel a few days before heading back to France: '. . . It is hard to leave behind such dear people, but you are brave as well as dear & it makes it less hard. It is an honour to be able to fight and do one's best for such a country & such dear people. Mother, I shall fight for you & come home for you & God will always look after me and make me strong . . .'

Returning to the front, Ball had clearly not lost his stomach for combat or his sharpness at the controls of his Scout. In the final two weeks of September he accounted for twenty-one enemy aircraft, including four hat-tricks. Flying patrol after patrol, it was during this period of intense combat that Ball realised that the cumulative effect of his experiences on his 'nerves' was more than just superficial. For Ball, the target in aerial combat had always been the aircraft, not the pilot, but on 21 September he broke with his own personal set of rules of engagement in a merciless attack on an enemy he had already destroyed. Having dispatched three aircraft to earth and with no others waiting around to chance their luck against the English ace, Ball spotted the wreckage of his victim in a field below. Immediately, he put his Nieuport into a steep dive and emptied two drums into the stricken machine in order, he wrote later, 'to make certain of the passengers'. It was an uncharacteristically bloodthirsty act on Ball's part as well as an unnecessary risk to himself. Back at the airfield he told the CO, Smith-Barry, that his bloodlust was unsettling him and that he was in need of a proper break. Over the next ten days, there was precious little evidence of Ball's shredded nerves either to his comrades or to the enemy, and he continued to fly and fight with the same courage and skill as always. It was a testament to his courage that, though now vulnerable and edgy, he forced himself to operate with the same degree of intense commitment as he had done when he was feeling on top of his game.

When Ball returned to Nottingham on 5 October, the homecoming of Britain's leading fighting ace triggered a frenzy of coverage in the local and national press. Ball was flattered but he loathed all the attention. He wanted to relax at home in the company of his beloved family, catch up with some old schoolmates, spend some time fishing and tending the garden. What he didn't want was to be reminded of the bloodshed in Flanders. After two weeks fielding newspaper interviews and replying to hundreds of letters from admirers, Ball took up a post as a flying instructor at a flying school where it was hoped his reputation and expertise would inspire waves of new recruits on their way to France and Belgium. On 18 November, he went to Buckingham Palace to receive his Military Cross and his Distinguished Service Order and bar. A week later he was awarded a further bar to his DSO, making him the first airman to win a triple DSO.

In no time, the tedium of the training job began to drive Ball mad with frustration. Desperate to get back into front-line action, he began to fire off letters to influential contacts within the military and political establishment. He even wrote to Lord Northcliffe, the powerful newspaper magnate. Finally, six months after shooting down his last enemy aircraft, Ball was transferred to 56 Squadron, a new unit undergoing the final stages of training before being sent to the front. Among their number were Cecil Lewis, Gerald Maxwell and Arthur Rhys Davids, men who would also make great names for themselves by their exploits over the trenches of Flanders. The squadron was billeted at London Colney in Hertfordshire and it was while awaiting orders to fly out to the front that Ball fell in love with an eighteen-year-old beauty, Flora 'Bobs' Young. On the day before he left for France, barely two weeks into their whirlwind romance, the love-struck young-sters were engaged to be married. He also wrote a farewell letter to his family that day:

'I cannot leave dear olde England without a word of thanks to you. It is hard to leave such dear people, but you are brave as well as dear and it makes it less hard. It is an honour to be able to fight and do one's best for such a country and such dear people.'

By the spring of 1917, the Germans had the superior aircraft in the Albatros D111, but Trenchard, the RFC commander, still continued to pursue his highly aggressive policy towards the enemy. Every day British squadrons continued to fly deep behind enemy lines to seek out their foes. They suffered appalling losses. By the time Ball touched down at Vert Galand airfield on 7 April to resume combat duty, the life expectancy of a pilot at the front had plummeted to just seventeen days.

On arrival, Ball was presented with the new SE5 fighter to fly. With a top speed of 120mph, a ceiling of 17,000 feet, a Vickers machine gun on its central cowling and a Lewis on its top wing, the SE5 was a formidable beast – at least by specification. But Ball wasn't impressed, even after making his own modifications to it. He went to Trenchard himself and begged to be allowed to fly his Nieuport. As before, a compromise was reached: Ball was to fly the SE5 for squadron work, but was allowed to use the Nieuport for his own enterprises. Over the coming weeks, engineers made a series of alterations to the SE5, turning it into a first-class fighting machine, but even before the improvements Ball still succeeded in using it to devastating effect. One of the SE5's great virtues from the outset was that it had the capacity to absorb heavy punishment. With a pilot as durable and tenacious as Ball at its controls, the SE5 became a worthy adversary to the German Albatros.

In a letter to his fiancée, he wrote of an alarming encounter with an Albatros patrol shortly after his return to action. He had just shot down one aircraft and was engaging a second, flying as always straight at his rival with his finger squeezing the trigger, when: '. . . Well, Bobs, I thought it was all up with us and it was going to be a ramming job. But just as we were about to hit a bullet hit my engine and all the oil came into my face. For a short time, I saw nothing but when all got OK again, I looked down and saw the Hun going down out of control . . . Oh, won't it be nice when all this beastly killing is over and we can just enjoy ourselves and not hurt anyone. I hate this game, but it is the only thing one must do just now.'

His fellow pilot Cecil Lewis survived the war, became one of the founders of the BBC and wrote a brilliant account of his war experiences in *Sagittarius Rising*, the inspiration for the film *Aces High*. He vividly recalled the moment he watched Ball returning to the airfield after a dogfight:

We saw him coming in rather clumsily to land. He was not a stunt pilot, but flew very safely and accurately so that, watching him, we could not understand his awkward floating landing. But when he taxied up to the sheds we saw his elevators were flapping loose – controls had been completely shot away. He had flown back from the lines and made his landing entirely by winding his adjustable tail plane up and down! It was incredible he had not crashed. His oil tank had been riddled, and his face and the whole nose of the machine were running with black oil.

The men who flew with Ball recorded many stories of his awe-inspiring exploits. On one occasion he chased two aircraft as they fled back to their base. Infuriated that they refused his challenge to fight, he dropped a note over their airfield daring them to a fight at the same time and place the following day. To his surprise, the two Germans were waiting for him at the appointed hour but as soon as the dogfight got underway, three other enemy aircraft appeared out of the blue. Ball engaged them all, but each time he closed in on one, the other four forced him to take evasive action. Having exhausted his ammunition, Ball was in serious jeopardy as all five aircraft closed in for the kill and opened up on him. He appeared to have run out of feasible options when he put his Nieuport into a vertical dive, pretending he had been hit. With two enemy aircraft following him down, Ball made a deliberately rough landing in a field behind enemy lines to give the impression he was out of control. He slumped over his controls, feigning death or serious injury. When the two enemy aircraft landed nearby, the pilots jumped out and ran towards him, but just as they reached him Ball opened up the throttle and took off, giving them a wave and a smile as he climbed skyward.

In the trenches below the airmen, the infantry often sat for weeks and months before receiving orders to 'jump the bags' and charge the enemy lines. Their experiences bore out the saying about war being long periods of boredom, punctuated by short, terrifying bursts of action. But for the fighter pilots of the Great War, life on the front line meant relentless heart-thumping, nerve-shredding action, hour after hour, day after day. There were no periods of boredom; the men were either on leave or they were in the air fighting from dawn to dusk. Their nerves barely had time to recover from one patrol when, having rearmed and re-fuelled, they were straight back in the air, embroiled in a fresh round of dogfights. Any pilot claiming he was unfazed by the constant demands of combat on body and soul was either a liar, a fantasist or a madman.

The continuous patrols placed the pilots under more and more stress as the war progressed. By April 1917, the war in the air had changed beyond all recognition, even from Ball's last experience of it in the autumn. There were many more enemy aircraft in the skies and they were better, more deadly machines, too. A year earlier, the British had had to go looking for a fight, but now every time they took to the air, the aces knew they were going to be in an engagement. The realisation that every flight meant a fight added to the already overwhelming burden of worries sitting on the minds of the young pilots. Many bottled up their anxieties, but others, including Ball, admitted to the strain in their letters home, even if he hid the raw reality of his fears in words such as 'tired', 'fagged' or 'fed up' which pepper his letters home in this period.

It was with reluctance that Trenchard had bowed to all the pressure and agreed to allow Ball to return to front-line action. The young pilot had already exhausted his supply of narrow escapes many times over. As one of only a few publicly celebrated national heroes in an otherwise faceless war, Ball's death would be a blow to the morale of the nation and the Flying Corps. Trenchard is said to have come to a verbal agreement that Ball would remain in France for a month to lead and inspire the raw recruits of the new squadron. By 5 May, that time was up and the leading pilot of the Allied forces was just a day or two away from being granted an honourable retirement from front-line duties. That night, Ball the dutiful son, wrote yet another letter home, revealing how close he had come to being killed. His early letters are neat and ordered, but this one is an almost unintelligible scrawl:

I attacked two Albatros Scouts and crashed them, killing the pilots. In the end I was brought down but am quite OK. Oh! It was a good fight and the Huns were good sports. One tried to ram me after he was hit, only missed me by inches. Am indeed looked after by God. But Oh! I do get tired of always living to kill. I am really beginning to feel like a murderer. Shall be so pleased when I have finished. Well now for bed and bath. Cheer Oh! Dear Dad. Please give my dear mother a huge cheer oh! for me and tell her I'm doing my best for her. Tons of love, Albert

P.S. Do send me a few plants for my garden & greenhouse.

It was on the following day that Lothar von Richthofen, walking away from the wreckage of his plane, looked up to see his English adversary disappear into the gathering rain clouds. Four German officers were the only witnesses when, minutes later, the SE5 reappeared, upside down, its propeller motionless, leaving a trail of black smoke as it fell towards earth and slammed into the ground close to a farmhouse outside Annoeullin. By the time the four Germans had reached the scene, the young Englishman had been removed from the cockpit and was lying, dead but unmarked, next to his aircraft. A young French girl had pulled him from the wreckage and cradled him in her arms as his life slipped away. Aware from his personal belongings that the man lying before them was the 'English Richthofen', the officers arranged for the body to be taken to a field hospital where the examining doctor concluded that he had died from impact wounds caused by the crash: broken back, crushed chest, broken arm, three fractures to the leg and a number of abrasions. He had suffered no battle wounds. The Germans buried Captain Albert Ball with full military honours two days later in a service attended by British prisoners of war and a large crowd of locals.

The Germans declared that von Richthofen had fired the fatal rounds that accounted for Ball, but the evidence to support the claim doesn't stack up. All the individual witness accounts talk of a 'triplane' falling from the sky; Ball's SE5 was a biplane. An examination of the wreckage showed no significant damage caused by armaments and Ball had suffered no bullet wounds either. None of the evidence suggests that the English ace was shot down and it is far more probable that he had run out of fuel, suffered mechanical failure or that he had become disorientated inside the dense, low cloud and was unable to pull out of the fall when he re-emerged into the open.

The men of 56 Squadron at Vert Galand airfield waited anxiously for reports of Ball's fate. They clung to the hope that, just as he had done in the past, the fighter ace had been forced to land in a field and spent the night sleeping by his aircraft. Notes were dropped over German lines requesting information. But when no news came the following day, or the day after that, Ball was officially listed as missing in action. Three weeks later, the Germans dropped messages over British territory with news of his death. On 8 June, the *London Gazette* announced that Ball had been awarded the Victoria Cross. The President of France made him a Chevalier of the Légion d'honneur. His VC citation read:

For most conspicuous and consistent bravery from 25 April to 6 May, 1917, during which period captain Ball took part in 26 combats in the course of which he destroyed 11 hostile aircraft, brought down two out of control and forced several others to land.

In these combats captain Ball, flying alone, on one occasion fought six hostile machines, twice he fought five and once four. When leading two other British aeroplanes he attacked an enemy formation of eight. On each of these occasions he brought down at least one enemy.

Several times his aeroplane was badly damaged, once so seriously that but for the most delicate handling his machine would have collapsed, as nearly all the control wires had been shot away. On returning with a damaged machine he had always to be restrained from immediately going out in another.

In all, captain Ball has destroyed 43 German aeroplanes and one balloon, and has always displayed most exceptional courage, determination and skill.

Ball's parents received his Victoria Cross from King George V on 22 July 1917. Thousands lined the streets of Nottingham to watch a memorial service procession pass through the city centre. His mother was too distraught to attend and is said never to have spoken about her son's death up until the day she died in

1931. Ball's grave at Annoeullin remains the only one for an Allied serviceman in the German cemetery.

Like Noel Chavasse, the double VC-winning medic working in the trenches below him, Albert Ball showed sustained courage in the face of intense, relentless danger for very long periods of time. And like Chavasse, the flying ace was a gentle soul, more interested in tending his allotment behind the front line than he was talking about his remarkable aerial combat record. A single act of extreme valour is a noble and inspirational thing, but when a man carries out such an act several times in a day, and then day after day, month after month, with the exhaustion and stress of his efforts accumulating all that time, we are left lifted up in awe at the capacity of the human soul for such courage and self-sacrifice.

Ball was no madman or glory hunter; he was a quiet, serious, dutiful person from the heart of what today would be called Middle England. He was driven to push himself to the limits of human endurance out of patriotic duty and brotherly love for his comrades. On the ground, he may have been shy and retiring, even a little cold and reserved, but when he settled into the cockpit of his fighter plane behind a Lewis or Vickers machine gun, he became a ferocious warrior. He took no pleasure in killing fellow pilots; his prey was the plane itself. Ball accounted for dozens of enemy planes and was an inspiration for waves of young recruits rushing to join the fledgling Royal Flying Corps. But the bare statistics of his combat record tell us only a little about an incredibly brave young boy, barely out of school, and the terrifying world in which he operated.

King George V and Field Marshal Sir Douglas Haig led the glowing tributes after his death, but his fellow pilot in 56 Squadron, Cecil Lewis, probably put it best: 'Ball was a quiet, simple little man. He never boasted or criticised, but his example was tremendous . . . he was absolutely fearless.'

Flight Sergeant Norman Jackson

Flight Sergeant Norman Jackson could have stayed back at base on the night of 26 April 1944. Two days earlier, the twenty-five-year-old Londoner had flown his thirtieth bombing mission, to Munich, to complete his tour of duty. He had flown one more mission than the other six men of his regular crew after stepping in to help out when another crew's flight engineer was incapacitated. Jackson was one of a minority of Bomber Command crewmen to survive a full tour. Roughly one in every two active members of the organisation was killed. None of his mates at 106 Squadron of the Royal Air Force Volunteer Reserve would have held it against him had Jackson opted for the bar stool in their local Lincolnshire pub that evening – not least because he had just received a telegram from his wife Alma informing him that she had given birth to a son. None of them, however, were in the least surprised when he cheerfully volunteered for one more mission – 'just for luck'. A Lancaster crew was nothing if not a ferociously loyal and tight unit.

All of the men of Bomber Command – or boys in many cases – were volunteers, and their average age was just twenty-two. A month earlier they had lost more men in one night, during a raid over Nuremberg, than died in the entire four months of the Battle of Britain. Of the 125,000 who served in the organisation, 55,600 of them were killed and a further 18,000 were injured or captured. When it is taken into consideration that a sizeable number of those who served in Bomber Command were still in training or never flew a mission, the percentage of crewmen killed climbs to a staggering 60 to 70 per cent. Jackson may not have known the statistics, but he certainly knew the odds as he climbed aboard Lancaster ME669 that night.

Just after half past nine Jackson settled down at his instrument panel next to the pilot as the 15-ton bomber, carrying the same weight again in fuel and explosives, took off from RAF Metheringham for the thousand-mile round trip to central Germany. The aircraft was one of 215 Lancasters and eleven Mosquitoes heading for Schweinfurt, the home of Germany's ball-bearings industry and a crucial element of the Nazis' military infrastructure. All the regular crew members were aboard: the captain, Flying Officer Mifflin, the navigator, Flying Officer Higgins, the rear gunner, Flight Sergeant Johnson, the wireless operator, Flight Sergeant Sandelands, the bomb aimer, Flight Sergeant Toft, and the mid/upper gunner, Sergeant Smith.

Strong headwinds and inaccurate marking by the 'pathfinder' aircraft slowed the mighty bomber force. They were barely out of British-dominated airspace when they came under attack from fighter aircraft. The attacks intensified as the bombers approached the killing zone of the heavily defended skies over Germany. Searchlights criss-crossed the night sky, thousands of anti-aircraft shells pounded the air and enemy fighters swooped out of the darkness to strafe the armada of Allied aircraft.

Buffeted by flak and gusts of wind, Lancaster ME669 reached the target safely, dropped its bombs and turned for home. No one inside the plane needed reminding that a bombing mission was never over until the wheels of the aircraft skidded and jolted along the runway of their airbase back in England. They still had to run the gauntlet in reverse. In a short time the Lancaster had climbed to 20,000 feet, close to its ceiling, and the gunners were shivering in their cramped turrets, when a Focke-Wulf 190 screeched out of the gloom and riddled them with cannon fire. Jackson was no stranger to the terror of being attacked by enemy fighters. Four months earlier, on a trip to Berlin, the most heavily defended target of all, his aircraft was attacked but managed to splutter home with three severely damaged engines. On this occasion, Jackson was thrown to the floor, sustaining shrapnel wounds to the legs and shoulder. The starboard inner engine of the Lancaster burst into flames. Quickly back at his seat, Jackson pushed the button on his control panel to operate the engine's built-in fire extinguisher. The flames died down but just moments later they flared up again. An airman of his experience didn't need to be told that the fuel tank was in danger of exploding and destroying the aircraft.

Mifflin was struggling to control the damaged aircraft as the fire took hold. It was a desperate situation. If the flames weren't extinguished quickly, it was only a matter of minutes before ME669 fell from the sky. The pilot was just about managing to keep the giant bomber straight and steady when Jackson turned to him and suggested he try to put the fire out manually – by climbing out on to the wing with a hand-held extinguisher. In less extreme circumstances, the captain may well have wondered whether Jackson had completely lost his mind, but, with no time to lose and no other options, he agreed.

Jackson stumbled through the aircraft and pulled out a parachute from the stowage area, working as quickly as he could as the plane wobbled from side to side and the engines screeched to keep her airborne. Jackson pulled the ripcord of his parachute inside the fuselage while Higgins and Toft took hold of the chute and the lines. The plan was for the pair to feed out the lines as Jackson crawled along the wing. Stuffing a fire extinguisher inside his Mae West life jacket, Jackson opened the escape hatch above his head and pulled himself out on to the fuselage into the 200mph slipstream. The Merlin engine was still ablaze as he lowered himself down the side and hurled himself flat on to the starboard wing. Grabbing hold of the leading edge of the wing, he felt the freezing cold air bite into his fingers as he clawed his way towards the flaming engine.

Hanging on with one hand and with the flames licking his arm, he pointed the extinguisher into the engine cowling and began to douse the fire. He was succeeding in bringing it under control when the Lancaster banked sharply and cannon fire raked the aircraft once again. The German fighter was back. Jackson felt stabbing pains in his back and legs, forcing him to let go of the extinguisher. Flames engulfed the engine once again. The slipstream was more powerful than the winds of the strongest hurricane and when the aircraft turned sharply again, Jackson lost his grip and was swept backwards off the wing. Inside, Higgins and Toft clung on to the parachute cords as Jackson was dragged behind the rear gunner's turret, floundering like a fish on a line. Seeing that the cords were smouldering and hearing Mifflin's call to abandon the aircraft, his two crewmates quickly tried to let out the entire parachute before they baled out. Then, suddenly, Jackson was free of the aircraft and falling like a stone, a wispy trail of smoke rising above him.

The wounded flight engineer tried to extinguish the burning cords of the parachute and his smoking uniform but his hands were terribly burned. With the burn holes of his ragged parachute canopy getting ever bigger, he descended faster and faster to earth. A stand of large bushes broke his fall, and almost certainly saved his life, but both ankles were shattered on impact. With his right eye puffed up from burns, he lay in semi-conscious delirium and extreme pain for the rest of the night.

As day broke, Jackson crawled out of the bushes and, continuing on all fours, in agony from his severely burnt hands, he made it to the outskirts of a nearby village. There he was confronted by a German man, who spat at and abused him, calling him a 'Churchill gangster'. The young men of Bomber Command were not the most popular figures in Nazi Germany at the time. The man's two daughters brushed him aside to tend to the grievously wounded airman. Dragging him into their cottage, they bathed his wounds while their father went to fetch the police. Supported by one of the policemen, Jackson was forced to walk to the nearest town on his broken ankles. He was paraded through the streets before being taken to the local hospital. Some bystanders jeered him, others watched impassively as he staggered and hobbled along the road.

After ten months in hospital, Jackson finally recovered, although his disfigured hands were to trouble him for the rest of his life. He was taken to a transfer camp for Air Force prisoners near Frankfurt where he was interrogated before being moved to a regular POW camp. He made two attempts to escape before the camp was liberated by US forces in 1945. Four of his crewmates had managed to jump from the burning Lancaster. They landed safely, were rounded up and saw out the war as prisoners, but Flying Officer Mifflin, the captain, and rear gunner Johnson were killed. Four other Lancasters that took off from Metheringham that chilly spring night also failed to return.

Jackson told no one about his remarkable exploits to try and save the Lancaster and it wasn't until the war had ended and the remaining members of the crew were repatriated that the story came to light. Higgins and the others got together and recommended him for a decoration to recognise his extraordinary bravery.

His Victoria Cross was announced in the *London Gazette* on 26 October 1945. The citation was long, covering the facts of the episode in detail, and it ended with an acknowledgement that Jackson knew that even if he had succeeded in putting out the fire, he had little or no chance of making it back inside the aircraft.

. . . This airman's attempt to extinguish the fire and save the aircraft and crew from falling into enemy hands was an act of outstanding gallantry. To venture outside, when travelling at 200 miles an hour, at a great height and in intense cold, was an almost incredible feat. Had he succeeded in subduing the flames, there was little or no prospect of his regaining the cockpit. The spilling of his parachute and the risk of grave damage to its canopy reduced his chances of survival to a minimum. By his ready willingness to face these dangers he set an example of self-sacrifice which will ever be remembered.

King George VI presented Norman Jackson with his Victoria Cross at Buckingham Palace on 13 November 1945 alongside another great airman, the celebrated Group Captain Leonard Cheshire.

Jackson left the RAF on a disability pension of £2.00 a week and took a job as a travelling salesman for a Scottish whisky distillers. Adopted at birth, Jackson became a devoted family man when he and Alma settled in south-west London after the war, raising four sons and three daughters. Like so many of his generation, he never spoke about his heroics in the war. Whenever he went to a reunion, he didn't put his medals on until he was inside the venue. He died in March 1994 aged seventy-four and is buried in the Percy Road Cemetery, Twickenham. In 2004 Jackson's VC, one of just 182 awarded in the six-year conflict, was sold at auction for £200,000, a world record for a gallantry award and a price that surely would have embarrassed this deeply modest man.

During the war, all the RAF boys were fêted as the men who had saved the country during the Battle of Britain and then taken the fight to Germany in wave after wave of perilous bombing raids. The men of Bomber Command were used as a propaganda tool, raised up as a shining example of courage, self-sacrifice and patriotic duty. But after the war, no one wanted to know them. The surviving bomber crew heroes were shunted to the shadowy fringes of public consciousness, the memories of their dead comrades covered in a veil of embarrassment as the authorities moved to distance themselves from the moral scrutiny of a debate that still causes controversy today. Bomber Command's tactic of area bombing, which led to the deaths of hundreds of thousands of German civilians, was seen to undermine the moral high ground that the victors enjoyed after routing the Nazis. In his Victory in Europe broadcast on 13 May 1945 Prime Minister

Churchill neglected to mention the contribution Bomber Command played in bringing Hitler's regime to its knees. Yet five years earlier, he had declared: 'The fighters are our salvation but the bombers alone provide the means of victory.' While Britain's fighter pilots basked in the glory of national celebrity, of the tens of thousands of men who served in Bomber Command, only Guy Gibson and Leonard Cheshire became known to the wider public.

There is no debate about the devastation that Allied bombing raids came to wreak on Germany. The Luftwaffe's blitz of British cities at the outset of the war provided the original justification to respond with a bombing offensive of their own. A comparison of the figures shows that Germany was to pay a heavy price of retribution for their earlier attempts to break the spirit of the British people. The Luftwaffe's attacks are estimated to have killed 60,000 civilians; the Allied raids killed any number between 300,000 and 600,000. By the end of hostilities, Germany's seventy-five largest cities and towns had been reduced to rubble.

But for the men tasked to carry out the raids, many of them barely out of their teens, politics and ethics were not their problem. It was not for them to reason why or how. They were simply playing their part – and arguably the most hazardous part of all – in a massive national effort to save their country and liberate Europe from the stranglehold of fascist rule. How victory was to be brought about was a question for the politicians and the military commanders. They, the crews, dutifully donned their Mae Wests and flew off to Europe in the knowledge that there was a very strong chance they might never come home – men, like Norman Jackson, who volunteered to put himself through a thirty-first trip to hell out of loyalty to his mates and duty to his country.

In the 380,000 individual sorties flown, Bomber Command smashed the Nazi regime's military manufacturing capacity, thereby severely compromising the country's ability to fight on. The immense courage and sacrifice of the crews, many of them from the Commonwealth and other Allied countries, has never been properly acknowledged – until recently. After decades of campaigning by survivors, relatives and supporters of Bomber Command, the possibility of a national memorial to honour the young men has edged closer with political leaders backing plans for a monument in London's Green Park. To many, it is the very least that the free people of the United Kingdom can do to honour the boys who gave their lives in such numbers and did as much as anyone to defeat Nazi Germany and to shorten the bloody conflict in Europe.

Squadron Leader James 'Ginger' Lacey

'Scramble! Scramble! Scramble!'

The ear-splitting order burst over the tannoy of Middle Wallop airfield, startling the pilots out of their sleep. One or two members of the squadron were up and about but most were slumped in chairs or lying on the grass dozing outside the dispersal hut in the bright afternoon sunshine. The Sector Ops room had called through with the news that a large British supply convoy, on the last leg of its journey across the Atlantic, was coming under attack from Ju 87 Stuka dive-bombers out in the Channel. Immediately, the twelve pilots of No. 501 Squadron leapt to their feet and sprinted across the airfield in their fur-lined boots to the rows of parked Hurricanes.

Among them was a pale, sandy-haired young Yorkshireman, buttoning up his grey tunic over his long, heavy, white sweater as he raced and stumbled over the pristine new tarmac. Ground crew were waiting beside his squat 32-foot-long fighter as he climbed on to the wing and squeezed himself into the cramped cockpit. It was a hot day and the sweat was running as he adjusted his parachute and flying helmet and fastened his harness straps and oxygen mask. Pulling down his goggles and yanking on his gloves, the twenty-three-year-old former chemist's dispenser primed the 1,030 hp Rolls-Royce Merlin engine. It spluttered momentarily before roaring into life. Responding to its power, the twin-blade wooden propeller made a couple of slow revolutions and then burst into a furious spin.

After a rapid, last-minute check of the main controls, the pilot gave the thumbs-up to his mechanic. The wooden chocks were kicked from under the front of the wheels and he pulled out on to the runway and joined the procession of fighters streaming down the runway. One by one the Hurricanes gathered speed before lifting away and climbing steeply at almost 2,000 feet a minute into the clear blue sky above the north Hampshire countryside. He felt the familiar fluttering in his stomach as the wheels of the 3-ton fighter left solid ground and the voices of his colleagues crackled through his headset.

It wasn't long before the rolling, sun-kissed hills and fields of southern England gave way to the glistening silver of the

Channel. When they reached about 10,000 feet, the plummy voice of a BBC broadcaster introducing the latest music-hall tune cut through the radio traffic and crackle of his headsets. The original information from the ground controller located the convoy close to Normandy's Cotentin peninsula but the formation was barely halfway across the Channel when it saw the scene of the attack in the haze of the horizon. A swarm of small black dots, climbing and diving through the air, was just about visible against the glare of the sun. The outlines of the motley collection of ships below were more easily identifiable.

The young pilot had seen action during the Battle of France two months earlier and immediately recognised the symptoms of impending combat – an exhilaration mixed with terror as his stomach knotted, his mouth dried and his hands gripped the controls ever tighter. The Stukas were dropping vertically upon the merchant ships, their engines screaming with the effort, as the Hurricanes streaked to the rescue. Flying towards the sun, the British fighters were quickly picked up by the escort squadron of Me 109s, who immediately turned to engage them.

As they did so, the perfectly aligned formation of twelve Hurricanes broke in all directions to start hunting down targets individually. With the two sets of aircraft heading towards each other at a combined speed of 600mph, battle was joined almost instantly. A German fighter closed on the young Yorkshireman but before he had time to fix his target, the British fighter banked away sharply and the two became embroiled in an aerobatic game of cat and mouse as they sought to establish a good firing position. The RAF sergeant was a superb airman, and he led the German a merry aerial dance for a minute – but he was an even better marksman. He had no more than a second or two in which to react, but he made no mistake when the opportunity presented itself as he closed to within 100 yards of his adversary. With a three-second depression of the trigger, dozens of rounds and tracer fire spat out of the eight Browning machine-gun ports along the wings and raked the Me 109 along its engine cowling and fuselage as it shot past. The Hurricane turned sharply and came back to strafe it with a second burst. There was a brief pause before the German fighter turned on its back and plunged earthwards.

The Hurricane pilot pressed his goggles up against the Perspex of the cockpit canopy and watched the stricken aircraft spiral crazily towards its destruction, following its long trail of smoke as it grew ever smaller. From so high up, the splash as it hit the water and broke up was barely visible. When he looked down again seconds later, the only sign of his adversary was a smear of oil on the sea's surface. He wasn't aware of it at the time but Lacey had just scored his first victory in a mighty military contest that held the fate of his country and the free world in the balance. The Battle of Britain was underway. By the time it was over, not one of the thousands of Fighter Command pilots who took to the air over southern England could claim to have done more to have affected its outcome than James 'Ginger' Lacey.

* * *

Ten weeks earlier, Lacey and 501 Squadron, an Auxiliary Air Force unit, were based at Filton in the suburbs of Bristol when the call came to head for France without delay. Germany had launched its long-expected invasion of the Netherlands, Belgium and France. It was 10 May 1940, the same day that Winston Churchill took over from Neville Chamberlain as Prime Minister. A quarter of a million men of the British Expeditionary Force (BEF) were already on the ground in anticipation of the onslaught but more were needed to try and block the Blitzkrieg.

No. 501 Squadron was one of three sent to boost numbers of the Advanced Air Striking Force under Air Vice-Marshal Arthur 'Ugly' Barratt, the commander of all British Air Forces in France. Made up of eight squadrons of Fairey Battle light bombers, two of Blenheim medium bombers and two of Hurricane fighters, the AASF stood little chance against the might of the Luftwaffe. The squadron's sixteen Hurricanes, including the four reserve aircraft, flew through clear skies the following day on the second leg of the journey to reach the front. The Channel dazzled in the late afternoon sun as they began their descent over the lush green fields of northern France. But for the odd small plume of smoke, it made for a peaceful scene from above and gave no indication of the butchery being carried out by the German forces as they scythed a path through northern Europe and pushed towards the coast. One by one, the Hurricanes landed on a field outside the village of Bétheniville near Reims, bumping over the grass as they taxied into their parking position. One of the airfields used during the First World War, Bétheniville was a far cry from the smart surroundings of the new RAF aerodromes back home with their tarmac runways, spacious hangars and comfortable messes. Here there was not a single building for them or their equipment and stores. They were to eat and sleep under canvas and wash wherever they could find running water.

The sixteen pilots were nonetheless in high spirits as they stood by their Hurricanes joking about their primitive lodgings when they heard the approach of the two Bristol Bombay troop carriers and the Armstrong Whitworth Ensign airliner carrying their spare pilots, ground crews and other support units. The Ensign landed first, followed by one of the Bombays, and men were soon disgorging from both aircraft when the second Bombay came over the hedge at the far end of the field. It was about to touch down when the pilot suddenly pulled her nose up and put her into a steep climb. The aircraft stalled, tipped on its side and crashed into the turf with a sickening, metallic thud. It hadn't exploded on impact and Lacey and the others rushed towards the pile of twisted wreckage. They were greeted by a scene of carnage. Three men were dead, twelve seriously injured. The following day the squadron buried their friends in the local cemetery, but a bombing raid two days later chewed up the churchyard, leaving body parts scattered all around in a scene as macabre as it was harrowing. Burying their comrades once had been bad enough; burying them a second time was doubly distressing. It was an inauspicious start to the war for No. 501 Squadron.

Thirty-six hours later, Lacey was shaken awake in the dead of night. His section was on dawn patrol and after a quick cup of tea he and the other two pilots, all still half asleep, stumbled out of the HQ tent and climbed aboard their Hurricanes. Lacey had difficulty priming his engine and the other two took to the charcoal grey sky without him, assuming that he would be only a few seconds behind and would catch them up. When he finally managed to get airborne there was no sign of the other two aircraft and Lacey set out by himself to the area above Sedan where the Germans were advancing. The sun had appeared over the skyline to reveal another almost cloudless day when he arrived over the Ardennes town. With little sign of enemy activity, let alone a Blitzkrieg, Lacey turned away in search of the other two Hurricanes.

He was cruising at 20,000 feet, listening to the BBC Overseas Service in his earphones when, as he was squinting through the side of the cockpit, his heart jumped. It was the first enemy aircraft he had ever seen: a Heinkel III bomber. A split second later he picked out its escort, an Me 109 fighter which was faster and a better climber than the Hurricane and had a far higher ceiling. In that instant, the war became a blood-thumping reality for Lacey. He may have had hundreds of flying hours in his log book after his spell as an instructor with the Yorkshire Aeroplane Club and then in training with the RAF Volunteer Reserve but, unlike many of his German counterparts, he had no experience of aerial combat. More alarmingly, in training he had become accustomed to running through exercises in formation, but now he was on his own.

Neither of the enemy aircraft had spotted him when he tipped the Hurricane on its side, opened the throttle and swooped upon the Me 109 at 320mph. He closed to within 100 yards before squeezing the trigger and the Hurricane trembled violently as the eight machine guns raked the unsuspecting German. Streams of tracer tore through the morning sky and orange sparks flashed along the mottled livery of the fuselage as the rounds riddled their target. Almost instantly the Me 109 burst into flames and Lacey felt his Hurricane buck in the shock wave of the explosion. As his victim fell to earth, Lacey made straight for the Heinkel below. At almost 100mph slower, the lumbering bomber had no chance of escaping his British predator, but to make sure Lacey closed to within almost point-blank range before opening up. Pulling away as he took his finger off the trigger, he saw the wing of the Heinkel being torn from the fuselage. The aircraft turned over and spiralled to earth.

The pilots of the two other aircraft of his section were relieved to see him on his return to Bétheniville, but there was barely time to report his solo adventure before they were ordered to get airborne again. On this patrol, there were five Hurricanes in total and they were heading towards Sedan when they encountered a formation of half a dozen Me 110s. Not much was known about the operational capabilities of the Me 110, except that it was bigger and faster than the Hurricane and, with five machine guns and two cannons, it had greater overall firepower as well as the added benefit of a rear gunner, operating from the back of the cockpit. In these opening days of the Battle of

France the aircraft's fatal lack of manoeuvrability had yet to be discovered.

But the relative specifications of the two opposing models of aircraft were the last thoughts on the minds of the pilots as they set about each other. The Hurricanes broke out of formation, each falling upon a target. Lacey's dived as soon as he saw the approaching Hurricane. For several minutes, the two planes twisted and turned as the Me 110 tried to shake off the more agile Hurricane. Tracer fire from the rear gunner's retaliation fizzed over the Hurricane as Lacey stalked the German. The Yorkshireman was said to have perfect eyesight as well as a great facility for calculating speed, time and distance under pressure and he was using these benefits to great effect as he rattled the metalwork of his adversary with short squeezes of the trigger. The Me 110 absorbed the punishment without obvious complaint but a final burst into its engine brought its resistance to an abrupt end and it began to fall from the sky. Lacey was impressed to see the rear gunner still firing at him as he plunged to his death. For his actions this day, Lacey was later awarded the Croix de Guerre.

The fighting in France and the Low Countries intensified over the weeks that followed and flying became ever more hazardous for the overstretched RAF squadrons. Flying mission after mission, they moved from airfield – or, rather, from empty field to empty field – as the Germans tightened their grip on north-west Europe and pushed the British, French and Belgian troops back towards the coast. Sleeping under canvas or in farm outbuildings, the airmen and their ground crews lived a hand-to-mouth existence, washing and shaving in streams and rivers, haggling with locals for fresh eggs, meat and vegetables, and grabbing the occasional carafe of wine in a local café.

Anti-aircraft fire soon came to be the main threat facing them and the Germans were bringing in more guns by the day. Operating over enemy territory for the most part, each time the Hurricanes crossed the lines they were met with a ferocious barrage from below. The tracer fire streaked ever closer as the gunners found their range and hundreds of shells burst around them, buffeting the 3-ton aircraft with gusts from the shock waves. Clouds of smoke filled the air around them and shards of metal clanked and rattled the wings and the fuselage. On occasions, the force created by the flak was so intense that it was able to throw the squat British fighters upside down.

Two weeks after touching down in France, the situation facing the BEF was desperate. By 26 May the British and French armies were in full retreat, facing pulverisation under the jackboot of Hitler's advancing hordes. The evacuation at Dunkirk was launched, immediately attracting relentless bombing raids by the Luftwaffe as the Allied troops scrambled aboard the hundreds of ships and boats, military and civilian, coming to their rescue. Boulogne and Calais had fallen. The Belgian army had fought bravely to resist Hitler's Blitzkrieg but was close to collapse as it made a final stand near Ghent. No. 501 Squadron played its part in covering the retreat to the beaches when, the following day, it fell upon a formation of thirty Heinkel bombers heading for the British lines, and shot down fourteen of them. Lacey himself dispatched two bombers, closing to within a few dozen yards of each before unleashing his deadly bursts of fire. For this action, he was mentioned in dispatches.

After the Dunkirk evacuations were completed, and 340,000 men were rescued to fight another day, 501 Squadron was one of several that remained in northern France to continue the fight. On 9 June, Lacey's section of half a dozen Hurricanes clashed with a formation of Me 109s. All the aircraft scattered and a short fight ensued before the Germans turned tail. At the very moment Lacey scanned the skies around him and realised he was alone and had no idea where he was, the engine of his Hurricane started to make an unhealthy choking sound. Moments later, the aircraft started to shudder from nose to tail. The oil pressure was falling and the engine was heating up at a rapid rate. He had been hit and Lacey knew that at any moment the Hurricane was going to start tumbling to its destruction. Spotting what looked to be a wide open field below, perfect for a forced landing, he floated the spluttering aircraft to earth. It was only when he was about to touch down that he realised he was landing in a bog. As the undercarriage made contact with the ground, the Hurricane somersaulted and came to rest on its back.

On impact, Lacey was catapulted forward and smashed his head on the instrument panel. Though stunned, he was conscious enough to realise that he was hanging upside down, supported by his harness straps, and that the cockpit was slowly filling with water. He could smell the petrol as it leaked over the engine steaming in the water. He kicked frantically at the Perspex canopy of his cockpit, but, unable to manoeuvre easily in the cramped cockpit, his soft flying boots could make no impression. With the aircraft sinking inch by inch and the stench of fuel growing stronger by the second, Lacey had resigned himself to a hideous, claustrophobic death by fire and drowning when he fell unconscious.

When he came round, he was lying with his back in the water, staring into the face of a pretty French girl. Minutes later, some British troops arrived and, using a gate as a stretcher, carried him half a mile to an RAF ambulance. He had no idea how long he had been in the cockpit but was told that French farm workers had cut him free. Blood from his head wound had caked his face, but the injury wasn't serious and, after a few days under observation, he was allowed to rejoin the squadron.

Within forty-eight hours of his return to duty, the French had been defeated and the last remaining British forces quickly packed up their equipment and slipped back over the Channel. In the space of a month, Lacey and his young colleagues had gone from fresh-faced recruits to battle-hardened veterans, but their action-filled adventures in France were nothing more than a taste of what was to come.

On return to England, 501 Squadron had a quiet two-week spell based at Croydon airfield – Britain's principal airport at the time – and they were grateful for the opportunity to recuperate after a month of combat and living rough. The patrols they flew were largely uneventful and in between they slept for hours and enjoyed the generous hospitality of landlords and locals in the neighbouring pubs. By the time they transferred to Middle Wallop, they were eager for a return to serious action, but another two weeks passed with little 'trade' for their squadron. They beat off the attack on the convoy in the Channel but otherwise they saw more action in the village inns than they did in the skies above their heads. At the end of July the squadron was moved to Gravesend on the south side of the Thames Estuary, closer to the East End of London and therefore to the aerial front line.

Just a fifteen-minute flight across the Channel, the forces of the Third Reich were massing to invade. The moment France fell, Hitler ordered his generals to draw up the plans for the invasion of Britain, the only country standing in the way of his total domination of Western Europe. The plan, code-named Sea Lion, was to land 200,000 German soldiers along a 120-mile stretch of coast of southern England from Ramsgate in Kent to Lyme Regis in Dorset. A large armada of vessels, including 2,500 troop-ferrying barges, had been assembled in Belgian and French harbours.

Before Operation Sea Lion could be launched, it was imperative for the Luftwaffe to gain mastery of the skies. To do that, they had to destroy the Royal Air Force, the one service with the capability of inflicting severe damage on an invading force. Home advantage was a great strength for the British. They could see the country they were defending as they fought. What greater motivation to fight did a man need than to look down on the towns, villages and even the homes where his family and friends lived? They also had the practical advantage of being closer to their airfields. The German fighters could only remain over England for roughly twenty-five minutes before having to return to their bases to refuel. The RAF could also exploit the benefits of an excellent early-warning radar system and the intelligence provided by ULTRA through the decryption of enemy radio messages.

But no matter how well informed the RAF were going to be, they still had to defeat the enemy in the air and, on all other counts, in a comparison of their relative strengths, the Luftwaffe outscored the British.

Many of the German pilots were battle-hardened following campaigns in Spain (during the civil war) and more recently in France, Poland, Norway and the Low Countries. By contrast, the RAF pilots, bar a few dozen who had seen action in France, were hopelessly inexperienced, not to mention hugely outnumbered, by five to one. The Germans had technically the best fighter plane in the Messerschmitt Bf 109, as well as the Messerschmitt Me 110 and the Stuka. They had 2,800 aircraft, hundreds of reserve pilots and tons of spare equipment parts and ammunition. The RAF had 600 fighter aircraft and 1,250 pilots. Founded four years earlier under Sir Hugh Dowding, the fledgling Fighter Command consisted of 29 Hurricane Squadrons and 19 Supermarine Spitfires. A further problem for the British was that they had to spread their resources all around the country and Fighter Command was broken down into four groups – one each to cover the north, south, east and west of the country. No.

11 Group, commanded by New Zealander Keith Park, was based in the South East and London and was expected to take the full force of Hitler's all-out attack from the air.

By the beginning of August, the War Cabinet, the military chiefs and the people of Britain all knew that if an invasion was to come it was going to have to come soon. Across the Atlantic, no one in the US administration was holding its breath for a British victory. The Americans had yet to join the war and, from where they were sitting, the odds looked heavily stacked in Germany's favour. The shadow of Nazi totalitarianism was creeping across the Channel. Britain looked doomed.

It was just as well for the fate of the free world that a few hundred young men in blue-grey tunics knocking back their beers in the pubs of southern England had other ideas.

The first phase of the Battle of Britain had taken place in the four weeks from 10 July when the Luftwaffe focused on offensive reconnaissance, softening up and probing the British defences ahead of a major assault. In particular, they targeted shipping convoys, coastal towns and radar stations. The attack on mainland England – the second phase – was going to come from all angles and the first line of the defence was the early-warning network alerting controllers to the raiders' approach.

As war loomed, a string of radar stations had been thrown around the coastline and they quickly proved to be a highly effective tool in the war in the air. German aircrews were continually surprised by the fact that almost every time they crossed the Channel a unit of British fighters was waiting to intercept them.

The physical combat may have been taking place in the air but an invisible, parallel war was taking place behind the scenes as an army of scientists and engineers on each side battled to gain supremacy over the other. Britain's early-warning system was a multi-layered network that made the most of the amateur and the professional, the sophisticated and the basic to get the upper hand on the raiders pouring towards her coast. Using radio intercepts, radar detection and volunteers from the Royal Observer Corps on the ground, the reports of enemy aircraft movements were passed rapidly down through a pyramid of departments to the Sector Operations rooms of each group of Fighter Command.

The staff in these Operations rooms, many of them members of the WAAF, were the unsung heroes of the Battle of Britain. Like the pilots, they worked through the day and night to the point of exhaustion. Collating and passing up-to-date information about the position and strength of the enemy, they gave the airmen the gift of long-distance vision and hearing. They talked them on to targets and warned them of approaching aircraft in a code which has since become part of the lore of the Battle of Britain: 'Angels 12', for example, meant 12,000 feet, 'bandits' enemy, 'vector' steer and 'pancake' land, refuel and rearm.

The system had been coping well, in spite of the damage inflicted on many radar stations in the previous four weeks, but on 12 August the network was presented with its greatest challenge of the battle to date when Germany intensified its attacks in preparation for a full-scale aerial assault the following day. It was shortly after midday and 501 Squadron were already in the air when the order came through to head to the Thames Estuary where 'bandits' were attacking a destroyer. No German plane better fitted the description 'bandit' than the Junker Ju 87 Stuka dive-bomber. Falling upon its target in a vertical dive, with its engines screaming, it was a potent sound and symbol of Nazi aggression and a terrifying sight for anyone on the ground caught within the splash range of its bombs. Although it was coming to the end of its operational life at the start of the war, it was still proving to be highly effective in the Blitzkrieg.

As 501 Squadron arrived on the scene, they were met with the spectacle of a dozen Stukas swooping upon the British ship, which was firing back with everything it had. Puffs of smoke filled the air and columns of water leapt up the sides of the destroyer as the bombs crashed around her. Ignoring the Me 109 escorts – they would have to wait their turn – the Hurricanes went straight for the Stukas. Within seconds, Lacey had taken down his first opponent. Two short bursts was all it took to send the bomber spiralling into the estuary. Weaving, diving, climbing, banking, spiralling . . . the swarm of different aircraft packed the skies with an aerobatic display that was at once stunning, stirring and terrifying to behold from the ground. The tracer fizzed around his cockpit as Lacey sought his next Stuka. Climbing as quickly as he could to get into a dominant position, he soon spotted his target but, at the sight of the Hurricane making towards him, the pilot of the Stuka jettisoned his bombs to lighten his load and turned down the estuary towards the North Sea. As Lacey chased it, the Stuka's rear gunner opened up on him and the tracer streaked past the cockpit and over the wings. Lacey responded with a squeeze on the trigger, killing the gunner at his first attempt. He closed in for the kill, raking the Stuka with eight streams of rounds from the gunports on each wing. Smoke began to pour from the Stuka's engine as it dropped from the sky.

On a day of frenetic activity in the air and on the ground, Lacey added one more kill in the afternoon when the squadron were scrambled to intercept a formation of fifty Me 110s and 109s. Back at Gravesend aerodrome, Lacey received the news that he had been gazetted for a Distinguished Flying Medal, awarded to non-commissioned officers and other ranks, for his actions during the defence of the Channel convoy three weeks earlier. But there was no time to celebrate as a formation of Heinkel He IIIs and Ju 88 bombers began to attack the airfield, forcing Lacey and his colleagues to dive for cover.

The following morning, Hitler's long-expected air assault finally came. Known to the Germans as 'Adlertag' (Eagle Day), it marked the beginning of the most intense period of action in the Battle of Britain. The German plan for the days that followed was simple: drive the RAF out of the skies, destroy its infrastructure on the ground and clear the route for the massive ground invasion force waiting for the order to set out across the Channel. Not since William the Conqueror assembled his army in Normandy some 875 years earlier had the freedom of Britain stood in greater jeopardy. With 870 long-range bombers, 300 dive-bombers and 900 fighters deployed to attack the South East,

Lieutenant Colonel Robert Blair 'Paddy' Mayne DSO & Three Bars. Many consider it a scandal that the Ulsterman was never awarded the Victoria Cross.

A monument to the men of the 1st Special Air Service, located at one of their training centres in Scotland.

Lt Colonel 'Blondie' Hasler (left), with Marine Bill Sparks, returns to Bordeaux for a memorial service to the Cockleshell Heroes, involved in Operation Frankton. Canoeing up the Gironde they attacked Axis shipping docked at the French harbour. Of the twelve who set out, Hasler and Sparks were the only two to survive.

Captain Albert Ball VC, DSO★★ holding the nose and propeller from his aeroplane. He has been described as Britain's Baron Von Richthofen.

Captain Albert Ball, standing in front of his plane, liked to close within yards of his target before opening fire.

Statue of Albert Ball in the grounds of Nottingham Castle.

Norman Jackson VC. His act
of courage was one of the
most remarkable of the war.

A Lancaster bomber. Jackson climbed onto the wing of his plane to extinguish an engine fire. It was his final mission.

Norman Jackson VC sitting in the cockpit of an Avro Lancaster Bomber during the Battle of Britain Memorial Flight in 1968.

World War II flying ace 'Ginger' Lacey (third from right, smiling broadly), inspects a silk scarf presented to him along with the first parachute manufactured in Australia to reach Britain.

Captain Edward Fegen, who went down with his ship, H.M.S. *Jervis Bay*, was awarded the Victoria Cross posthumously, after his bold actions allowed most of convoy HX-84 to escape.

The *Jervis Bay*, a converted merchant ship stood no chance against the mighty pocket battleship *Admiral Scheer*.

The German battleship *Admiral Scheer*, one of the most formidable ships Germany had ever produced.

Lt Commander Malcolm David Wanklyn (pictured) is one of Britain's great unsung heroes. Many consider him to be the greatest submarine captain of all time.

H.M.S *Upholder* sunk over 130,000 tonnes of axis shipping heading for North Africa.

Hitler expected the battle to last no more than a week. To maximise the pressure on British defences, the Germans sent in high- and low-level raids to different targets at the same time. They also mobilised two hundred aircraft based in Norway and Denmark to attack the north and east of England, thereby forcing the British to divert and dilute their relatively meagre resources.

In the following weeks, the skies over Britain became the scene of the most intense air fighting yet witnessed. The pilots of 501 and the other fighter squadrons of 11 Group were flying between four and eight missions a day. A nervous population watched from below as Hurricanes and Spitfires streaked into the skies, the bombs fell among them and hundreds of flaming aircraft spiralled to their destruction into fields, villages and towns. Hitler became increasingly infuriated that Hermann Goering's Luftwaffe was taking so much time and effort to secure the victory he had taken for granted. But it was tantalisingly close; for weeks, the Battle of Britain and the fate of the country hung in the balance. The people could only pray and hope as a dwindling band of raw pilots, many of them barely out of school, took the fight to the Luftwaffe and kept the invasion force at bay across the Channel.

The strain on Lacey and the other pilots during this period was immense. Fatigue was as great a danger as the enemy himself. Even the slightest dulling of a pilot's reactions could mean the difference between living and dying. Flick through archive photographs from the Battle of Britain and you see dozens of images of young airmen lying outside their huts and hangars, heads off to one side, mouths open, waiting for the scramble order to rouse them from an almost comatose stupor and back into the fray.

The summer of 1940 was beautifully hot, the nights were warm and Lacey took to sleeping under the wing of his aircraft during the height of the battle. Like others, he did this partly so that he could scramble more quickly but also because he had developed a habit of vomiting every time he heard the tannoy being switched on to order the squadron into the air. The adrenaline surging through his system over the past weeks was playing havoc with his mind and body. Sleeping in the hut, he often didn't make it to the toilet in time. Sleeping next to his aircraft, he was able to roll over, spew up his guts and then jump straight into the cockpit.

By the time Prime Minister Winston Churchill stood up at the dispatch box in the House of Commons on 20 August 1940, the RAF had lost more than two hundred fighters and one hundred pilots in the fighting. 'The gratitude of every home in our island, in our Empire, and indeed throughout the world except in the abodes of the guilty goes out to the British airmen who, undaunted by odds, unweakened by their constant challenge and mortal danger, are turning the tide of world war by their prowess and their devotion,' he boomed. To prolonged cheers from all benches of the packed House, he continued: 'Never in the field of human conflict was so much owed by so many to so few. All hearts go out to the fighter pilots, whose brilliant actions we see with our own eyes day after day.'

What Churchill didn't know as he spoke was that the Battle of Britain was still two or three weeks from reaching its height.

The pattern of fighting continued for the next two weeks and by the end of the month the situation facing 11 Group, and therefore the whole country, had become desperate. Many RAF and radar stations, maintenance facilities and factories had been badly damaged and Fighter Command was being forced to use small, ill-equipped civilian airfields where squadron bases had been bit badly. The supply of spare parts was stretched to the limit while the overworked, shattered ground crews working in the open were taking heavy casualties in the raids. The rate of destruction of Hurricanes and Spitfires now outstripped their production of replacements and the training of pilots to fly them.

There was even talk of pulling the fighter squadrons back north of the Thames, but Dowding and Park knew that such a move was exactly what the Germans had planned. They were in no mood to surrender the merest degree of the air superiority their men had been fighting so hard to preserve, but they knew better than anyone that the current rate of attrition was unsustainable. Had Hitler and the Luftwaffe commanders fully understood quite how close Fighter Command was to breaking point, then the course and outcome of the Second World War might have been entirely different.

The Germans had their own problems which shaped their tactical and strategic thinking. Their losses had been far higher than expected and their bomber squadrons in particular had suffered terribly at the hands of the Hurricanes and Spitfires, forcing their commanders to transfer more squadrons of fighters to serve as escorts. Morale among the enemy bomber crews plummeted by the day as more and more of them were shot out of the sky. Lacey played his part in puncturing that morale when he shot down a Dornier Do 17 over the Kent coast and scored a 'probable' with a second. The rest of the squadron accounted for a further twenty-two bombers during the day.

As in the Great War, the system of scoring kills was complicated and unreliable. At the end of a day in which they had flown as many as eight missions, attacked an endless stream of aircraft and then collapsed back at the airfield, it was difficult for the pilots to recall how many they had destroyed or damaged. The fighting was frantic and relentless and many pilots didn't bother to record their victories unless they were asked to submit a combat report. Often they were too tired or it was simply that no one asked them for days. As a result, many victories were never recorded and the question of who was the successful pilot or which squadron can never satisfactorily be answered. Not that the pilots themselves cared. It wasn't a game for them. They were interested only in getting airborne, staying alive and wreaking as much havoc as possible on the swarms of bombers and fighters attacking their homeland. It was only after the war that military and aviation historians became interested in totting up the scores.

On 25 August, Britain delivered an audacious message of defiance into the heartland of Nazi Germany when a bombing raid was launched on Berlin. Goering had boasted to Hitler and the German people that no enemy bombers would get within striking distance of the Fatherland. The shock waves from the attack reverberated not only through the streets of the capital but also in the corridors of the Reichstag. The raids caused only minor physical damage but it was a symbolic blow that showed that the British, even with their backs to the wall, still had the capacity, the will and the daring to go on the offensive and take the fight into the heart of Hitler's empire.

The last week in August and the first two of September saw the Battle of Britain reach its height as Hitler ordered the Luftwaffe to intensify its assault and smash British defences once and for all. The last two days of August saw especially heavy fighting as German aircraft poured over the Channel in wave after wave of massive formations.

On 30 August the Germans launched major attacks on the south coast as well as the port of Liverpool and equipment produc-tion factories at Luton and Radlett, in Hertfordshire. In mid-morning, 230 aircraft in three waves darkened the skies of Kent and Sussex at half-hourly intervals. For the first time in the battle, all ten of 11 Group's fighter squadrons were ordered to scramble to meet the threat. It was the heaviest day of fighting so far and the onslaught continued until nightfall. No. 501 Squadron was sent up to intercept one formation of more than one hundred bombers and escorts as it approached the Dungeness headland on the Kent coast. Flying straight into the midst of them, Lacey got the better of an Me 109 and a Heinkel before he ran out of ammunition and was forced to take evasive action from the section of fighters he had been engaging.

Once Lacey was back in the air again after rearming and refuelling, the ground controller's voice announced that another huge formation was heading up the Thames Estuary towards London. The Commanding Officer, Squadron Leader Harry Hogan, ordered his Hurricanes to form up for a head-on attack. As the two units raced towards each other, the CO gave the order to fire and keep firing while holding their formation as they flew through the massed rows of German bombers and fighters. It was growing late in the day and by coming down-sun from the west they had the advantage of taking the Germans by surprise. One moment the skies ahead were clear to the German pilots, the next they were filled with twelve Hurricanes bearing down on them at pace. The ninety-six gunports of the British fighters opened up from point-blank range, scattering the Germans' neat formation in all directions and allowing them to close in on the raiders one at a time.

As soon as the two formations collided, Lacey's Hurricane was riddled by a long burst of machine-gun fire which damaged his wings and stopped his engine. Oil squirted over the cockpit Perspex, obscuring his vision as he banked way, chased by a German fighter which continued to rake his aircraft as it descended. When the Me 109 pilot turned away in search of further targets, Lacey realised that the wind was in the right direction and that he had just enough altitude to glide his stricken aircraft back to Gravesend. As he brought it in to land, the ground crew were standing by the runway open-mouthed. They were staggered that such a severely damaged machine was in the air at all, let alone being landed with textbook perfection by a young pilot who appeared no more shaken up than if had been out on a gentle Sunday afternoon spin. Walking round the Hurricane to inspect the damage, they counted eighty-seven bullet holes as well as half a dozen larger holes caused by the lumps of machinery that had torn through its skin.

The next day, the Luftwaffe launched an even bigger assault and fighting raged from eight in the morning till dusk. Fighter Command had 37 aircraft shot down and 12 pilots killed – its heaviest daily toll to date – in addition to 40 RAF personnel killed and 22 injured on the ground. The odds against the British, already very long, were stretched even further over these days. Accustomed to engaging four or five aircraft at a time, the Hurricane and Spitfire pilots were now taking on as many as eight or ten at a time. Many of the old characters around the airfields had gone, replaced by fresh-faced recruits straight out of training. Some didn't even last a day. The battle had reached a critical juncture. Every pilot and aircraft lost added to the operational burden of those that remained.

No. 501 Squadron was down to the bare bones with just seven serviceable Hurricanes available when the call came in the afternoon to intercept a massive attack on Hornchurch aerodrome north-east of London. Up against two dozen Dornier Do 17 bombers and as many Me 109s, the Hurricanes were hopelessly outnumbered, but they went at the German formations head-on, forcing them to break in all directions. Lacey latched on to a lone Me 109, raking its fuselage with a short, deadly burst as he went after it in a near-vertical dive. The German fighter plunged into a fuel depot, sparking an explosion.

The Hurricanes successfully beat off the attack but a follow-up raid on the aerodrome that evening caused enough damage to render it unusable for a short period. At the end of a day which had seen wave after wave of German formations swarming over the Channel, the RAF claimed that 70 enemy aircraft had been shot out of the skies with 34 'probables' and 33 damaged. Lacey claimed three of the probables and one damaged to add to his one confirmed kill. A further fifteen German planes were shot down by anti-aircraft fire. After the war both sides revised down the figures they had inflated for propaganda purposes, but in either set of statistics the RAF carried the day.

As the pressure from the Luftwaffe intensified, so too did the doggedness of the RAF. But something was going to have to give soon. The relentlessness and exertion were unsustainable as the fighting continued without respite into the first week of September. The British lost roughly two dozen aircraft a day and the Germans about twice that, but, with far fewer aircraft available to them, the RAF losses, as a percentage, were far greater than their enemy's. Another week of such attrition and Fighter Command would be close to breaking point.

It was at this critical moment that the Germans switched strategies in what historians have come to regard as the turning point in the battle.

After attacking the RAF airfields of the South East for over a fortnight, Hitler and his commanders believed they had caused enough damage to Fighter Command to launch Operation Sea Lion within a week. But with time running out and Hitler eager to invade Russia before winter set in, the Germans opted to attack London rather than carry on its policy of bleeding the RAF.

On 7 September, the Blitz began. The bombardment was to continue almost every day for the next nine months as German bombers laid siege to the capital and other major cities and towns around the country. Tens of thousands of civilians would die and thousands of buildings be destroyed, but Hitler and his military chiefs had made the wrong tactical call. In the short term, the respite granted to the Fighter Command stations gave the RAF the time to repair, regroup and come back at the Luftwaffe even harder. And, in the longer term, the spirit of the British was never broken by the aerial hammering. If anything, by bringing the war into the streets and houses of the people, it strengthened the mood of defiance.

It had also become easier for the RAF to marshal its resources to the greatest effect.

Defending dozens of targets spread over a wide area, Fighter Command's elasticity had been stretched to snapping point. But now that they knew exactly where the Germans were heading, the Spitfire and Hurricane squadrons merged into larger forces and succeeded in disrupting many of the German formations before they could reach their targets.

The day before the Blitz began, Lacey was ordered to take a week's leave. With extreme fatigue taking its toll as the battle wore on into its seventh week, the exhausted pilots were sent away in rotation to allow them to come back fresh and hungry for more action. When he returned to duty on 13 September, the squadron had been posted to Kenley in the southern suburbs of London.

It wasn't long before Lacey was airborne again – on a very important and dangerous solo mission. Buckingham Palace had just been bombed by a Heinkel – the royal residence was bombed seven times in all during the war – and the government was determined that such a provocative, morale-sapping breach of national defences would not go unanswered. In order to seize back the propaganda initiative, it was imperative that the culprit was shot down. There was one big problem: the weather was atrocious. Heavy, low cloud sat over southern England, making flying conditions hazardous and the observation of targets impossible. Unwilling to order an airman into such menacing skies, the Sector Ops room asked for a volunteer to chase down the offending bomber. The request was made in the knowledge that whoever undertook the mission would have no chance of landing and would be forced to bale out.

Lacey instinctively put his hand up. He claimed he was interested in experiencing the novelty of baling out. Within minutes he was climbing through the towering columns of cumulonimbus cloud that blanketed the landscape. As the radar operators and interceptors hunted the Heinkel remotely, the voice of the ground controller talked Lacey on to his target, guiding him to all points of the compass, but he could see little beyond his propeller and the tips of his wings 'The visibility was very poor and at times the rain was very heavy, and there was 10/10 cloud at 500 feet', the Air Ministry combat report states. They had almost given up the chase, when, out of nowhere, he caught sight of it, right underneath him. It was no more than a fleeting glance through the slightest break in the cloud, but Lacey was in no doubt that it was his prey. At this stage he hadn't seen the surface of the earth for the better part of two hours and didn't know whether he was over land or sea when he went in for the kill.

Lacey put the Hurricane into a dive and raked the tail of the plane with a short burst, killing the rear gunner who slumped forward over his gun and setting fire to the port engine. Over the next few minutes, the lumbering bomber tried to shake him off, banking left and right, losing height then climbing, but Lacey stayed with him, firing bursts as he closed to within 50 yards. The dead gunner was pulled away and another crewman took his position and immediately opened up on the Hurricane. The rounds tore into the bottom of the cockpit, ripping out the radiator and setting the engine on fire. Lacey only had a few moments before the Hurricane would begin to fall but he kept firing until he had emptied the rest of his ammunition into his adversary. The flames were leaping around Lacey's legs as he watched the Heinkel fall to earth. Opening the cockpit canopy, he leapt into the cloud, somersaulting through the air, out of control, before he finally managed to get hold of his parachute ripcord. The canopy billowed open, slowing his fall with a sharp jolt as the smoke from his burning clothes wafted over him. The cold, damp air was a soothing balm for the burns to his face and legs.

As Lacey emerged from the cloud, he saw his Hurricane, trailing thick, black smoke, smash into the ground in a ball of flame. He floated to earth to be greeted near the village of Sutton Valence by a member of the Home Guard sticking a double-barrelled shotgun in his face. With an accent as broad as the Humber Estuary, it didn't take Lacey long to convince the elderly volunteer reservist that the two of them were fighting on the same side. What remained of his scorched trousers had fallen away during his descent, and dressed only in his underpants and flying boots from the waist down, he was taken to the hospital at Leeds Castle in Kent, a short journey from where he had landed.

There, he refused to be put into a hospital bed, insisting he had to get back to Kenley to let the squadron know he was alive. With all the phone lines down, he was worried his mother would be informed that he was missing. The doctor let him go on the proviso that the ambulance took him straight to the medical centre at the base to have his burnt legs attended to. On reaching the gates of the camp, now wearing a new pair of trousers to cover his wounds, he sent the ambulance on its way and reported to the CO and made himself available for the next sortie.

On 15 September the Germans threw everything they had at the RAF in a final bid to destroy Fighter Command's resistance and launch the amphibious invasion of the south coast. But after seven days of re-equipping and repairing, the RAF, with six hundred Hurricanes and Spitfires in service, was as strong now as it had been at the outset of the battle. Over a thousand German aircraft appeared over southern England throughout the course of the day, concentrating their attacks once again on the capital, with smaller raids on Southampton and Portland.

There was one major attack in the morning and one in the afternoon and on each occasion British fighters succeeded in shooting down or driving off most of the bombers before they reached London. The city still suffered extensive damage, especially south of the Thames, but it was a resounding victory for the RAF. They had shot down thirty-five bombers and twenty-five fighters and damaged countless others, inflicting the highest daily losses on the Germans since 18 August. Lacey accounted for three of those victories and damaged a fourth aircraft. He was awarded a bar to his DFM for his efforts.

Two days later, codebreakers decrypted a message carrying news that Hitler had postponed Operation Sea Lion indefinitely. His much-vaunted air force had failed to secure the air supremacy that he had taken for granted. Ever since, 15 September has been celebrated in the United Kingdom as 'Battle of Britain Day'.

The threat of imminent invasion was over but the struggle in the skies above Britain went on for a further six weeks as the Germans continued to pound her cities. No. 501 Squadron remained on the front line and on the day that Hitler was calling off the invasion they became embroiled in a series of clashes along the Kent coast. During one dogfight over Dover, the squadron had become scattered and was ordered to regroup over Maidstone. On his way there, Lacey spotted fifteen Me 109s below him and, unable to resist the temptation, he tipped the wing of his Hurricane and swooped upon them.

As the Hurricane hit its maximum 330mph, the G force wrenched at his body and made the aircraft shudder from nose to tail. It was only when he was right on top of them that he realised the Messerschmitts were travelling far slower than he had calculated. Before he had time to react, he found himself hurtling straight through the formation, exposing himself to the combined firepower of the entire squadron. The Germans opened up on him at once, filling the air with thousands of rounds, and Lacey felt the thud of bullets strafe the entire length of his aircraft.

Now out of control, the Hurricane stalled and began to fall. Lacey unfastened his harness straps, threw back the hood of the cockpit and was immediately sucked from his seat. Just as he had done four days earlier, he tumbled through the air, fumbling for the ripcord of his parachute. He had just entered thick cloud when he managed to open it and began the slow descent to earth. When he emerged from the cloud he was pleasantly surprised to see that once again he was falling to within walking distance of the beautiful Leeds Castle. Lacey was meant to be resting after treatment to his burns and the doctor who had sent him to hospital earlier in the week was less than delighted to find the same young sergeant standing before him once again.

Lacey added a further half a dozen victories to his tally before the Battle of Britain came to a close at the end of October. The battle marked the first defeat of Hitler's forces since hostilities had started fourteen months earlier. For the first time since tanks had rolled into Poland, the military commanders of the Third Reich machine had set themselves a major objective and been driven back. The failure showed the British people that Nazi Germany was not invincible. More importantly, it showed the Americans that Britain had the stomach to fight on. Crucially, by keeping Hitler out, it left Europe with a springboard from which an invasion of the mainland could be launched in the future.

During the greatest air battle the world had ever seen, the Royal Air Force lost around 800 planes and the Luftwaffe 1,300. A total of 2,353 pilots from the UK and 574 from overseas fought in the Battle of Britain; 544 were killed and a further 791 lost their lives later in the war. To qualify as one of 'The Few', a fighter pilot had to have flown just one operational sortie during the period 10 July to 31 October 1940. Sergeant James 'Ginger' Lacey, the chemist's dispenser from Wetherby, flew dozens and shot down more enemy aircraft in the battle than any other pilot in Fighter Command.

Lacey finished the Second World War as the RAF's sixth highest scoring ace, on twenty-eight victories. He was also credited with four probables and nine damaged. James 'Johnnie' Johnson was the leading British fighter pilot of the conflict with thirty-eight, but there is no doubt that, had he been given the opportunity, a pilot of Lacey's tenacity and skill would have added significantly to his tally. As it was, after a relatively quiet nine months flying in bomber escorts and coastal patrols, he was appointed chief instructor of the Special Attack Instructors School and then spent much of the rest of the war in the Far East where his squadrons experienced little aerial combat.

He remained in the RAF after the war and had reached the rank of squadron leader before retiring in March 1967. For the rest of his working life he ran an air freight business. He died on 30 May 1989, aged seventy-two. He remains little known beyond RAF circles, and the only individual memorial to one of Britain's great heroes in one of her greatest battles is a small plaque in the Priory Church of St Mary, Bridlington, Yorkshire.

ROYAL NAVY

ROYAL NAVY

Captain Edward Fegen

When Captain Edward Fegen squinted through his binoculars and caught sight of a small black smudge on the hazy northern horizon, he knew that, in all probability, he and his crew had only a matter of hours to live. It was the afternoon of 5 November 1940 and his ship, HMS *Jervis Bay*, was roughly halfway across the North Atlantic in the midst of the thirty-seven merchant ships she was escorting. Spread out over several miles in rectangular formation and churning through the cold sub-Arctic waters at 9 knots, convoy HX-84 was carrying tons of vital materials for a nation clinging on for dear life against the might of Nazi Germany.

The Battle of Britain had been raging for the better part of four months. Although the RAF had out flown and outfought its numerically superior foes in the skies over southern England, no one had called an official end to the battle. The country remained braced for an invasion at any time. Frustrated by Spitfires and Hurricanes, Hitler turned his attention to London and the country's other major cities in an effort to bomb the British into submission. The British turned off their lights, disappeared into their Anderson shelters and listened to hundreds of thousands of Luftwaffe bombs raining down on their communities. So long as they had food to eat and weapons to fight with, however, they were not going to capitulate.

Winston Churchill had captured the mood of defiance four months earlier: '. . . We shall fight on the landing grounds, we shall fight in the fields and in the streets, we shall fight in the hills; we shall never surrender!' But in the very next sentence of his rousing speech, the new Prime Minister acknowledged that the country depended for its survival on its lines of supplies: '. . . and even if, which I do not for a moment believe, this island or a large part of it were subjugated and starving . . .' With all the will in the free world, Britain could not fight on with empty stomachs and bare armouries. The country was under assault on two fronts: from the air and on the sea – in the North Atlantic. Defeat in either theatre would almost certainly have led to a Nazi triumph over the island nation, the last country in Western Europe standing up to the threat.

The Battle of the Atlantic began the moment Britain declared war two days after German troops poured into Poland. After years of building up their navy to rival the British fleet, the

Germans dispatched eighteen U-boats, two pocket battleships and a fleet of torpedo boats and minelayers from their bases in the North Sea and the Baltic. Immediately, British convoys began suffering huge losses. In the first nine months of the war, the German navy was sinking an average of 200,000 tons of Allied shipping per month. From June 1940 that figure had more than doubled. German planners had figured that Britain would fold if they were able to increase the destruction to 600,000 tons a month. Unpatrolled by the overstretched navies of Britain and Canada, the waters of the mid-Atlantic were the favourite hunting ground of the U-boat 'wolf packs'.

During this period, only the pilots of Fighter Command were doing as much as the seamen of Britain's Merchant Navy to help the country fight another day. Poorly paid civilian volunteers, and working some of the most unforgiving seas on the planet, the merchant crews ploughed their unarmed, heavily laden ships through howling gales and waves of up to 90 feet as they ran the gauntlet from Canada. They sailed under constant threat of an ambush by the U-boats of a highly motivated Germany navy that was sinking their ships for fun – and against one of the *Kriegsmarine*'s advanced warships they stood virtually no chance of survival.

With millions of people threatened by starvation, and no equipment to keep up the fight, Britain would quickly be convulsed by social upheaval and her government forced to sue for peace. In that event, there would be no platform to launch a counter-attack and the United States, were she ever minded to join the fight, would have had no chance of victory in Europe. The shadow of

Nazi totalitarianism would darken the whole of Western Europe. This was the grim prospect facing the free world as Fegen watched the menacing black shape growing ever larger as it powered towards the thirty-seven vessels he had been tasked to protect.

Captain Theodor Krancke, the captain of the *Admiral Scheer,* had taken advantage of a violent winter storm to slip past the Royal Navy blockade through the Denmark Strait between Iceland and Greenland and into the killing zone of the North Atlantic. German intelligence had indicated that a large British convoy was scheduled to reach the unpatrolled waters of mid-ocean over the coming days – and this was his one opportunity to fall upon his prey. A few days later and the convoy was to be met by Royal Navy escorts and brought safely into port. Riding waves of up to 100 feet, the 616-foot *Scheer*, one of the most formidable warships of the time, came close to capsizing as giant breakers crashed into her sides. Only her reinforced superstructure saved the ship from breaking in two across the beam. Dozens of crewmen filled the sickbay with an assortment of broken limbs, deep gashes, concussion and heavy bruising after twenty-four hours of relentless pounding by the violent seas.

The *Admiral Scheer* was an exceptional ship. Commissioned in 1933 with sister ships the *Deutschland* and *Graf Spee*, no other warships in the world, except for a handful of ageing British battle cruisers, could match them for speed and firepower. With six 11-inch guns and a top speed of 27 knots, the *Scheer* had the muscle to outgun most ships and the speed to outrun slower but more heavily armed ones. These 'pocket battleships', as they were dubbed at the time, were one of Germany's many ingenious answers and a two-fingered salute to the draconian restrictions imposed on the country's military development after the First World War.

Any new ships built by the Germans were limited to a displacement of 10,000 tons so that they would never pose a serious threat to the larger ships of the Royal Navy and other forces. The Germans appeared to play by the rules, but not all was what it seemed. Knowing that a 10,000 ton ship would be blown apart by the force of its own huge guns, the designers packed in an extra 3,600 tons of metal to beef up the *Scheer*'s structure. With a muzzle velocity of almost 3,000 feet per second and a range of 21 miles, the ship's big guns were a formidable threat to smaller ships with lesser range. When Allied observers questioned the integrity of these new ships, the pride of the *Kriegsmarine*, the German authorities brushed them off with a contemptuous sneer, effectively saying to the League of Nations, 'OK, so what are you going to do about it?'

Once the *Scheer* had survived its passage through the Arctic storm in the Denmark Strait, Krancke stopped the engines and mustered the 1,150-strong crew. He spelt out their mission: to destroy a massive British convoy. Heading for a square of ocean, roughly 100 by 100 miles where the British were thought to be, Krancke then ordered the engines to full speed.

The Royal Navy was still the most powerful maritime force in the world at the outbreak of war but it had been cut back harshly over the previous twenty years. Its resources were so stretched around the globe in defence of the Empire that the service was barely able to spare any ships at all to escort the Atlantic convoys. To plug the gap, the Admiralty was forced to requisition fifty commercial cargo liners and convert them into fighting ships, known as Armed Merchant Cruisers (AMCs). With a handful of small guns and little or no real armoured protection, these ships stood no chance against real warships, U-boats or even the better equipped enemy AMCs. To the men who sailed them, AMC stood for Admiralty-Made Coffin. Their main purpose was to intercept enemy merchantmen.

The *Jervis Bay* was one such AMC. Though large at 549 feet and displacing almost 14,000 tons, 15 knots was her maximum speed. With dozens of wooden compartments, her crew feared she would go up like kindling under fire. The 6-inch guns that were installed had been in use since the turn of the century. The oldest of them had seen action in the Boer War. The crew was made up of roughly three dozen Royal Navy regulars and 220 others, a mixture of reservists and other volunteers – most of them from the Merchant Navy.

On 1 April 1940, a new commanding officer took over the *Jervis Bay*. He was Edward Fogarty Fegen, a man of noble Irish ancestry and impeccable Royal Navy stock. Fegen could trace his family history back to the eighth century. Since 1778, every male member of the family had chosen a career in the Royal Navy. Born in Portsmouth, within sight of the masts of the harbour's warships, he was involved in the first naval battle at sea in the Great War and by the outbreak of the Second World War he had twenty years' experience under his belt. Respected by his peers and adored by his men, Fegen was a commanding officer in the style of Nelson. A warrior eager for the fray, he never asked his men to carry out a task he wasn't prepared to undertake himself. A recurring phrase in the observations made about him was that he had 'no regard for his own safety' but an almost bottomless concern for that of his men. Shortly after taking command of the *Jervis Bay*, he addressed the crew and made the following statement of intent: 'So far, we haven't seen any real action, but I promise you this much: if the gods are good to us and we meet the enemy, I shall take you in as close as I possibly can.' In other words, if there was so much as a sniff of a fight to be had under his command, the *Jervis Bay* would be straight in among it. The fighting talk thrilled the ship's company.

On the night before the *Jervis Bay* and the thirty-eight ships of convoy HX-84 set out from the bustling port of Halifax on Canada's Nova Scotia coast, a rumour had spread through the town that the *Admiral Scheer* had broken into the North Atlantic. Halifax was a hotbed of intrigue at the time; rumours about German activity on the convoy surfaced every day in the dockside bars and warehouses. The latest news was dismissed as more scuttlebutt as the ship's company boarded the *Jervis Bay* and – little did they know it – prepared to set out on a course for what was to become one of the most famous naval engagements of the twentieth century.

The weather was clear but cold when the first of the convoy's thirty-eight ships moved out of Halifax harbour and took up position a few miles off the coast. They formed up in four long ranks with 600 yards between each ship, and nine short columns with

400 yards separating each ship from the one in front. After two days their Canadian navy escort turned for home, as was standard practice, and left the convoy to fend for itself in the mid-Atlantic, before the Royal Navy picked them up on the other side, ten to twelve days later. In among the cargo of the convoy were 126,000 tons of petroleum products (including vital supplies of aviation fuel for the RAF) and over 42,000 tons of steel. Other ships were rammed to the gunwales with desperately needed provisions such as meat, dairy products, flour, canned food, wool and almost 5,000 feet of pit props for Britain's overstretched mining industry.

One of the smaller ships was forced to return to Halifax with engine trouble, but for the other thirty-seven and their armed escort, the first week was plain sailing. There was not a U-boat or torpedo boat in sight, let alone, as rumoured, the awesome pocket battleship the *Admiral Scheer*. In no time at all, they would be making contact with their Royal Navy escort and be guided safely into port.

Lieutenant Pietsch climbed into the cockpit of his Arado Ar 196, a small seaplane used for the observation of enemy ships. He was catapulted from the decks of the *Admiral Scheer* into a sky of broken cloud. On his first mission he found nothing in the great grey expanse of the North Atlantic, but half an hour into his second flight his observer caught a glimpse through the clouds of the neat formation of Allied freighters. Returning to ship, he waggled his wings as he began his descent on to the water. The officers watching from the bridge knew straight away that Pietsch had found their prey. The plane was winched on board, and the excited pilot went straight to Captain Krancke and handed him a map with an X planted in the middle of a featureless ocean of blue. Krancke set the ship's course, and rang down to the engine room, calling for full speed. He lit up a large cigar and weighed up the options open to him.

By his calculations, the *Scheer* would be in contact with the convoy within three hours, at dusk. The question then was when to attack: did he attack straight away and risk some of the ships escaping under darkness or did he wait until the morning and pick them all off one by one? The risk with the latter plan of action was that the convoy would be that much closer to Royal Navy vessels. What's more, his on-board meteorologist was warning of worsening weather, poor visibility and heavier seas that would give the convoy a greater chance of escape. By the time he had finished his cigar, Krancke had made up his mind. He ordered an immediate attack. The announcement triggered a wave of nervous excitement through the ship's company as the 1,150 men set about clearing the decks and lashing down and stowing any object capable of moving.

At about a quarter to four, one of the convoy ships reported a smudge of smoke on the horizon. It was most probably the smoking remains of the *Mopan*, a 5,400-ton refrigerated banana boat, owned by British firm Fyffes, that had just been blown out of the water by the *Admiral Scheer* as she cut her way through the swelling ocean. The Germans took the crew prisoner and set about destroying the boat, sending over a quarter of a million bananas to the bottom of the sea. The dawdling of the *Mopan*'s captain as his crew slowly lowered their lifeboats into the sea infuriated Krancke. Precious killing time was slipping away.

The *Mopan* had passed the convoy a few hours earlier. Why her skipper, Captain Sapsworth, failed to send a brief warning signal to the Allied freighters on encountering the battleship remains a subject of controversy. The *Mopan* radio operator had only to send the letter 'R' – meaning raider – to alert the convoy and give them time to scatter. Some crewmembers claimed that, panic-stricken by the sight of the battleship, the captain ordered the operator not to transmit for fear the *Scheer* would pick up the message and immediately blow the banana boat to smithereens with all hands onboard. Sapsworth refused to comment on the matter after the war and took the mystery to his grave. More sympathetic commentators have suggested that the captain's reluctance to transmit the signal saved the lives of his crew and bought the convoy time.

As the *Mopan*'s crew were taken prisoner, the man with the responsibility of protecting the convoy paced the port side of the bridge of the *Jervis Bay*, his binoculars glued to the pencil-lead skyline to the north. The sun had set and the relative safety of darkness was just over an hour away, but his fellow officers could see from his intense concentration that Captain Fegen was sensing trouble. A second small dot had appeared on the horizon and it was growing perceptibly larger by the minute. The bridge soon identified it as a battleship. The question was whose battleship: Germany's or Britain's?

The general consensus was that it must be British. The Royal Navy's surface fleet was far larger and more active in the North Atlantic. German warships were a rare sight; U-boats were the principal threat to Allied shipping. A tense ten minutes followed before serious doubts about its identity began to emerge. The order was given: 'Sound action stations!' As the alarm rang, there followed a scene of orderly pandemonium. The crew dropped whatever they were doing and ran to their guns and other positions. Those who had been washing or sleeping bounded through the ship barefoot or in a state of semi-undress. Most of the men, unaware of the drama unfolding on the bridge, thought they were about to be put through yet another of Fegen's drills to keep them on their toes.

Fegen yelled at his signalmen to 'make the challenge' to the ship to reveal her identity. Three times the signals crew flashed the invitation by Morse through the gathering gloom, each time on a bigger light than the one before. But each time there was no reply and the tension on the bridge rose a notch higher. When the 36-inch searchlight failed to yield a response, one of the officers, peering through his binoculars, uttered the words no one wanted to hear: 'It's a pocket battleship.'

It was at this moment that everyone on that bridge understood the fate that awaited them. It was just a question of how much of a fight their captain was prepared to put up. In line with Royal Navy convention, there was never any possibility of surrendering, no matter how great the mismatch between the two ships. Few captains had greater concern for the welfare of their men than Fegen, but his assignment was to protect the convoy to the best of his ability; his ship and his men were his second responsibility. So it was that he took the decision, there and then, to sacrifice the *Jervis Bay*. To give the other thirty-seven ships the best chance to scatter, he had to buy them as much time as possible. To waylay the mighty German battleship, Fegen knew he and his men were going to have to suffer a horrifying slaughter.

'Full speed ahead!' Fegen bellowed into the voice tube. Awe mingled with foreboding as the crews of the convoy ships watched the converted passenger liner accelerate out of the formation and head straight towards one of the most fearsome warships ever launched. At the same time, he ordered the signalmen to hoist the white/red/yellow/white flags telling the convoy to get ready to scatter. As the *Jervis Bay* surged through the waves for a confrontation that could only bring her death and destruction, the four guns towards the bow of the ship began firing at the German vessel. They were still several miles out of range, but the shells were not expected to find their target; they were more a statement of intent, saying, in effect: 'We're going to fight you to the death.'

When the gap between the two ships had narrowed to about ten miles, Krancke turned the *Admiral Scheer* to port so that the two giant 11-inch guns and the secondary guns on the starboard were lined up against the British escort. In silent dread, Fegen and the men on the bridge looked through their binoculars and the mounted telescope and saw a series of pinprick flashes on the horizon. On the *Scheer* the noise of those guns was ear-splitting; the violence of the recoil rocked the ship and sent men sprawling to the deck. Twenty-three agonising seconds passed before the huge shells crashed 40 yards short of the *Jervis Bay*'s bow. The sea erupted, sending up towers of water higher than the top foremast. A wave of water crashed over the bow, drenching every man and smearing faces with an oily deposit from the debris of the explosion. A splinter from one shell decapitated a crewman. As the second salvo thumped into the water just behind the *Jervis Bay*, bracketing the ship with near perfect precision, Fegen ordered Verey rockets to be launched indicating the convoy ships should scatter. It was every ship for herself now.

The third salvo from the pocket battleship found its target with devastating effect. A huge flash burst over the foredeck, and the foretopmast fell backwards towards the bridge just as a second shell landed further back – all but on the bridge. The massive explosion tore Fegen's left arm almost clean out of the shoulder socket and several other officers were killed outright. The 600-pound shell from the 11-inch gun also effectively annihilated the greater part of the ship's offensive capability, destroying the range-finder, fire-control system and the bearing director. The radio room was shattered, and three men lay dead in there. The generators were gone, leaving what remained of the ship's main instruments without power.

In the surrounding waters, there was bedlam as thirty-seven ships, each left to their own devices, turned this way and that as their captains quickly tried to work out the escape route that gave them the best chance of escape. It was, they would have reasoned, surely just a matter of minutes before the Germans had done for the lightly armed, poorly protected escort ship. In a subsequent report into the engagement, one of the convoy captains summed up the view of the entire convoy when he wrote that, at the sight of the *Jervis Bay* 'steaming in to sure slaughter to save the rest of the convoy', he felt a glow of 'inspiration and defiance'.

The crews of all thirty-seven ships lit smoke floats and dropped them over the sides in an attempt to confuse the enemy and cover their flight, but this served only to hinder their own manoeuvring in the gathering gloom. Several ships came so close to colliding that the men could make out the accents of the crews passing by.

The only damage caused to the *Scheer* thus far in the engagement was self-inflicted. The sheer force of the big guns' recoil had damaged the ship's radar, leaving the bridge dependent on the more basic equipment of its range-finder and bearing director. Once darkness had blanketed the North Atlantic, Krancke would have only his searchlights to seek out his prey. There was now even greater urgency on him to hurry up and sink the *Jervis Bay* and set out in pursuit of the precious convoy ships. One of the vessels, he was convinced, was a major troop-carrier and he was eager to get after her. This was the *Rangitiki*, the largest ship of the convoy at almost 17,000 tons. When the *Jervis Bay* rushed forward to confront the Germans, she cut in front of the *Rangitiki*, convincing Krancke that the escort was trying to protect her. In fact, the New Zealand cargo liner was carrying seventy-five mostly civilian passengers, plus tons of wool, meat and cheese.

Krancke constantly manoeuvred his ship into position to bring as much firepower as possible to bear on the fearless escort ship. Wave after wave of devastating broadsides rocked the German warship back and forth in the water and created a boom of sound heard for miles around. Each time, the kickback from the 11-inch guns sent those men not holding on to railings hurtling backwards. Within twenty minutes of the opening salvoes, the *Jervis Bay* was a maelstrom of fire, acrid black smoke and twisted metal. Dozens of dead and hideously injured and burnt men lay across what remained of her decks.

The men ferried the injured into the *Jervis Bay* sickbay as fast as they could but, as the pounding continued, one giant shell scored a direct hit on the converted passenger salon, triggering an inferno that engulfed the scores of men undergoing or awaiting treatment. As 5 November drew towards its furious, bloody conclusion, the crew were still able to crack jokes about it being a Bonfire Night as good as any they had witnessed. Amidst the infernal chaos, one crewman, seeing that the White Ensign of the Royal Navy had been destroyed, climbed the mast and tied on a replacement. No gesture can have better summed up the crew's pride and defiance.

The gun crews were firing back and, though all their shells fell well short of the German raider, they were still having a decisive effect on the engagement. Captain Krancke was not going to go after the convoy until he had seen off the *Jervis Bay*. Had he known quite how long the converted liner and her redoubtable crew were prepared to slug it out, he may well have opted to ignore her and head straight after the wealth of booty that was melting into the twilight at all points of the compass.

Holding on to his severed arm with his right hand to stop it from falling off, Fegen grimaced through the pain as he did what he could to keep his ship taking the fight to the *Scheer*. With shrapnel and spall flying across the decks, most of the vessel in flames and over half his crew either dead or maimed, the captain moved among the survivors offering words of encouragement. Several miles away, his opposite number shook his head and marvelled at the character of a captain whose men continued to fight through such appalling slaughter. The Royal Navy captain, he noted, must have a 'touch of Nelson' about him. 'He must be a commander with such authority over his men that they are prepared to follow him to certain death in a hopeless fight.' But as Krancke marvelled, Fegen was killed by the next shell to hit the bridge.

Krancke continued to use his big guns, refusing to get too close to the escort ship in case the *Scheer* received a hit in a key area that might imperil his escape. He knew the Royal Navy ships would soon be surging out of Scapa Flow in the Orkneys and heading towards them at full speed. But every minute the *Jervis Bay* held out was another minute bought for the fleeing convoy ships. Krancke could see that the floating wreck of the British ship was aflame from bow to stern. His gunners were hammering it with dozens of shells and yet it refused to go under – and what's more, it was still firing back! The rising star of the *Kriegsmarine* was nonplussed. It didn't make sense. No ship, he mused, should be able to survive such a ferocious battering for so long. What he didn't know was that the convoy escort had been fitted with hundreds of empty 45-gallon barrels in her holds and it was these that were keeping her afloat.

The *Jervis Bay*'s navigation officer, Commander George Roe, had taken command of the ship following the death of Captain Fegen. He had to decide how long he was prepared to expose the surviving members of the crew to the slaughter. The whole superstructure of the ship was ablaze, fires had broken out below and water was pouring in through holes blown by the shelling. The engines were out of order, the steering had gone, they had no means of communication and the last of the guns had finally fallen silent. Roe had seen that the German captain had shown no sign of leaving the *Jervis Bay* until she was settled on the bottom. He therefore gave the order to abandon ship.

At roughly the same time, Krancke ordered some of his gun crews to start targeting the fleeing cargo ships. Staying within the vicinity of the *Jervis Bay*, the *Scheer* sank two ships in rapid succession. Krancke's original plan had been to make short work of the escort ship and then wheel around the convoy ships, destroying them one by one. Had the *Jervis Bay* sunk within twenty minutes, as he had expected, the *Scheer* would have picked off at least half of the convoy ships, given the range of its big guns and being much the fastest vessel of them all. But distracted by the *Jervis Bay*'s pig-headed refusal to go under and with his radar out of action, Krancke decided to dash south, the direction in which he believed most of the convoy had fled.

In an inferno of fires and bursting shells, the remnants of the crew of the *Jervis Bay* set about trying to find undamaged boats and rafts in which to escape. Scattered up and down the ship, the men were still dying in numbers, most of them caught by flying metal splinters. Roughly two dozen of them had found their way to the back of the funnel where two life rafts were kept.

The smaller one was damaged but still had most of its flotation barrels attached beneath it. As it was lowered into the swollen, ice-cold waters below, the raft suffered even more damage as it crashed against the hull and smashed into the water, reducing its size to 10 by 5 feet. Leaping over the railings, the men dropped 45 feet into water so cold that for several seconds they were unable to breathe or move with the shock. They splashed and scrambled through the rising waves and clambered aboard the small piece of flotsam. Within minutes, seventeen men had squeezed on to the broken wooden platform, all of them standing up to create more room, clinging on to each other for warmth and balance. The raft was so overburdened that it sank beneath the surface and the water lapped at the men's knees. Other survivors thrashed around the boat, but there was nothing that could be done for them. There was no room for them. Fearing that the raft would be sucked under by the sinking escort ship, the men paddled furiously with their hands to get away from the hull.

Above them, amidst the belching smoke and flames and the roar of explosions, a second group of men was labouring to move the larger raft that had managed to escape undamaged from the onslaught. Measuring 10 by 15 feet with six 45-gallon drums lashed to the timber, it was almost impossible to drag it over the mangled deck, lift it up and lower it over the railings. As some of the men heaved at the dead weight, others dragged dead and wounded comrades out of their path. More were felled by shrapnel before they finally managed to lower the wooden craft into the water. Dozens of men leapt overboard, disappearing with a splash under the breathtakingly cold swell. The stronger swimmers scrambled aboard her, leaving many others – perhaps as many as three dozen – desperately clinging on to the side or treading water nearby.

A third group of men, meanwhile, had congregated around the jolly boat, stowed away on the port side of the main deck. The wounded were helped into the 18-foot craft before it was lowered into the churning waves. Four of them began rowing away as fast as possible from the blazing mother ship. Like the two rafts, the jolly boat was full to capacity and beyond. Groaning with men, the little boat displaced so much water that the sea was no more than a few inches below the gunwales. The men baled constantly as their craft receded into the night. They had barely reached a safe distance from her when the *Jervis Bay*, now completely engulfed in flames and its ammunition exploding in all directions, tipped up and slid under the waves in a cloud of hissing steam. As the 616-foot-long ship plummeted the four miles to the ocean bed, the extinguishing flames took away the last of the light. Rammed with men, many of them badly injured, the three tiny craft were quickly enveloped in darkness on an increasingly angry sea.

Soaked through in air temperatures just above freezing, they huddled together for warmth, praying that the Royal Navy rescue ships would find them before it was too late. But for some, hope and willpower were not enough to resist the combination of wounds and hypothermia. When they died, their bodies were put overboard, freeing up space for a handful of men in the water who, insulated from the cold by the slick of oil on the surface, had managed to survive far longer than they had expected. The less fortunate were soon overcome by the cold. As the night wore on, the men did their best to keep each other alive. The more physically able slapped the faces of those drifting in and out of consciousness. They sang classic British songs including 'Roll Out the Barrel' and 'There'll Always Be an England' as loud as their enfeebled state allowed them. The three craft drifted their own ways, lashed and semi-submerged by the rising ocean. On the larger of the rafts, forty men clung on to each other and the wooden planks beneath them as they were tipped and tossed by waves reaching 15 feet. When a man was washed off, he needed all his diminishing strength to claw back on board.

On seeing the scatter signal from the *Jervis Bay*, Sven David Olander, skipper of the Swedish freighter *Stureholm*, had immediately swung his ship in a north-westerly direction. Filled with admiration at the sight of their escort ship going straight for the pocket battleship, he sped away from the scene as fast as he could in his 4,600-ton freighter, carrying almost 7,000 tons of steel and iron. But his conscience quickly began to eat away at him as he watched the plumes of smoke and flashes of gunfire grow ever smaller on the darkening horizon. He knew there was a chance that some of the crew would escape the slaughter as she finally surrendered to her inevitable fate. He had had enough experience of the cruelty of the North Atlantic to know how they would be suffering. He therefore summoned his crew.

It was one of the golden rules of the Atlantic convoys that no ship went to rescue the survivors of another, for fear that it should meet the same fate. But in a moving appeal, he put it to his men that they should go back for the survivors, letting them decide on the matter in a vote. A forest of hands rose before him. Olander smiled and swung his ship back round.

It was shortly after eleven o'clock, roughly four hours after the *Jervis Bay* had gone down, that the men in the jolly boat saw the dark bulk of the *Stureholm* looming above them. At first they thought she was a German ship, come to take them prisoner, but on hearing friendly voices the twenty men let out a collective roar of joy. One by one, they climbed the ropes of the Jacob's ladder to safety with the Swedish crewmen carrying the most badly injured on their backs.

There was no doctor on board but the Swedes did what they could for the injured, giving up their sleeping quarters and emptying their first aid kits. Dry clothes and strong spirits were handed out to all as the search for more survivors continued deep into the night. It seemed highly unlikely that anyone could withstand the rising winter gale for such a length of time, but at half past three in the morning the Swedes came across the larger raft. Thirty-six men, numb and delirious with cold, nursing an assortment of wounds, were taken aboard. Alerted by the survivors that there had been one other raft to escape the carnage, the *Stureholm* continued to comb the rough grey waters.

It was something of a minor miracle that the little raft was still afloat. Splintered and shattered even before it was lowered into the pounding waves of a violent sea, and with only one empty drum to keep it afloat, it had just enough buoyancy to keep the torsos of the men above the water. Alerted by the flashing of a torch, the crew of the *Stureholm* were astonished by the sight of twelve men, apparently sitting in the water. One by one they plucked them into the sanctuary and warmth of the freighter. Risking their own lives all through the night, Olander and his crew ultimately rescued 68 of the *Jervis Bay's* 265-strong crew, though three of them were found to be dead on being carried aboard and were buried at sea shortly afterwards. Six days later the ship arrived safely back at Halifax and the most seriously wounded were taken to hospital.

By the time the *Stureholm* had turned for Canada the *Admiral Scheer* was surging south at full speed, trying to put as much grey water between them and the British ships sent to hunt the German raider. After a delay caused by communications problems, eleven British ships, including the battle cruisers *Hood* and *Repulse* and six destroyers, slipped out of Scapa Flow to start the hunt. The *Scheer* had sunk a further three convoy ships before deciding to make a run for it.

A total of five unarmed merchant ships was a paltry return for the pocket battleship. The German crew would have been expecting to sink three times that number. The shark had swam into a huge shoal of fish but it had left hungry. Thanks to Fegen and his men, hundreds of lives were saved and hundreds of thousands of tons of vital provisions were able to reach British ports over the coming days. Had the majority of the convoy been lost, the blow to British morale would have been immense. The *Scheer*'s attack did still have a heavy impact on the country's war effort. All convoys were postponed while the hunt for the battleship continued and those ships that had already left port were turned back. For two weeks no convoys set out from Canada, pushing an already desperate Britain closer to the brink of collapse.

After the long-drawn-out assault on the *Jervis Bay* and the merchant vessels, Krancke had become worried about his ammunition levels. In the three and a half hours since the assault began, the *Scheer* had fired over 220 heavy shells and 550 medium-sized ones, amounting to almost half his entire supply. The British destroyers would annihilate the *Scheer* if they caught up with her, and Krancke knew he was going to need every last one of his remaining shells to give his ship even the slightest chance of survival. Nor had his ship and crew escaped the encounter unscathed. The recoils from her mighty guns had caused significant damage to the ship's operational capability and put thirty injured men in the sickbay, most of them suffering from broken bones and concussion. The British dispatched even more ships in separate task groups to join the hunt, putting twenty-six to sea in total, but the delay at the outset proved crucial and the *Scheer* was able to slip through the net. After two weeks, the hunt for the pocket battleship was abandoned.

The *Scheer* powered into the South Atlantic, rounded the Cape of Good Hope and reached the Indian Ocean in early February, attacking enemy merchant ships along the route. On 21 February, Krancke received a message from Erich Raeder, Grand Admiral of the German Fleet, announcing that Hitler had awarded him the Iron Cross, and ordering the ship back to Germany. When she arrived back at Kiel six weeks later, Krancke and his crew were right to feel delight and relief at having evaded the British once again. The remainder of the war was relatively uneventful for the *Scheer* and she was kept in port or sent on less hazardous assignments as the Allies began to dominate the war at sea. After so many narrow escapes she earned a reputation as a lucky ship, but her good fortune finally ran out on the night of 9 April 1945 when six hundred Allied bombers pounded the dockyards at Kiel. The *Scheer* was hit several times and capsized. After the war she was dismantled by the occupying British who used the bare bones of her remains as the foundation for a new car park.

No man followed the action involving the *Jervis Bay* more closely than King George VI, a former naval officer himself. He asked the Admiralty to recommend Fegen for the Victoria Cross, the only one that would be awarded for convoy defence during the war. The king wrote in his diary: 'I have awarded Captain Fegen the Victoria Cross posthumously. When he attacked the *Admiral Scheer*, he knew he was going to certain death.' Two days earlier Winston Churchill paid tribute in the House of Commons, saying that the spirit of the Royal Navy had been 'exemplified in the forlorn and heroic action . . . fought by the captain, officers and ship's company of the *Jervis Bay* in giving battle against overwhelming odds . . .' Eleven of the surviving crew members were also awarded medals. In his testimony to the Admiralty's Board of Enquiry, Temporary Lieutenant Wood, the most senior surviving officer by the end of the ordeal, said: 'Everyone behaved magnificently. The calm way in which Captain Fegen carried on with his job during the action was an inspiration to everyone. His immediate turn toward the enemy was exactly what we expected of him.'

Like miners and dockers, Britain's merchant seamen were essential to Britain's survival in the desperate days following the outbreak of war, but, unlike many of their land-based compat-riots, they chose not to exploit their vital importance to the country by taking industrial action. Facing immeasurably greater peril than any workers back home, the seamen risked a hideous death to keep Britain's essential supplies coming. By the time hostilities drew to an end, 30,000 merchant seamen had lost their lives and 2,500 of their ships had been sunk. As civilians, the merchant seamen were effectively volunteers. In the long conflict of the Second World War, many heroes emerged in many theatres, but no group can have passed into history more unsung than the remarkable men of Britain's Merchant Navy and the Royal Navy volunteers.

And none more remarkable than Captain Fegen and the crew of the *Jervis Bay*.

'Sheer senseless destruction to send a cockleshell like the *Jervis Bay* up against the might of a pocket battleship,' wrote Alistair MacLean in *The Lonely Sea*, a collection of true stories about life at sea. 'One feels, however, it would be unwise to voice such thoughts in the presence of the men from convoy HX-84 ... The *Jervis Bay* moved out into the path of the *Admiral Scheer* and died so they might live.'

Lieutenant Commander Malcolm Wanklyn

'I have often looked for an opportunity of paying tribute to our submarines. There is no branch of His Majesty's Forces which in this war has suffered the same proportion of fatal losses as the Submarine Service. It is the most dangerous of all services. That is perhaps the reason why the First Lord tells me that entry into it is keenly sought by officers and men.' Winston Churchill to the House of Commons in September 1941.

Malta was an island under siege when the *Upholder* stole silently into the Grand harbour on 14 January 1941 and manoeuvred into her berth in Lazaretto Creek beneath a towering limestone cliff. The small submarine had only been there a few days and was in the dockyard preparing for her first patrol when swarms of German Stuka dive-bombers launched their most ferocious attack to date.

The main objective of the raid was to sink the aircraft carrier *Illustrious* which was undergoing repairs after suffering extensive bomb damage in an earlier attack. The *Upholder* was in the neighbouring berth when the screeching Stukas swooped out of the blue skies, raining bombs on the fleet below. Every ship in harbour returned fire, adding to an already deafening uproar of explosions and rattle of gunfire. The *Upholder* fired back at the low-flying bombers with its three machine guns mounted on the bridge but in the ten-minute assault it seemed only a matter of time before she took a potentially catastrophic hit as the shower of ordnance fell around them. So high were the walls of water being thrown up by the bombs that the gun crews of the *Upholder* were unable to see the giant carrier right next to them. Seventeen Axis planes were shot down in the frenzied assault.

When the huge clouds of dust and smoke cleared and the drone of the bomber engines faded into the distance, the defenders emerged to inspect the damage. They were stunned to discover that *Illustrious* had taken no direct hits and suffered only relatively minor damage from bombs exploding beneath the surface of the water. Incredibly, the *Upholder* had also managed to escape without a scratch. In the words of every man who witnessed the furious bombardment it was a 'miracle' that so many bombs, dropped from so low, had failed to hit so large a target sitting motionless in the water.

It was as much enormous luck as stout defence and poor aiming by the bombers that had saved them. It had been a mighty close call. A neighbouring merchantman, the *Essex,* suffered thirty-eight casualties when her engine room was hit and it was only the thickness of her bulkheads that prevented a truly catastrophic explosion. There were 4,000 tons of torpedoes and ammunition on board the *Essex* and, if that had taken, there would have been little hope for *Illustrious* or *Upholder*. Three days later, the giant carrier weighed anchor and raced for the relative safety of the Royal Navy base at Alexandria while *Upholder* made the final preparations for her first offensive venture in the Mediterranean. The Germans were left rueing their botched attempt to sink one of Britain's capital ships, but as events were soon to prove the real disaster was missing the little submarine berthed alongside.

Germany never dared to risk its surface ships in open conflict with the Royal Navy during the Second World War. Though reduced in size and power between the wars, the British fleet was still the largest in the world and it had a weight of tradition and experience that no other navy came close to matching. Put bluntly, in an open sea confrontation the Royal Navy would have blown the *Kriegsmarine* out of the water – and Hitler knew it. The Nazis therefore focused their efforts on their submarine fleet, dispatching it into the North Sea and the Atlantic to cause as much havoc as possible against the merchant ships bringing vital supplies from North America.

British submarines were denied the opportunity of inflicting the same degree of pain on their foe because, being largely land-locked, Germany was not dependent on the ocean for its supply routes. Much of what the country needed to survive and that its armed forces needed to fight could be transported by road, rail and air. And with no German warships to attack either, the first year of the war was a frustrating period for crews of the Royal Navy Submarine Service desperate to get into the action. The country was being squeezed on all fronts but they were unable to make a meaningful contribution to its defence.

That all changed dramatically in the second half of 1940.

When Italy entered the war in June, Mussolini's forces in Libya began threatening Egypt and, with it, Britain's control of the strategically vital Suez Canal. All the advantages lay in the favour of the Axis powers at this stage of the conflict in the Mediterranean. They enjoyed near-total air superiority in the central area of the sea and their supply lines from southern Italy were no more than a couple of hundred miles long. Britain's supply ships, meanwhile, had to flog six thousand miles around the Cape of Good Hope and up through Suez. To compound the difficulties for the Allies, the Axis supply routes to North Africa were roughly one thousand miles from the British fleet bases at Gibraltar and Alexandria. In order to protect and support the British and Allied troops in North Africa, the enemy's supply of reinforcements, equipment and provisions had to be disrupted. Failure to do so would hand victory to Hitler and Mussolini in North Africa and seriously undermine Britain's overall war effort. The problem was that, without air cover, it was unwise for the ships of the surface fleet to expose themselves to constant attack.

Submarines were therefore the only answer, but when the war in the desert erupted there simply weren't enough of them in theatre. Those that were in place, valiantly though they fought, weren't up to scratch. They were too big and too old – and to make life even more challenging, the British rules of engagement prevented them from attacking ships thirty miles beyond the coasts of Italy and North Africa. In the second half of 1940, nine British submarines and 448 lives were lost, most of them victims of the extensive mine-laying operations of the Italians.

With the war in the desert intensifying by the week, it was not a day too soon when ten U-Class submarines, a new generation of vessels, were dispatched to Malta to join the 10th Flotilla. *Upholder*, commanded by Lieutenant Commander Malcolm David Wanklyn, was among the first to arrive at the tiny British colony. Over 6 foot tall, Wanklyn was an unlikely looking submariner; quietly spoken and modest with a gentle sense of humour, he seemed unlikely warrior material. But 'Wanks', as he was inevitably and affection-ately known, had an air of authority about him that commanded the unwavering loyalty and respect of all who served with him. Having volunteered for the Silent Service eight years earlier, Wanklyn had plenty of experience and his arrival in Malta delighted Captain 'Shrimp' Simpson, commander of 10th Flotilla, or the Fighting

Tenth as it came to be known. Wanklyn had impressed Simpson when he had served as his first lieutenant in peacetime. The two had become great friends as well as trusted colleagues.

The situation in Malta and the Central Mediterranean was a desperate one when *Upholder* arrived. Lying sixty miles south of Sicily and 210 north of Tunisia, Britain's small island colony had been under attack from the air for over six months and would continue to be so for another twenty-two. Since June it had been the Italian bombers of the *Regia Aeronautica* carrying out the raids, but the arrival in the region of the far more formidable Luftwaffe squadrons marked the beginning of a massive increase in the scale and frequency of the assaults. Malta was battered by bombardments on an almost daily basis.

Smaller than the Isle of Wight, its importance to Britain's wider war effort cannot be overstated. If the British lost Malta, in all probability they lost North Africa and, with it, the Suez Canal, the vital link to India and the Far East as well as the oilfields of the Persian Gulf. Italian and German aircraft launched more than 3,000 raids in total, dropping over 16,000 tons of explosive on the island. Thirty thousand buildings were destroyed. The fact that only 1,500 Maltese were killed was thanks to the protection provided by the tunnels dug deep into the island's thick limestone. Malta's British defenders and the local inhabitants refused to be broken and, at the height of the siege, King George VI was moved to make the unprecedented step of awarding the entire colony the George Cross to '. . . bear witness to a heroism and devotion that will long be famous in history'. The protection of

Malta in effect amounted to the defence of Allied territory in North Africa – and the only way to do that was for British submarines to sink as much enemy shipping as possible.

To the surprise of his crew and to the consternation of his commanders back at base, Wanklyn's first attacks on enemy shipping ended in failure. With torpedoes at a premium, owing to the constant bombardment of Malta, stocks were low and every single one fired had to count – and Wanklyn's first four, half his complement for the patrol, were all wide of the mark. The target had to be worth it, too; there was no point in attacking a ship heading north from Africa that in all likelihood was going to be empty after disgorging its load. The torpedoes had no homing devices so a successful attack was down to the marksmanship and mathematical calculations of the commander. Stroking his thick black beard, Wanklyn showed no sign of the frustration he must undoubtedly have been feeling as his fourth shot raced harmlessly past its target.

At first light two days later, he was presented with an opportunity to make amends. Gentle waves lapped *Upholder*'s 191-foot hull as it sat on the surface. An 8,000-ton German transport ship, later identified as the *Duisberg*, was spotted, accompanied by an armed merchantman. This time there was no error. The two torpedoes raced away at 35 knots at twelve-second intervals towards their target just under a mile away. The crew of the *Upholder* waited in silence in the hot, fetid atmosphere. The seconds ticked by and a full minute passed before the shuddering thud of explosive impact rocked the sub and echoed through the hull. As the crew cheered, Wanklyn took hold of the voice tube and calmly made the order to dive. After lying low for two hours, Wanklyn raised the periscope and saw the water pouring over the decks of his victim as she began to sink beneath the waves.

For the next forty-eight hours, the *Upholder* prowled the waters of the Central Mediterranean in search of prey. On the afternoon of 30 January the ASDIC (sonar detection) operator picked up telltale signals. A convoy of two large supply ships, complete with escort, was soon confirmed through the periscope. The *Upholder* closed in for the kill but Wanklyn had to act quickly before the faster-moving convoy got away. One thousand yards was the ideal range because it provided a good chance of hitting the target and gave the enemy ship little time to take evasive action. They had under a minute from spotting the torpedo tracks to manoeuvre to safety and for a large ship that was often difficult. On this occasion, Wanklyn unleashed his remaining two torpedoes at one of the transports from 4,000 yards, the outer limit of his range. At the moment of firing, he realised he had been spotted by the escorting destroyer, which was turning in their direction. 'Dive! Dive Dive!' came the order over the voice tube. Leaving only a slight ripple on the surface, the 600-ton sub had barely disappeared from sight when the first depth charges, hurled by the chasing ship, began to crash around them. It was the first time the crew had experienced the nauseating terror of a depth-charge attack. They knew better than anyone that there was no pleasant way to die in a submarine, but there was little they could do but sit and hope and trust in their commander. The explosions grew louder and louder as the destroyer closed in.

This was the moment Wanklyn revealed to his men his gift for remarkable composure under the most intense pressure. Those of a nervous disposition need not apply to the Royal Navy Submarine Service and it was a great boost for the morale of the thirty-strong crew to see their commander looking no more hassled than if he had been wrestling with a tough crossword clue, stroking his beard and calmly issuing instructions. When being hunted, the human impulse is to get away from the danger as quickly as possible, but a submarine commander must fight that instinct because movement gives away location. Often the best hope of evading the predator on the surface was to go very slow or stop altogether – and that is precisely what Wanklyn did. Whenever the destroyer stopped, so did he. When it moved, so did he.

For a quarter of an hour, but what felt like an eternity to the young crew bottled up inside their cramped vessel, the lethal game of stop and start went on as the German escort stalked its prey, looking out and listening for signs of its presence in the waters below. Each of the twenty-four depth charges dropped reverberated through the submarine, shuddering the walls and equipment, shattering light bulbs and rattling the nerves of the men cooped up inside. But thanks to Wanklyn's steady nerve, the *Upholder* carried the day. After descending to 150 feet, she set course for Malta and slipped away through the dark depths at her maximum 10 knots. The U-Class submarines, a great improvement on the previous generation, had many qualities but speed was not one of them.

Given the glowing reputation that preceded Wanklyn's arrival in Malta, it was as much a disappointment as a surprise to his peers when his next three patrols ended in expensive failure. Of the thirty torpedoes that Wanklyn had fired in his first four patrols only one had hit the target. Part of this could be put down to poor decision-making, but much of it was just plain bad luck and design deficiencies of the torpedo itself which had a tendency to veer off course in all but the calmest of seas. No one rated Wanklyn higher than the Commanding Officer of the 10th Flotilla, but even 'Shrimp' Simpson was forced to contemplate the unthinkable of removing him from his post. After the war, Simpson wrote that his friend's 'torpedo expenditure without result was actually making me wonder whether such a poor shot could be kept in command'. If the *Upholder* were to return to Malta after her next patrol with no kills registered on her black and white Jolly Roger flag hanging from the conning tower, then Wanklyn's career as an active submarine commander was certainly all but over.

The commander knew his job and reputation were on the line when the *Upholder* slipped out of Malta's Grand Harbour and headed out to open sea on 21 April. For four days they hunted for targets without success until, on the afternoon of the 25th, lurking close to the Tunisian coast, they spotted a large merchant vessel with an armed escort. Wanklyn went straight for them, closing at full speed before firing two torpedoes from about 700 yards. Thirty seconds later one of the torpedoes, loaded with 320lb of TNT, crashed into the side of the vessel, wreaking instant devastation. The reverberations from the explosion were so intense that over half of *Upholder*'s light bulbs were shattered.

A few days later, Wanklyn was ordered to finish off a transport ship and destroyer escort that had been abandoned after an attack by Royal Navy surface ships. The stricken vessels were foundering in the rich hunting grounds around the Kerkennah Bank, twenty miles off the coast of Tunisia. It was going to be a tricky, dangerous task that would demand skilful seamanship to weave through the labyrinth of hidden sandbanks. Wanklyn chose the transport ship, called the *Arta*, as his first objective but he quickly discovered that the waters were too shallow. Not wishing to risk wasting torpedoes on her, he edged the *Upholder* alongside and put a party on board to lay demolition charges. The *Arta* had clearly been abandoned in haste as most of the German troops' equipment was still lying around, including helmets, uniforms and weapons – souvenirs to which the men liberally helped themselves. On the decks there was row upon row of trucks, motorbikes and cars destined for Rommel's Afrika Korps.

When the charges were detonated, the ship burnt furiously, lighting up the area for miles around, and Wanklyn decided it would be safer to return in the morning to dispose of the destroyer which lay in even shallower, more treacherous waters. They surfaced at first light but as they inched towards the destroyer, they grounded on a shoal just 15 feet below the surface. It was soon broad daylight and, with vast concentrations of enemy in the vicinity, their situation was a perilous one. As the engines heaved and groaned with the effort of pulling the sub clear, the crew waited nervously for the approach of aircraft. To the undisguised relief of the occupants within, none appeared and the *Upholder* finally managed to wriggle clear and dive to safety.

Back at base, Simpson had received news of a convoy scheduled to leave Naples for Africa on 1 May. The *Upholder* was ordered into position. All morning the crew scoured the sea for their prey, scanning the horizons and listening out for sonar activity. Patience was an essential quality for a submarine commander and, early in the afternoon, Wanklyn's was rewarded when five transports and four destroyers were sighted. The weather was poor and the sea rough, making it very difficult to keep the sub at the right depth and to observe targets by periscope. All the same, Wanklyn wasted no time in getting his torpedoes away. The customary nerve-shredding wait followed as the sleek, self-propelled weapons, laden with their deadly payload, streaked towards two of the ships whose profiles were overlapping. Suddenly, the *Upholder* was convulsed and the hull rang with the shock waves from three hits in rapid succession. The two ships, totalling 10,000 tons, were destroyed.

When the *Upholder* entered the harbour at Malta, Wanklyn ordered the upper deck crew to don the German helmets they had captured and to hoist the German ensign below their Jolly Roger. Simpson, the flotilla commander, was given a guard of honour by submariners armed with German weapons. No one in the assembled group smiled more broadly than Simpson. Wanklyn, his protégé, had finally delivered on his rich promise.

After a short 'run ashore', which he spent fishing and riding around the island in a pony and trap, Wanklyn was ordered to head to the east coast of Sicily to attack traffic heading south through the Strait of Messina, separating the Mediterranean's largest island from the toe of Italy. The patrol began inauspiciously when a loaded torpedo sprang a leak, triggering a major upheaval in the cramped hull to remove the 16-foot-long, 1½-ton missile and replace it with one in good working order. But a far greater problem surfaced three days later when the ASDIC system failed, seriously compromising the boat's ability to detect enemy ships and escape a depth-charge attack. No one inside the hull needed to be told that the already high level of risk they faced had just doubled at a stroke.

A few hours later, they received a signal carrying news that a convoy was setting out for the Greek port of Patras. The *Upholder* prowled the waters for its prey for a day and a half and Wanklyn was about to surface to refresh the air inside the stinking, fetid atmosphere of the hull when the convoy was spotted. There were two tankers and one tramp steamer and Wanklyn closed on them as fast as he could. Firing three torpedoes from a range of four miles he could barely make out the targets against the backdrop of land. Two of them missed the convoy and exploded along the rocky coastline but one hit home, seriously damaging and probably destroying a

4,000-ton tanker. With depth charges from the convoy's escort landing in their wake, Wanklyn didn't wait around to see if his victim was going to the bottom.

Two days later, Wanklyn caught sight of two tankers, one of which appeared to be sailing under the red, white and blue of the French tricolour, presenting him with tough moral dilemma. If it was a Vichy ship, then it was neutral and should be allowed to pass, but if it was working for the Axis powers then it was a legitimate target. The clock was ticking and Wanklyn had just seconds to decide whether to attack as he consulted his *Booth's* shipping guide. Neither names appeared in the listings as French vessels. Wanklyn erred on the side of suspicion and fired off three torpedoes at the rear tanker. One found its target. After an almighty explosion, the 5,000-ton ship quickly began to sink. Wanklyn's instincts proved to be sound: the tanker, the *Damiani*, was Vichy French but it was sailing under Italian charter. As expected, the escort destroyer raced after the *Upholder* and an aircraft joined the search for the British predator. Without an ASDIC to pinpoint the location of their pursuers, Wanklyn and his crew were going to need all their skills of seamanship to get away. The *Upholder* dived to 150 feet and the now familiar, nerve-jangling game of escape and evasion began. Wanklyn weaved and twisted through the depths, giving his hunter on the surface the runaround all afternoon. Twenty-six depth charges were dropped but none came close to finding their target before Wanklyn gave them the slip once and for all and escaped to less hazardous waters.

The following evening, the sun had just set and the horizon was glowing orange and pink when First Lieutenant 'Tubby' Crawford pulled his eyes away from the periscope. He couldn't quite believe what he was seeing. It was the dark silhouette of a huge ocean liner heading south, surrounded by five destroyers. The size of the escort could mean only one thing: the liner was packed with troops heading to reinforce Axis forces in North Africa. Rommel's Afrika Korps were gaining the upper hand in the Western Desert conflict at the time and were laying siege to Tobruk, where thousands of Allied troops were holed up.

Closer inspection revealed the twin funnels of a further three giant troop ships. With night falling, Wanklyn had to act quickly, but he was handicapped in a number of respects and an attack was fraught with risk. He had no sonar-listening gear and observation through the periscope was made all but impossible by the combination of rapidly fading light and a heavy swell that obscured the sight lines. To be sure of hitting the target, there was only one realistic option – to get in as close as possible. With five destroyers on the scene to launch a counter-attack, Wanklyn knew the odds were stacked against the *Upholder* as he ordered the attack.

In the gathering gloom, Wanklyn had virtually no idea where the escorts were as he headed straight for one of the liners, whose giant bulk could still be made out. As he was about to fire the torpedoes, one of the destroyers appeared out of nowhere at full speed. Wanklyn immediately ordered 'diving stations!' and the *Upholder* escaped being rammed by a matter of yards. Undeterred by the shock, Wanklyn lined up the troop ship and fired. On this occasion, the crew didn't have to wait long for the thud of the explosions. The 18,000-ton *Conte Rosso*, carrying three thousand Italian soldiers and crew, quickly began to break up and sink. Barely had the first explosion erupted against the hull when the depth-charge counter-attack began – and it was by far the worst they had experienced so far, made all the more harrowing by the knowledge that they had lost all sonar detection capability.

As Wanklyn plotted their escape route, a bombardment of underwater explosions rocked the *Upholder* from all directions. The walls shook, glass tinkled, insulation debris rained down and the men crouched forward with their hands over their heads, waiting for the worst. As they lay still in the water, the crew could hear the amplified roar of the destroyer's propellers above their heads. The only sound inside the *Upholder* was the quiet voice of their commander as he issued instructions to switch course and alter the depth and speed of their course. Many inside the boat that night admitted after the event to quivering with fear as the deafening explosions burst around them. For one man, the tension was too much to bear. They were 150 feet under the water when the signaller made a sprint for the conning tower and tried to unlock the hatch. He was dragged away and had to be restrained.

Over the course of their two-hour escape, thirty-seven depth charges fell around the British submarine but, relying on nothing but his instinct and experience, and to the astonishment and relief of his crew, Wanklyn succeeded in throwing off his trackers and weaving a path to safety. Only a fellow submariner could fathom the courage, skill and composure shown by the *Upholder*'s commander on the evening of 24 May 1941 and none of his comrades in the Silent Service were surprised to learn that he had been awarded the Victoria Cross for his efforts. Today, the attack on the *Conte Rosso* is regarded as one of the greatest in the history of submarine warfare. The Italians suffered heavy casualties: 1,600 of them went down with the ship. But it was as much the escape as the attack itself which earned Wanklyn the plaudits. 'The failure of his listening devices made it much harder for him to get away, but with the greatest courage, coolness and skill he brought *Upholder* clear of the enemy and safe back to harbour', his citation noted when it was 'gazetted' six months later. His was the first VC of the war awarded to the Submarine Service.

By total tonnage sunk, Wanklyn was now Malta's leading ace, but the *Upholder*'s triumphant return to harbour was soon overshadowed by an accident that left two of the crew dead when they were overcome by carbon monoxide fumes from a leaking torpedo.

The nerves of the *Upholder*'s crew, already frayed from their experiences, were shredded still further during the attack on the *Conte Rosso* and it was with great relief that they slipped back to the relative safety of Malta and climbed ashore to stretch their cramping limbs. But there was little respite in harbour. The constant air raids meant the submarines had to spend much of their 'rest' period sitting at the bottom of the sea. Even without the terrors of a depth-charge attack or an aerial bombardment in harbour, life on a submarine was an extremely trying experience. Not seeing daylight, sometimes for weeks on end, had its own depressing effect on the crew. Ill health was a constant problem. In the thin, rotten air inside the hull, bugs and viruses were in constant circulation among the crew. When the boat surfaced, those who went up on the bridge would invariably be soaked from the waves and would not dry out until they returned to harbour however many days later. The vast majority of crewmembers were smokers, but cigarettes were strictly prohibited on the grounds that they used up valuable oxygen. Men lived in the torpedo stowage compartment, taking it in turns to sleep between the racks alongside their deadly cargo or on the decks. Tinned rations were basic and were heated by one of the ratings, usually the gunlayer, adding to the already putrid stench in the atmosphere. There were no washing facilities. The boat's three toilets couldn't be flushed, or 'blown', until night-time in case the effluent gave away their position. A man farts on average twenty-five times a day – multiply that by thirty (number of crew) and then by seven (for a week-long patrol) and you can get some idea of the conditions inside the long, slender tube with less space than a London underground carriage.

Anthony Kimmins, the actor, film director and producer, was a correspondent during the war and he wrote an account of life on board *Upholder* that was broadcast on the BBC and published in a series of newspapers and magazines in Britain and overseas.

'The amount of sleep you put in is quite amazing,' he said. 'It is largely because of the lack of oxygen when submerged. You don't notice it much at the time, but if you strike a match towards the end of the day, you will find that it just flickers and goes out. There is, of course, no exercise to be had in the terribly cramped quarters, and during the twenty-four hours you will probably move only a few paces – and yet you are always hungry and, oddly enough, by the end of the patrol you have probably lost weight.

'The routine seldom varies: sleep – eat – a spell on duty – sleep and eat. The only differences between day and night are that during the daytime, while you are running submerged and clear of the effect of the waves, it is all very still and quiet. At night when you surface under cover of darkness to charge the batteries, you are rolling and pitching to the sea . . .'

Fifteen to twenty patrols was considered to be the maximum that a submarine crew could endure before the cumulative strain took its toll. But if Wanklyn was feeling any adverse effects as he and his crew entered their sixth month of operations, he certainly wasn't showing it. If anything, his nerve and daring were stronger than ever. By the end of July 1941, the *Upholder* had notched up an impressive 70,000 tons of enemy shipping. Their victims were mostly merchant vessels carrying supplies and troops but on 28 July Wanklyn was presented with the prospect of claiming a major military scalp when two cruisers, each escorted by a destroyer, appeared in the search periscope racing across the horizon over three miles away at roughly 28 knots. It was temptation beyond resistance for the *Upholder*'s commander.

Hitting a fast-moving target at such distance demanded marksmanship of the highest order. Making rapid mathematical calculations, factoring in speed, time and distance, Wanklyn unleashed a full salvo of four torpedoes at twelve-second intervals. The clock ticked away minute by minute as the four 'fish' sliced through the waves at 35 knots towards the dark silhouettes above the waterline. As they sat and waited, the crew knew they were in for a bumpy ride home if any of the torpedoes were to find their target. The attack was a long shot in every respect but after four minutes two huge explosions rumbled through the depths. They had struck the *Guiseppe Garibaldi*, causing serious damage that stopped the 10,000-ton cruiser dead in the water.

Almost instantly, the escorting destroyer threw up a smoke screen to protect her from further attack and then turned sharply and headed straight for the *Upholder* at full speed. For a full fifteen minutes, forty depth charges shook the deep waters around them, several falling very close to the 30-feet limit within which the submarine was not expected to survive. The knowledge that their lives lay in the hands of the coolest, most capable submarine captain operating in the Mediterranean brought only modest reassurance to the terrified crew as the boat was buffeted from side to side and the roar of explosions echoed around the metal walls. As ever, Wanklyn guided the *Upholder* to safety, but the danger was not yet over. As they made their way back to base, the *Upholder* found herself in the thick of one of the many minefields that the Italians had strung out along their coastline. The sound of the mine cables scraping along the side of the sub did little to settle the jitters of the men within. But Wanklyn negotiated a route to safety. Short of walking on the water above them, to the crew there appeared to be no maritime miracle their commander could not perform.

Two weeks later, the *Upholder* slipped out of Malta once again and headed for the rich feeding grounds around the coast of Sicily. They had already accounted for one merchant ship when, on the seventh day of the patrol, three tankers appeared in the sights of the search periscope. Wanklyn needed no second invitation and fired off a full salvo of four torpedoes, two of which hit the target with spectacular results. Two destroyers immediately came after them from opposite directions, trapping the *Upholder*. The enemy counter-attack was the most furious they had experienced so far with sixty-one depth charges – forty-three of them in eight minutes – bursting around them and battering the boat with a force that no one inside thought she could withstand. In addition to the usual shower of light-bulb glass, lumps of insulation once again rained down on the crew.

On 1 September the *Upholder* returned to base after a gruelling twelve days at sea for a two-week break. Never had a run ashore been more welcome for the increasingly exhausted crew. The following day, back in Britain, awards to eleven of the men were announced in the *London Gazette*. Among them was a Distinguished Service Order for the commander, whose Victoria Cross had yet to be announced. The 10th Flotilla's most successful sub set out on her fourteenth patrol on 16 September, edging that much closer to the total number of patrols that most people in the Service had come to regard as the maximum that a crew should be obliged to suffer. Even the bravest of men have their limits. On this occasion, four members of the flotilla were dispatched – *Upholder*, *Ursula*, *Upright* and *Unbeaten* – to intercept a fast-moving convoy of troop-carrying liners that intelligence sources said were scheduled to leave the Italian naval port of Taranto for Tripoli on the Libyan coast. Such a precious cargo would undoubtedly be given a formidable escort. The news of the convoy had reached Malta at very short notice and there was a frenetic scramble to load up before the four boats slipped out of the harbour and headed north towards Italy's south coast as fast as their slow-moving boats would allow them.

It was still dark, but not long before daybreak, when the outline of the three hulking liners, *Neptunia*, *Oceania* and *Vulcania* and their large escort became visible in the bright moonlight of a clear sky. There was a heavy swell and the *Upholder* bounced around as she cut through the waves and closed in on the unsuspecting troop-carriers. Wanklyn's attack on the *Conte Rosso* has been described as one of the greatest in submarine warfare. The one he executed on this occasion is considered by many to be *the* greatest – and it was all the more brilliant because he was operating under a serious disadvantage after the boat's gyro compass had stopped working. That meant he had to use his far less reliable magnetic compass to find his way in the dark and penetrate the heavy escort of six destroyers. The *Upholder* slipped through the protective net unnoticed and was at the outer limit of its range, yawing wildly in the swell, when Wanklyn chose to pounce.

Waiting until two of the liners had overlapped, thus doubling his chances of a successful strike, he fired off four torpedoes which streaked away across the dark waters. Time appeared to slow as the crew waited and waited before two explosions in quick succession shook the sea. The first destroyed the massive propellers of the 20,000-ton *Oceania*, bringing her to a grinding halt. The second was even more devastating as it ripped a massive hole in the side of *Neptunia*, which quickly began to take on water. In normal circumstances, the sub would go into 'diving stations' and disappear beneath the surface as quickly as possible to escape the inevitable depth-charge attack, but not on this occasion. As *Neptunia* began to sink, hundreds of troops began throwing themselves into the sea, forcing the escorting destroyer to abandon its hunt for their attacker in order to rescue the survivors of the blast.

Unable to flee the scene, *Oceania* had become a sitting duck for the British submarines lurking in the grey light of daybreak – but only if they were able to evade the attentions of the destroyers. At dawn, the *Upholder* moved in for the kill but just as they were preparing to fire they were spotted by one of the destroyers and forced to dive. Wanklyn's next move was breath-taking in its daring and courage. Realising that the destroyer prowling the surface had wrecked his chance of an attack along that line, the *Upholder*'s commander took the sub under the target itself, swung round, resurfaced and unleashed a second salvo. Eight minutes later, the giant liner had disappeared beneath the waves. In the space of a few hours, Wanklyn had accounted for more enemy men than all the Allied submariners in the entire six-year period of the war in the Mediterranean.

Even before news of the successful attack had reached him, Admiral Cunningham, Commander-in-Chief of the Mediterranean Fleet, had signalled this message to the Admiralty in London. 'Every submarine that can be spared is worth its weight in gold,' he said. In Berlin, Hitler now had even greater reason to complain to Mussolini about the failure of the Italian navy to protect his troops. No submarine commander had done more to disrupt the efforts of the Afrika Korps than Lieutenant Commander Wanklyn. After the war, General Fritz Bayerlein, Rommel's Chief of Staff, said: 'We would have taken Alexandria and reached the Suez Canal had it not been for the work of your submarines.'

Over the coming months, the *Upholder*'s Jolly Roger flag, flown by the subs on their return to harbour to signal their latest successes, gradually filled up with symbols of enemy ships they had destroyed. The early failures were now a distant memory, overshadowed by the mounting tally of tonnage sent to the deep.

On 6 April 1942 the *Upholder* headed out into the open seas for her twenty-fifth patrol – her last before she was to return to Britain. During sixteen months of operations in the Mediterranean, Wanklyn had sunk or damaged nineteen supply ships, sunk two U-boats, damaged one other and caused extensive damage to a cruiser and a destroyer. In all, he had accounted for 133,000 tons of Axis shipping, making him the leading submarine commander of the conflict. He had sunk a third more shipping by tonnage than the most successful American commander.

The prospect of sailing for home for an extended period of leave had lifted the mood of the shattered crew. Cheerful banter filled the living compartment and control room as she pulled out of Malta's Grand Harbour for their last patrol before heading home to their families.

The first mission was to drop two Arab agents on the shoreline of Tunisia's Gulf of Sousse. Captain Robert 'Tug' Wilson of the Royal Artillery, deployed as a 'special commando', ferried them ashore in his Folbot collapsible canoe, towing the men in an inflatable rubber dinghy. *Upholder* waited offshore anxiously before Wilson emerged from the darkness after completing the drop. The *Upholder* moved on to rendezvous with *Unbeaten*, another of the 10th Flotilla's subs, in order to transfer the Army officer. The two boats met in the gloom of first light. Shortly before Wilson climbed into his canoe to paddle across, Wanklyn dashed off a letter to his wife Betty, then staying with her parents in Perthshire, and asked him to post it on his return to England. ' . . . You would be amused if you knew just how this one is going to reach you,' he wrote. Wanklyn had not seen his wife or three-year-old son Ian for over a year and the upbeat tone of the letter reveals his yearning for home, family and relaxation. 'Well darling, count up the days, they are not so many. Only 59. All my love is for you sweetheart and the affection for Ian who is yours and mine only. Every your devoted David.'

The letter arrived a few weeks later – a few days after Betty received the following message from the Admiralty:

Madam,

I am commanded by My Lords Commissioners of the Admiralty to inform you that they have learned with great regret, that the ship of which your husband ... is in command is seriously overdue and considered to have been lost, and that your husband has accordingly been reported as missing. No details are at present available concerning the presumed loss of the vessel, and some time may elapse before it becomes possible to come to a definite conclusion regarding your husband's fate ...

The letter ended with a polite request not to pass on the news in case it fell into the hands of the press and provided the Germans with a propaganda coup.

Though his wife refused to accept the fact for many weeks to come, the greatest submarine commander of the Second World War was dead.

In fact, there has never been a 'definite conclusion'. To this day, the fate of Wanklyn and the *Upholder* remains a mystery. There have been a number of theories. After transferring Wilson to the *Unbeaten*, the last recorded movements of the boat show her moving south-east towards Tripoli. A signal had been sent from Malta ordering her to form a patrol line with two subs to intercept a convoy. Some say the boat came to grief in a minefield off the Libyan capital, but a commander of Wanklyn's experience is highly unlikely to have blundered into such an obvious danger zone. Another possibility is that the *Upholder* finally fell victim to a depth-charge assault but German and Italian records reveal no evidence of anti-submarine patrols in the area that night.

A third line of investigation suggests she was sunk by the *Pegaso*, an Italian torpedo boat, protecting a convoy. The *Pegaso*'s commanding officer reported attacking a British submarine with depth charges, adding that he had rejoined the convoy after his ship's echo-direction finder could detect no further activity below the surface. But this is doubtful, too, as it took place more than one hundred miles from where Wanklyn was meant to be. The commander of the *Upholder* was a hunter by instinct and, although it is not impossible that he had headed off to richer hunting grounds in search of prey, the distances involved suggest it was unlikely. In truth, all we can say for certain is that Wanklyn and his crew died a horrible death under the glassy, calm surface of the Mediterranean. Whatever caused the fatal blow, it doesn't take much imagination to picture the horror of the scenes inside the hull as the water rushed through the compartments and the boat began to plummet to the seabed, thousands of feet below.

Submarine losses had been mounting at the time, but the news of the *Upholder*'s suspected demise was still greeted with disbelief in Malta. In the sixteen months since arriving at the besieged colony, Wanklyn had built up an aura of invincibility and his brother officers struggled to come to terms with the fact that he and his crew were gone. In the following days, a stream of signals was sent out, but there was no response. The Commanding Officer of the 10th Flotilla paid his old friend a glowing, poignant tribute that was communicated to his grief-stricken wife in a letter from A. V. Alexander, the First Lord of the Admiralty, officially announcing the loss of the *Upholder* with all hands.

Simpson said Wanklyn's '. . . brilliant record will always shine in the record of British submarines and in the history of the Mediterranean Fleet in this war . . . it seems to me that Wanklyn was a man that the nation can particularly ill afford to lose. His modesty, determination and exceptionally fine character made him a natural leader, who received automatically the loyalty and a maximum effort from all who served with him. As an example of this, during the past year, two or three worthless scamps have been drafted to *Upholder*, never again to appear at the Defaulter's table.' Even the serial troublemakers couldn't fail to be inspired by the man.

Few outside of the Royal Navy have ever heard of David Wanklyn, but to the men of the Silent Service, then and now, he is one of the few men in the annals of our military history who truly deserve to be described as a 'legend'. With a Victoria Cross and a DSO with two bars, he was the most highly decorated of all Royal Naval personnel in the conflict, yet he achieved none of the celebrity of other war heroes of the day. Wanklyn is arguably the most unsung of all our heroes; and the Submarine Service in which he fought with such daring and courage, is arguably the most unsung of all significant units in the Armed Forces. At the outbreak of the Second World War there was an old-fashioned attitude among some within the Navy that submarines were somehow not fair play, even in the heat of a bitter global conflict with the country facing ruin and the free world under threat of domination by Nazi Germany and Imperial Japan. Traditionalists clung to the view expressed by Admiral Sir Arthur Wilson at the turn of the century that the submarine warfare was 'underhand, unfair and damned un-English'. The devastation caused by German U-boats to our merchant fleet compounded the sinister image. Sneaking up on a ship and taking her out with a torpedo simply wasn't cricket. While German U-boat commanders returned to cheering crowds in harbour and to saturation media coverage, their British counterparts slipped back home unnoticed.

Wanklyn never received the public acclaim his remarkable exploits so patently deserved, but he had certainly won over any remaining submarine sceptics in the Admiralty, prompting their Lordships to pay a tribute almost unprecedented in the long, glorious history of the Royal Navy.

The Official Admiralty communiqué announcing the loss of the *Upholder* shows the awe and admiration in which Wanklyn and his devoted crew had come to be held:

It is seldom proper for Their Lordships to draw distinction between different services rendered in the course of naval duty, but they take this opportunity of singling out those of H.M.S.

UPHOLDER, *under the command of Lieutenant Commander Wanklyn, for special mention. She was long employed against enemy communications in the Central Mediterranean, and she became noted for the uniformly high quality of her services in that arduous and dangerous duty. Such was the standard of skill and cool intrepidity set by Lieutenant Commander Wanklyn and the officers and men under him that they and their ship became an inspiration not only to their own Flotilla, but to the fleet of which it was part and Malta, where for so long it was based. The ship and her company are gone, but the example and the inspiration remain.*

The ship and her company are gone but the example and inspiration remain.

For the Royal Navy Submarine Service, Lieutenant Commander Malcolm David Wanklyn and the crew of the *Upholder* are very much 'still on patrol'.

Author's Acknowledgements

First I would like to thank Niall Edworthy, without whom this book would never have existed. His enthusiasm and attention to detail has never waned and his passion for all things military have driven this book forward from the start.

I would also like to thank my editor Ben Dunn for all his help and support, wicked sense of humour and the occasional beer.

And lastly I would like to thank my good friend and advisor, Lord Waheed Ali.

Publisher's Acknowledgements

A great debt of gratitude is owed to the Chavasse family and St Peter's College, Oxford for their permission to quote from Noel Chavasse's letters home in World War One. We must also thank a great many people at various archive resources and institutions who have been so generous in giving their help and advice during the research of this book, especially the staff at the National Archives in Kew, Matthew Little at the Royal Marines Museum in Southsea, George Malcolmson at the Royal Navy Submarine Museum at Gosport, Philip Grover from the Manuscripts Collections at the Pitt Rivers Museum, Oxford where the Chapman Papers are held, Colin Harris at the Bodleian Library, Oxford, the Nottinghamshire Archives for permission to quote from the letters of Albert Ball (References DD/1180/1 and DD/1180/2), the Green Howards Museum in Richmond, Yorkshire, the Department of Research at the Royal Air Force Museum in Hendon, the Royal Norfolk Regimental Museum in Norwich and Squadron Leader Patrick Edworthy (Ret'd) for his help on the Ginger Lacey chapter.

List of Illustrations

Lieutenant Colonel Freddy Spencer Chapman
British Diplomatic Mission to Lhasa 1936-37, 1998.131.399,
Copyright Pitt Rivers Museum
British Diplomatic Mission to Lhasa 1936-37, 1998.131.378,
Copyright Pitt Rivers Museum
©TopFoto

Captain John Randle
©TopFoto

Captain Noel Chavasse
© Pictorial Press Ltd / Alamy

©TopFoto
Getty Images
© Maurice Savage / Alamy

Sergeant Major Stanley Hollis

Getty Images
AFP/Getty Images
Courtesy of The Green Howards Museum

Lieutenant Colonel Blair 'Paddy' Mayne

©TopFoto
© Hugh Maxwell / Alamy

Lieutenant Colonel Herbert 'Blondie' Hasler

Getty Images

Captain Albert Ball

Getty Images
© CORBIS
© Tracey Foster / Alamy

Flight Sergeant Norman Jackson

Getty Images
Popperfoto/Getty Images
© Trinity Mirror / Mirrorpix / Alamy

Squadron Leader James 'Ginger' Lacey
Getty Images

Captain Edward Fegen
©TopFoto
Popperfoto/Getty Images

Lieutenant Commander Malcolm Wanklyn
Courtesy of The Submarine Museum
Courtesy of The Imperial War Museum Collections

Bibliography and Further Reading

Captain Albert Ball VC, MC, DSO***

Maurice Baring, *Flying Corps Headquarters 1914–1918*, Heinemann, 1930

Chaz Bowyer, *Albert Ball VC*, Crecy Publishing, 2002

Alan Clark, *Aces High*, Weidenfeld & Nicolson, 1999

Ira Jones, *King of Air Fighters: Biography of Major 'Mick' Mannock VC, DSC, MC*, Greenhill Books, 1989

Cecil Lewis, *Sagittarius Rising*, Frontline Books, 2009

Joshua Levine, *Fighter Aces of WWI*, HarperCollins, 2009

Lieutenant Colonel Freddy Spencer Chapman DSO

Ralph Barker, *One Man's Jungle: A Biography of F. Spencer Chapman DSO*, Chatto & Windus, 1975

Brian Moynahan, *Jungle Soldier: The True Story of Freddy Spencer Chapman*, Quercus Publishing, 2009

F. Spencer Chapman, *The Jungle Is Neutral*, The Reprint Society, 1950

Captain Noel Chavasse VC*, MC

Ann Clayton, *Chavasse, Double VC*, Pen & Sword Military Books, 2006

Selwyn Gummer, *The Chavasse Twins*, Hodder & Stoughton, 1963

Lyn MacDonald, *They Called it Passchendaele*, Penguin Books, 1993

A. M. McGilchrist, *The Liverpool Scottish 1900–1919*

Commander Edward Fegen VC

Gerald L. Duskin and Ralph Segman, *If the Gods Are Good: The Sacrifice of 'HMS Jervis Bay'*, Crecy Publishing, 2005

Admiral Theodor Krancke and H. J. Brennecke, *Pocket Battleship*, Tandem, 1975

George Pollock, *The Jervis Bay*, William Kimber, 1961

F. Tennyson Jesse, *The Saga of San Demetrio*, HMSO, 1942; 2007

John Winton, *Convoy: Defence of Sea Trade*

Lieutenant Colonel Herbert 'Blondie' Hasler DSO, OBE

James D. Ladd, *Commandos and Rangers of World War II*, St Martin's Press, 1978

C. E. Lucas Phillips and H. G. Hasler, *Cockleshell Heroes*, Pan Books, 1970

Ewen Southby-Tailyour, *Blondie: Founder of the SBS and Modern Single-Handed Ocean Racing*, Pen & Sword Books, 2003

Bill Sparks, *Cockleshell Commando: The Memoirs of Bill Sparks, DSM*, Pen & Sword Military Books, 2009

Sergeant Major Stanley Hollis VC

Antony Beevor, *D-Day: The Battle for Normandy*, Penguin Books, 2010

Roger Chapman, *Beyond Their Duty: Heroes of the Green Howards*, Friends of the Green Howards Museum, 2001

Max Hastings, *Overlord: D-Day and the Battle for Normandy, 1944*, Pan Books, 1985

Mike Morgan, *D-Day Hero: CSM Stanley Hollis VC*, The History Press, 2004

Geoffrey Powell and John Powell, *The Green Howards: Three Hundred Years of Service*, Pen & Sword Books, 2002

Sergeant Norman Jackson VC

Patrick Bishop, *Bomber Boys: Fighting Back 1940–1945*, Harper Perennial, 2008

Max Hastings, *Bomber Command*, Pan Books, 1999

Kevin Wilson, *Men of Air: The Doomed Youth of Bomber Command*, Phoenix, 2008

Squadron Leader James 'Ginger' Lacey DFM*
Richard Townshend Bickers, *Ginger Lacey, Fighter Pilot*, Pan Books, 1969

Patrick Bishop, *Battle of Britain: A Day-by-Day Chronicle, 10 July–31 October 1940*, Quercus Publishing, 2009

Stephen Bungay, *The Most Dangerous Enemy: A History of the Battle of Britain*, Aurum Press, 2009

Geoffrey Wellum, *First Light*, Penguin Books, 2003

Lieutenant Colonel Paddy Mayne DSO***
Stephen Bungay, *Alamein*, Aurum Press, 2002

Brigadier John, Durnford-Slater, *Commando: Memoirs of a Fighting Commando in World War II*, Greenhill Books, 2002

Malcolm James [Malcolm Pleydell James], *Born of the Desert: With the SAS in North Africa*, Greenhill Books, 2001

John Laffin, *Raiders: Great Exploits of the Second World War*, Sutton Publishing, 2003

Gavin Mortimer, *Stirling's Men: The Inside Story of the Original SAS*, Weidenfeld & Nicolson, 2004

Hamish Ross, *Paddy Mayne*, The History Press, 2004

Captain John Randle VC
John Colvin, *Not Ordinary Men: The Story of the Battle of Kohima*, Pen & Sword Books, 2003

Leslie Edwards, *Kohima: The Furthest Battle*, The History Press, 2009

Fergal Keane, *Road of Bones: The Siege of Kohima 1944*, HarperPress, 2010

Julian Thompson, *Forgotten Voices of Burma: The Second World War's Forgotten Conflict*, Ebury Press, 2009

Lieutenant Commander David Wanklyn VC, DSO**

Jim Allaway, *Hero of the Upholder*, Periscope Publishing, 2004

Richard Compton-Hall, *Submarine Warfare: Monsters and Midgets*, Littlehampton Books Services Ltd, 1985

Richard Compton-Hall, *HMS Upholder*: Warship 16 Profile

Sydney B. Hart, *Submarine Upholder*, Amberley Publishing, 2009

G. W. G. Simpson, *Periscope View*, Macmillan, 1972

John Wingate, *The Fighting Tenth: The Tenth Submarine Flotilla and the Siege of Malta*, Periscope Publishing, 2003

Research Institutions

Bodleian Library, University of Oxford
Green Howards Museum, Richmond, North Yorkshire
Pitt Rivers Museum Manuscript Collections, Oxford
Royal Norfolk Regimental Museum, Norwich
RAF Museum, Hendon
National Archives, Kew
Nottinghamshire Archives, Nottingham
Royal Navy Museum, Portsmouth
Royal Navy Submarine Museum Archive & Library, Gosport
Royal Marines Museum Archive & Library, Southsea

Index